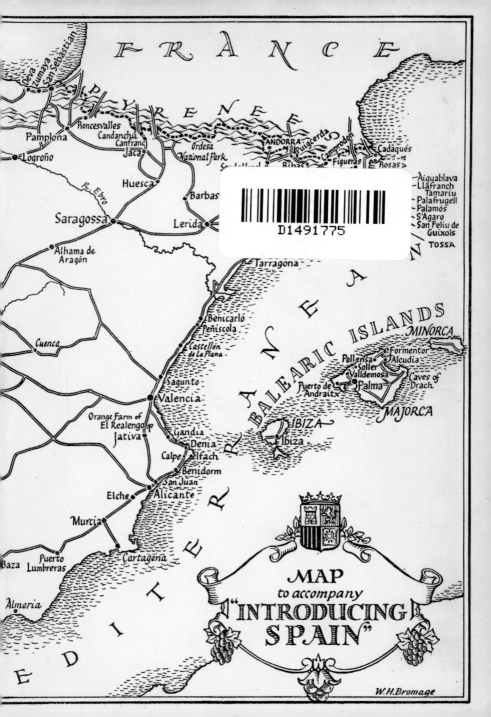

IN ARDUIS AUDAX

HELEN & MICHAEL
OPPENHEIMER

INTRODUCING SPAIN

Seville street scene during the Spring Fair

INTRODUCING SPAIN

by
CEDRIC SALTER

METHUEN & CO., LTD., LONDON
36 Essex Street, Strand, W.C.2

First published June 5th, 1953
Second Edition, revised, 1954

To
LUCAS DE ORIOL
For being my idea of a Friend

2.1

CATALOGUE NO. 5470/U

PRINTED IN GREAT BRITAIN

CONTENTS

ILLUSTRATIONS

ACKNOWLEDGEMENTS

I WISH to express my sincere thanks to Don Luis Bolín, Director General del Turismo until June 1952, and to his successor, Don Mariano Urzaiz y Silva, Duke of Luna, who have not only supplied me with most of the illustrations for this book, but have given me their generous encouragement and assistance in writing it.

I am also grateful to Don Antonio Gil-Casares for countless 'lifts' to different parts of the country by ATESA —the bus and car-hire company of which he is Managing Director, and to Mrs. Phyllis Fischer for her miraculous ability to read my manuscript.

My wife, too, deserves much credit for having patiently endured my maddening tendency to stay in bed and refuse meals when trying to write.

Plates 9, 13, 17, 18, and 22 are from photographs by Exclusive News Agency Ltd.

INTRODUCTION

THE tragic limitation of the British foreign travel allowance to £50 has naturally produced a crop of books in which the emphasis is exclusively upon finance, which, though ingenious, add little to the normal holiday-maker's knowledge of Spain.

Some of their authors recorded that they were 'living intensely and adventurously' as a result of staying exclusively in 'fondas', or inns, where there was no plumbing. Personally I have never found that the proximity of normal sanitation in any way impaired my own capacity for enjoyment.

They also seemed to consider it essential, even when they possessed motor transport, to undertake long cross-country journeys by third-class railway trains, arriving hot, dirty, late, and tired, but apparently fired by the hope of soon greeting some other equally intrepid compatriot with the traditional:

'Dr. Livingstone, I presume.'

Now I have periodically travelled third class by train, not only all over Spain but throughout the Balkans and Near East, as I have also travelled by car, plane, and first-class Pullman, according to the current state of my very fluctuating fortunes.

My recommendation is: Travel third if you are obliged to do so, but *not* for 'fun'. Mortification of the flesh was highly thought of in the Middle Ages, but in the twentieth century people who indulge in it are classified by psychoanalysts as masochists and put in 'rest homes' for treatment. To suffer unavoidable discomfort courageously is a very great virtue, but to feel that you have been clever because you have chosen an uncomfortable way of travelling, when a more agreeable method was available, is just plain dumb!

If economy were essential, our literary heroes could have bought a 'kilometrico' ticket and have travelled second class for the price they paid in order to travel third; and if they had applied for a journalist's pass they could have obtained a reduction of no less than 60% on the normal fares. Such practical measures for saving money might not have been so 'adventurous', but they would, in my opinion, have been a great deal more sensible.

Additionally, if expense is the supreme consideration, the only practical thing is to make sure of the kind of place in Spain that you want for your holiday and then stay there—when even a tiny travel allowance will go a very long way indeed—and not to spend money on needless third-class railway fares.

Proof that a very large number of people wish to visit Spain has been provided by the many hundreds of letters from both sides of the Atlantic that I have received and answered during the last two years, mostly from people whom I have never met, and all asking for holiday information about the country. Analysis of this correspondence revealed that visitors are never disappointed with a holiday in Spain *if* they know in advance more or less what to expect. Unfortunately, some people—aided and abetted by the travel agent's more highly coloured posters —form a mental picture of Spain which bears only the vaguest resemblance to reality, and when they find something quite different from what they expected, they feel—understandably, if unreasonably—that the country has 'let them down'.

Of course, there were a few hard cases, such as the lady who wrote to me indignantly complaining that she had not been able to get a good cup of tea during her entire stay, but the overwhelming majority of those who failed to have one of the most memorable holidays of their lives failed because they expected something quite different from what they actually got. Many went to San Sebastian expecting to find it filled with languorous ladies being serenaded by muscular baritones, and were annoyed to find that it was rather like Atlantic City or Brighton. One tired and obviously thwarted business-man complained that he had walked through Madrid all of one evening without seeing a single gipsy girl dancing 'flamenco' in the streets.

Others went to Asturias in spring and complained that it was snowing, and still others decided to 'do' Andalusia in August and went down with heat-stroke.

Fairly early on in this varied correspondence it struck me that practically no one, when subsequently reporting their impressions, appeared to agree upon what they had found in Spain in even the smallest particulars.

Now, however different their personal tastes may be, a group of individuals visiting France, Italy, or Switzerland will return and tell a tale that, though varied, can with a little imagination be fitted into the same general picture.

Not so with Spain. 'People were so courteous' was followed by 'The Spaniards were so rude'; 'Everyone seemed so happy', one writes, and his companion says, 'Everyone seemed so sad'; 'I have never seen so much comfort and luxury since before the War', one exclaims, 'and the food was good and plentiful'; then 'the people seemed poor and half-starved' immediately complains another. Everyone simply could not be right, and it took me a little time to discover the explanation.

Spain, unlike most places, is not a fixed quantity, but emerges in the form that the personality, character, and tastes of each individual encourage.

Summing up, it seems that people do not realize that Spain is territorially the largest country in Europe except France; that it is the most mountainous except Switzerland; and that parts of it are as different as Scotland is from Egypt, racially, scenically, and climatically.

The object of this book is to try to prevent these quite needless disappointments. In it I propose to show a definite but not overwhelming interest in pictures, scenery, ancient buildings, music, local customs, history, and so on, but I shall also assume that my readers are equally, if not more, interested in food, wine, fishing, shooting (or hunting if you come from the other side of the Atlantic), dancing, fiestas, bull-fights, comfort, bathing, expense, and, above all, in the people in whose country they propose to be, and in how to get the best out of them and so out of their holiday.

Quite often I shall devote more space to a place that your tourist agent will never have heard of, such as El Paular, Riaño, or Ifach, than I do to Easter Week or the Annual Fair in Seville.

Where this is the case it is because I believe that, for a certain kind of person, the former may provide a holiday that it is impossible to find elsewhere, whereas more than enough has already been written about the latter to ensure that visitors to the Andalusian capital know exactly what to expect.

I could have written it as a personal journey, though it is, in fact, the result of many journeys, as I have been going to Spain at intervals since my first foreign newspaper assignment to 'cover' the Civil War, and since 1948 I have made it my home. Personal adventures have been omitted, and anecdotes are employed only in order to illustrate the character of the people, upon some slight understanding of which the real success or failure of your holiday must depend.

I believe that almost everyone has his or her own special holiday castle somewhere in Spain, but few know just where to find it. It is there, among the blue mountains, tawny plains, and pale ochre cities, where storks gather on crumbling walls to clap their beaks voicelessly at dawn and sunset. You may find it in the wild rhythm of flamenco music, flung in the face of a blazing moon by harsh gipsy voices, or in the enchantment of small rocky islands, set in a sea that looks like blue tussore silk. I really believe that it is there waiting for you, and I should be very glad indeed if I felt that this book had helped you to find it.

PART I

GENERAL INFORMATION

I

LANGUAGE, CLOTHES, AND GENERAL BEHAVIOUR

BY and large, Spanish is a far easier language for the Anglo-Saxon to pronounce than is French—and it is the pronunciation that really matters.

An English friend of mine, whose French was the envy and admiration of all who were at school with him, returned from his first visit to Paris and confessed:

'As you know, my French is pretty good. My trouble was that all the French people I met had such extraordinary accents!'

The essential factors in pronouncing Spanish, so that the Spaniards who were not educated in Britain or America can understand you, are far more constant than in French.

Here, very briefly indeed, are those bare principles:

All 'A's are long—not quite -ar, but very nearly.

'E' (as in French) is like a short 'a' (as in 'make').

'I' (also as in French) is like a short 'i' (as in 'prison'—never as in 'private').

'O' is shorter and sharper (as in 'shot').

'U' is almost like 'oo' or 'ou' (as in 'frugal'—never as in 'dun', 'doubt' or 'trouble').

'B' and 'V' appear to be almost interchangeable in Spanish —so much so that 'automobile' is written 'automovil'.

'C' is softer and often becomes almost 'th'—thus 'reducido' (reduced) is pronounced 'raydoothido'.

'G' at the beginning of a word is usually pronounced as an 'H'—thus 'General' (general) is pronounced 'Hayneral', and 'George' as 'Horhay'.

'H' usually (but not quite always) is silent—thus 'habitación' (bedroom) is pronounced 'abitathion'.

'J' is always a rather guttural (Arabic) 'H', thus 'junta' (committee) is 'hoonta(r)' and 'justo' (exact) is 'hoosto'.

3

Double 'L' is always pronounced 'LY', thus 'murallas' (walls) is 'mooralyas' and 'caballero' (gentleman) is 'cabalyairo'.

'Ñ'. In addition to the ordinary 'n', which is pronounced as in English, the Spanish language possesses the letter 'ñ'. This is always pronounced 'ny'—thus 'niño' (boy) or 'niña' (girl) are pronounced 'neenyo' and 'neenya'.

'RR' is rolled more than in English.

'V' is so soft as often to be indistinguishable from 'B'.

'W' does not exist in Spanish and, when Spaniards meet it, they usually treat it as a 'V'. Thus a friend of mine, by the name of Wallace, always found it easier to leave messages with Spanish servants saying that Señor '*V*al-yath-ey' had called!

'Z' is almost always pronounced 'th'. 'Manzanilla' (a kind of dry sherry) becomes 'Manthanilya'.

A fairly general peculiarity is that a 'd' at the end of a word is dropped—thus 'Madrid' is pronounced 'Ma(r)dre(e)', and you will get nowhere by asking whether you are on the right road for Madri*d*.

Certain peculiarities at first will tend to bother you. One is that Spanish has only the one word—'mañana'—to signify both 'to-morrow' and 'morning', so that in order to say 'to-morrow morning' you must say 'mañana por la mañana'. It is also impossible to say 'last week' in Spanish, the phrase being 'la semana proxima pasada'—literally, 'the next (nearest) week (to us) of those that have passed'! Although 'hervido' means 'boiled' and 'huevos' means 'eggs', you will probably be met by a blank stare if you ask for 'dos huevos hervidos' (two boiled eggs) for your breakfast, as the phrase is 'dos huevos pasados por agua', i.e. 'two eggs that have been passed through water'. Why? Presumably for the same reason that we pronounce -ough as 'uff' in 'tough', as 'oo' in 'through', and as 'ow' in 'bough'!

Other oddities are the fact that everyone in Spain has two surnames, using both his father's and his mother's. Thus, if your father's name is John Smith and your mother's Emily Jones and they christened you Edward, your letters, if you were a Spaniard, would be addressed to:

SEÑOR DON EDWARD SMITH Y JONES

—though the Señor Don (equivalent to our Mr. or Esqre.) would be written Sr.D. and the 'y' (and) would disappear, except on formal occasions.

When asked for my 'second surname' (mother's maiden name) by a Spanish official I once replied (rather facetiously, I fear) that as my parents had been considerate enough to get married before my birth my mother's surname, as far as I was concerned, had always been the same as my father's. He took it well, so I gave him an opportunity for a come-back by asking him why they bothered with their mother's maiden name, particularly as it only kept it alive for one more generation in any case. He replied, 'We all like to think that we know who was our father, but, after all, we only have the word of one woman to go by, whereas there are usually witnesses to prove who are our mothers—so we make absolutely sure of at least one name being correct.'

As in French, it is apt to cause embarrassment if you say 'I am hot'. Instead one says, 'Tengo calor'—'I have heat'.

Another small peculiarity of the language was once painfully revealed to me when I was sitting out a dance with a most attractive, English-speaking, Spanish girl. While pondering upon the next move in the game, I sneezed suddenly and, after thanking her for the courteous 'Jesus' (pronounced 'Hayzus') with which such occurrences are greeted in Spain, I added my apologies. Smiling sweetly, she knocked me breathless by saying, 'I believe you are badly constipated'. Panic seized me that my little secret should be so apparent that it could be read upon my face like this, even by a comparative stranger. I defended myself only indifferently against the charge—and romance was at an end.

Only later I learned that the Spanish word for a cold in the head is 'constipado'.

I fell into a similar trap when, at a Spanish cocktail party,

B

I was asked whether I had recently seen a girl with whom it was known that I had been on very friendly terms, but with whom I had since quarrelled. I intended to say, 'Yes, I met her the other day, and she seemed to me to be pretty (bastante) embarrassed (by the meeting)'. Unfortunately, I translated the English word 'embarrassed' with the Spanish word 'embarazada', which means 'pregnant'. My reply therefore was, 'Yes, I met her the other day, and she looked to me to be pretty pregnant'—which struck my audience as ungallant in the circumstances.

A small oddity is the entire absence of a Spanish word to translate 'shy'. Discussing the point with a Spaniard, he offered me 'timido' and 'vergonzoso', but I insisted that the former implied fear and the latter shame—since the Spanish word for shame is 'verguenza'. As he looked blank I said:

'No, not fear or shame, but the sensation that you felt, at the age of fourteen, when you were suddenly introduced at a party to a couple of girls of, say, fifteen or sixteen.'

'What did I feel?' he puzzled, sincerely trying to be helpful. 'Why, nothing except a resolution to get them alone in the linen cupboard at the first possible opportunity.'

It dawned on me then that there is no word for 'shy' in Spanish simply because no Spaniard has ever yet felt shy!

Occasionally I am asked, 'How should we behave at a religious procession, or when sight-seeing in a church, in Spain?'

I do not think that this presents much of a problem if you use normal common sense, but I have known ardent Protestants panic at the imagined alternative of either compromising their beliefs or appearing disrespectful. As a procession passes, Spaniards will probably fall on their knees in the street, and all will cross themselves, but tens of thousands of non-Catholic tourists attend every year, and no one would dream of taking offence because they fail to do the same. I think that at such moments ordinary politeness would cause a man to take off his hat and put out his cigarette, while a woman would stand respectfully silent for the few minutes until the procession had passed on its way.

Personally I took off my shoes and socks in order to visit the Shwee Dagon Pagoda in Burma; publicly washed my feet and put on special shoes in order to explore the Omayad Mosque in Damascus; took off my hat when attending a Protestant marriage; and tried hard to remember to keep it on when attending a Jewish one. By doing so I in no way denied or weakened my personal religious beliefs, and I have very little sympathy for those whose faith is so frail that they are afraid to be civil towards the faith of others.

However, in visiting churches in Spain people do occasionally offend without intending to do so. There misunderstandings occur principally over the regulations as to clothes, which are different from those enforced not only in Protestant churches but even from those current in the churches of less strictly Catholic countries such as France.

For reasons best known to themselves, but for reasons which (since no one is obliging us to visit their churches) I think we should observe, the Spanish ecclesiastical authorities require a man to wear long trousers, a jacket covering his arms, and a closed collar, preferably with a tie. They require a woman to wear stockings, something (a handkerchief will do) on her head, and, if she is wearing a *décolleté* or sleeveless dress, a scarf covering her chest and arms. The simplest thing for a woman is to slip on some kind of sleeved jersey, which is not much of a hardship as, even in the height of summer, the interiors of Spanish churches are cool. If a service is going on, good manners suggest that you keep out of the direct line between the altar and the congregation and, if you are obliged to cross, a slight reverence towards the altar is considered respectful.

As it happens, the half-dozen or so 'incidents' between tourists and local Spanish Church authorities which occur every year are nearly always with Catholic French visitors, not with Protestant or Episcopalian British or Americans.

I myself saw a Frenchwoman enter a church on the Costa Brava during a service, wearing a loose wrap over a two-piece bathing-costume *and* smoking a cigarette. She was politely asked to leave, but refused, loudly and angrily, and was finally removed, gently but forcibly, and squawking like a spavined hen. Personally, I should have liked to put her in jail for the night—not for religious reasons (as I do not think the Almighty can be insulted by a silly woman, whatever she may do), but in the hope that in future she would reserve her bad manners for exhibition in her own country. The incident was duly reported in the French Leftist Press as affording another example of 'the modern Spanish Inquisition'!

Sea-side clothes are a little less obvious, and the explanation, therefore, a shade more complicated. Since all questions of public morality are in the hands of the Church, rules and regulations do exist which, if enforced, would oblige you to take your swim looking as though you were arrayed to celebrate a Gala Night in Galashiels, *circa* 1897. Fortunately these rules are never fully enforced, and in most places they are totally ignored, except for a few ultra-religious individuals who observe the Church's opinions on the matter through moral conviction, not authoritarian compulsion.

The strictness with which these regulations are enforced depends upon the local Civil Governor, who is urged to severity only on what we may call town beaches. Thus there is usually a uniformed 'snooper', undertaking what is known as 'the navel patrol' on the crowded urban beaches of San Sebastian, Valencia, Barcelona, Cadiz, and other big cities, but in such places as the Costa Brava and Majorca you can bathe in exactly what you would wear at the sea-side at home. In San Sebastian there are two beaches, that for the general public being controlled, but that for the 'diplomaticos extranjeros' (foreign diplomats) being morally beyond redemption! The snag arises most often in connexion with your costume between the beach and your hotel. This may be only 100 yards, but you may run into trouble if you do not put on (and do up) a bathrobe of some kind or another the moment you leave the beach itself, particularly so if you wish to have a drink in a café, or buy some cigarettes, en route.

By and large, the Spanish do not like 'shorts', either male or female, off the beach, and for men 'slacks' are advisable for sightseeing in any town. Women wearing trousers off the beach are apt to be pursued by 'wolf whistles', though they have become far more general in the last year, chiefly for feminine pillion-riding on motor-cycles.

Here again it is French visitors who get into trouble more often than British or Americans—and I must say that even to me some of these transparent nylon costumes do seem more suitable for the Folies Bergères than for the street.

In this connexion it is only fair to record that stuffiness about beach-wear is infinitely worse, and far more ferociously enforced, in Portugal than it is anywhere in Spain. For example, you will probably not see a single male in Spain wearing a 'top' to his bathing-costume, whereas your appearance without one on the beach at Estoril, outside Lisbon, will most surely result in your being ignominiously marched to the local police station, *and* fined anything up to £12 10s. However, Portugal, being a member of NATO, the incident will not feature in the foreign Press to the same extent as did the recent case of the ejection of the French woman from a Spanish church, to which I have referred.

This greater formality in the matter of clothes is observable in everyday city life in Spain as well as at the sea-side. A man will not take off his jacket in the street, a restaurant, a café, or in a cinema or theatre, whatever the temperature may be. The custom is being relaxed in offices that have no direct contact with the public, but is still the general rule.

Smoking is not permitted in any cinema or theatre in Spain, which is something of a hardship to the modern chain-smoker, though there are frequent intervals during which he can indulge his vice.

Hat manufacturers in Spain must have a thin time, as not one person in ten, man or woman, of those you will see in the street, ever wears one. For women going to church there is the universal 'mantilla'—the fine black lace veil worn, most attractively, over the hair, and afterwards tucked into the handbag. In fact the only occasion when hats are worn is for some society cocktail or bridge party, and applies to an infinitesimally small section of the population.

I must be forgiven for dealing in this chapter with things that may seem trivial, but it is ignorance of just these small everyday differences in popular customs that occasionally worries new visitors to Spain, and may even obscure their appreciation of much more important matters.

In conclusion, therefore, a word about time and money. We base our lives on the precept that 'time is money', and strive to give the impression that we are permanently in a dynamic whirl of industry, even when on holiday. Not to be busy—or at least not to appear busy—is to admit ourselves a failure, and we consider it our duty to drive ourselves unceasingly towards the twin heaven of super-tax and duodenal ulcers. In this the Americans are even more determined than the British—though we are fast adopting their attitude. We are all familiar with the film character who arranges to be telephoned every three minutes by his secretary so as to impress his visitors with the success of the enterprise in which he is engaged.

Now, to understand the difference, you may take it from me that the really successful man in Spain seeks just as assiduously to give a visitor the impression that he has absolutely nothing to do.

There is more in this than immediately meets the eye. He assumes that you know that he is the boss, and his attitude is that his affairs are so perfectly arranged that he can safely leave the temporary direction of the enterprise to lesser lights. The impression he wishes to convey is that little men must rush about and worry, but that the really successful can afford to take their momentary leisure when it pleases them—and the implied compliment is that it could never please him more than when in your company.

To this fundamentally different basic pose must be added the fact that to every Spaniard his personal, intellectual and emotional happiness is infinitely more important than is his business success. Obviously some degree of business success is essential in order to be free to enjoy life, but success is only the means to an end, and not (as is so often the case with ourselves, particularly after the habit is once formed) an end in itself.

Two further things give many foreigners the entirely false impression that Spaniards are lazy and unbusiness-like. In fact, though they do not as a rule drive themselves as remorselessly as we do, they work quite as hard. These two things are the unusual office hours, and the better-class Spaniard's dislike of a 'bargain'.

When a visitor calls at a Madrid office at 5 p.m., and is told that the boss is not expected back from lunch until 6 p.m., he not unnaturally exclaims, 'When do these people do any work?' The answer is the following: in winter from 10 a.m. until 2 p.m. and again from 6 p.m. until 9 p.m.—making a seven-hour day, but (and this is so often forgotten) for six, and not for five days a week, as Saturday, except for Government departments, is a full working day and the week is therefore of forty-two hours.

During July, August, and September, when everyone is taking his annual month's holiday, these hours are often from 8 a.m. until 2 p.m., giving a thirty-six-hour week, the reason being that the heat between 2 p.m. and 7 p.m. is often insupportable in an office. In most offices in London people work from 9.30 a.m. until 1 p.m. and from 2 p.m. until 5.30 p.m.—i.e. seven hours a day for five days, giving a thirty-five-hour week. But in Spain there are no odd quarters-of-an-hour off for tea!

Incidentally, Spanish firms are obliged by law to give their employees fourteen months' salary every year—one extra on July 18th, to help with the cost of the summer holidays, and the other on December 21st, to ensure that the New Year and 'Reyes' (January 6th, when Spanish children get their Christmas presents) are duly festive.

The generally held belief that because the Spanish workers are denied the right to strike they are at the mercy of their employers could not be farther from the truth—in fact the reverse is rather the case. If you take on an employee in Spain it is virtually impossible legally to get rid of him (unless you actually catch him rifling the till) without being called up before the 'sindicato' concerned and made to pay him at least six months'—and often a year's—wages.

This different design for living obviously means a different time-table for meals and sleep, and these are worth noting.

In Madrid and Andalusia meals tend to be later than elsewhere, but as a general rule the following holds true everywhere:

Breakfast (if at all) when you ring for it, but rarely before 9 a.m.

Lunch. Beginning at any time between 2 p.m. and 3.30 p.m. and ending at about 4 p.m., so as to allow for two hours' rest or sleep.

Dinner. Beginning at any time between 9 p.m. and 10 p.m., and finishing at 11 p.m., or even later.

These meal-times obviously produce a similar change in the hours for cinemas and theatres. A 'matinée' begins in Spain at 7 p.m., and the ordinary 'evening' show at 11 p.m.

Similarly, shops open from 9.30 a.m. until 1.30 p.m., and from 5.30 p.m. until 8.30 p.m., though this varies slightly from town to town.

Do not be surprised, therefore, if a Spaniard suggests that you meet for a cocktail to-morrow 'afternoon', and turns up at 9 p.m.

The Spanish business-man's distaste for bargaining leads to many misunderstandings. One, at which I happened recently to be present, may illustrate the point. The firm concerned had rented a car to a very rich American visitor who, having completed a tour, had called to pay his bill.

AMERICAN (to the Manager of the Accounts Department): How much do I owe you?

MANAGER: At the agreed rate of 10½ cents per kilometre for 1,620 kilometres, that will be $170.10.

AMERICAN: Buddy, that's a lot of dough—I'll make you a proposition.

MANAGER (whose English is good, but limited): Thank you, sir! A proposition about what?

AMERICAN: A business proposition. Listen, what do you say to $125 *cash* in full settlement?

MANAGER (worried): You mean that there has been some miscalculation as to the number of kilometres you have driven? I am sorry, but I thought that you had checked the meter yourself.

AMERICAN: To hell with the meter. Look, I'll meet you— $150 cash.

MANAGER (working hard): You mean you do not wish to pay more than $150. I must ask the Managing Director.

AMERICAN: Sure, I don't *want* to pay anything, but I am offering $150 in settlement. Ask your boss what he thinks of my proposition.

The Manager retires for a five-minute conference with the Managing Director, and returns full of sympathetic smiles.

MANAGER: Everything is all right, sir. The Managing Director says that you need not pay *anything* now, and we will send you the account next month at your New York address. (He drops his voice to a confidential tone.) He also told me to say that if you are temporarily short of cash, I may advance you $100 or so to help you over your present difficulties.

[Exit American making strange sounds.]

MANAGER: Poor fellow! he is worried about money.

The following day $170.10 was delivered in cash, and the Manager's only comment was:

'There now, I am glad! That must mean that the money has arrived for that nice American who could not pay his account yesterday.'

I thought it kinder not to explain that he had probably made an enemy, rather than a friend, for his firm!

Tipping, which seems to worry many people, obviously varies

according to the character of the place, but, as a general rule, tip often, but in small sums.

Do not forget that a Spaniard, of the type that will accept a tip, is probably earning at the most 1,500 pts a month (roughly £13 10s. or $37). On discovering this fact, people are apt immediately to assume the most terrible poverty, since it would be impossible to maintain life on that in Britain or the United States. It is, of course, very poor indeed; but, then, prices for most essentials in Spain have been kept down by the Government's policy of increasing wages only very gradually. As a result, many articles in Spain are cheaper to-day than they were in 1946, and the position of the man earning 1,500 pts a month (if he is a Spaniard and not a visiting foreigner) would correspond to that of an Englishman earning £6 or £7 a week.

Returning to tips, therefore, do not spoil the market by translating into Spanish money the tip you would give at home for a similar service.

I know that if you gave a bell-boy a tip of 2d. or 2½ cents at home you would probably be lynched, but in Spain it is enough.

Similarly, with restaurant waiters do not forget that 12% has been already added to your bill for service and, consequently, unless it was a large party, the addition of 5 pts is sufficient.

Railway porters and taxi-drivers in all countries 'try it on' with foreigners, but 5 pts per large piece of luggage is generous for the former, and when without luggage the addition of 1 or 2 pts to the fare is all that is required.

Beggars, lottery-ticket sellers, and itinerant musicians do not expect more than 20 centimos, and café shoe-shine boys should be given not more than 3 pts—and keep an eye on their ambition to tack on a pair of rubber soles while you are not looking, an old trick you may have met before and elsewhere!

Travellers' cheques can be changed at any bank and, at a discount of about 1 pt to the pound or dollar, in most first-class and all luxury hotels.

Petrol, or 'gasolina', is now cheaper in Spain than it is in Britain and there is no rationing. The quality of 'gasoline' is poor, and if you have a highly-tuned engine it might be advisable to buy some 'plomo' (lead), as the pink, higher-octane stuff is called, which is obtainable only in the big towns.

In general, Spaniards are extremely courteous (if you are to them), and this slightly old-world manner is to be found as much among shabby and penniless labourers as among the highly educated classes. Do not be surprised therefore if, upon admiring your Spanish host's home, he gently corrects your use of the word 'your' with the phrase:

'*Su* casa—your house' (as well as mine).

At the same time you might spoil the gesture if you took him at his word and inquired when you might take possession!

Similarly, do not take him literally when he begs you, at the moment of your departure, 'to place him at the feet of your wife'.

It is only a convention—but an agreeable one—smacking of a more gracious age.

In this, as in many things, Spain is still eighteenth century, and this as much as anything else may be the reason why visitors are rarely indifferent to the country—they either love it or hate it. I know that the story has been told of other people, but apparently I really was guilty, at the age of four, of refusing a seat facing the engine of the train and of replying to the query, 'But don't you want to see where you are going?' with a firm, 'No, I want to see where I have been.'

Spain, like myself, is more attracted by the past than by the future, and it is nonsense to attribute this to cowardice or lack of ambition. She prefers her age-old folk-dancing to boogie-woogie, and her old, familiar, leisurely round of 'fiestas' to tearing around every week-end from pub to pub in a fast car.

Perhaps it is that Latins are more realistic and less idealistic than Anglo-Saxons, and they feel that the atomic age holds out even less hope of happiness for the future than belonged to them in the recent past. They believe in 'progress', but are less convinced than the Anglo-Saxons that all change is necessarily for the better.

This is probably not a conscious idea, but you will find

in Spain, as in very few other places, that people seem to draw upon their deep emotional and intellectual roots in the past, and do not share our enthusiasm for 'the latest' thing. It constitutes both a strength and a weakness, but for the harassed holiday-maker of the twentieth century it makes a spiritual change quite as profound as the merely physical one produced by his journey to a strange land.

II

HOTELS

A LARGE number of people, including myself, have nasty, suspicious minds. I am aware, therefore, that too frequent eulogies of the Spanish State Tourist Bureau may lead to the assumption that they are paying me so much a line!

Alas! they are not: but the fact remains that they have got the hotel business more effectively under control than is commonly the case with government departments in any other country. This tends enormously to simplify the problems of the foreign tourist or visitor to Spain. It simplifies matters, because no stranger needs to trust exclusively to his own judgement in selecting his hotel, but is free to make his individual discoveries without being financially 'stung' during the process.

Briefly explained, the system is that every hotel in Spain is officially classified, and its prices are fixed annually according to that classification. 'Pensions' or boarding-houses are also listed. In all cases the prices are fixed for a room alone, and for the room together with all meals for twenty-four hours.

Many friends reply to this information by saying:

'Fine, but do the hotels stick to these official prices?'

The answer is that if they do not it is your own fault. By this I mean that its category is prominently displayed in every hotel, and the price that it is entitled to charge accordingly certain. If an individual hotel manager charges you more than he is entitled to do, and you pay him what he asks, then you are thereby doing both yourself and other tourists a grave injury. The exchange rate at the moment of writing is 109 pts to the pound and 38 to the dollar. The system of hotel classification is as follows:

Luxury Hotels
    180 pts a day with full pension.   100 pts for room only.
Class 1a (which includes all the State-run Paradores and Albergues)
    140 pts a day with full pension.   70 pts for room only.

Class 1b
100 pts a day with all meals. 50 pts for room only.

Class 2
75 pts a day with all meals. 35 pts for room only.

Class 3
55 pts a day with all meals. 25 pts for room only.

Pensions (Luxury)
75 pts a day with all meals. 35 pts for room only.

Pensions (First class)
55 pts a day with all meals. 25 pts for room only.

To all these prices must be added 12% of the total for service.

The procedure to follow, if you find that these prices have been exceeded, is to point out the error to the Manager. If he does not make the desired change, then inform him that you propose to send the receipted bill to the Director General del Turismo, at Medinaceli 2, in Madrid, together with your official complaint. I have never yet heard of a case where this did not achieve the desired result.

The system is water-tight if it is properly applied, but you may hear a certain amount of wailing from hotel Managers that the prices fixed by the 'Turismo' do not permit them to retire as millionaires at the age of 50. This may or may not be true—but it is an issue to be settled between the hotel Manager and the Tourist Department, and no concern of yours.

It is true that in Catalonia, where the price of everything, including food, is at least 25% higher than it is anywhere else in Spain, the hotel Managers must be hard put to it to observe the regulations, and the indications are that the maximum prices quoted here may have to be increased for next season. However, even so, they will not be increased by much, and the system will remain unchanged.

It must be remembered, however, that there are the few occasions already mentioned when hotel prices are legally increased and, as in the case of Easter Week in Seville, may even be doubled. Equally, it must be remembered that the system cannot protect you against 'extras', though if the price charged for them is unreasonable it is usually worth while either to report it to the 'Turismo' or to threaten to do so until you secure a reduction.

Do not get the impression from the foregoing that hotel Managers are worse in Spain than they are anywhere else. On the contrary, they are better than in Italy and France, for example, but there is always the dishonest individual, and it is simpler to know your rights.

As a matter of psychology I would recommend that you point out to the erring Manager any departures from the straight and narrow way of virtue in an amiable, rather than in a threatening, manner. He will know that the threat is there without its being specified in words—and better results are usually obtained in all countries when an individual is not made to 'lose face' by being openly accused of having unsuccessfully tried to pull a fast one on you!

As soon, therefore, as you know the places at which you will be staying, consult the Spanish Tourist Bureau's booklet entitled *Los Hoteles de España*. It is in Spanish, but you do not need to know the language to look up the alphabetically listed name of the town you want, and to perceive the significance of the signs L, 1a, 1b, 2, 3 placed against the names of the different hotels.

Do not get all hot and angry about some apparent error in your bill until you have established the justice of your grouch, and bear in mind that a meal 'à la carte', wine, tea, mineral water, or an egg for breakfast, are all 'extras', and so are liable to certain luxury taxes, which can quickly push up the total. In these respects you are 'on your own', and the Tourist Bureau cannot do much to help you—so keep an eye on those 'extras'.

In conclusion, a word on cleanliness.

The Spanish are one of the cleanest peoples in Europe, and you will be very unlucky indeed if you meet a flea. I am one of those unfortunate people who obviously taste delicious, and if there is anything that bites within a mile, it can be relied upon to clap its little hands and abandon all other potential free meals in my favour. This, I can assure you, was a source of distress in the Balkans, Turkey, and China, and the fact that I have travelled the length and breadth of Spain in summer and winter and have never even been nibbled, really does mean something!

In very small country inns—known as 'fondas'—the sheets may often look peculiar, but this is only because they have not been ironed or starched. However, they have not only been washed in the local stream or river (which presumably might not be clean, though it is usually melted snow) but have been hung over a bush or shrub in the blazing sun, which is guaranteed to kill any normal germ or parasite.

When you get below the 1b Class you may occasionally find the lavatory a little primitive, and this, I have discovered, worries some people a good deal. Not to put too fine a point on the matter, the important thing is whether or not it is smelly. If so, then raise hell with the manager; if not, it will not hurt you temporarily to accept the conditions which your own grandparents, however rich they may have been, would, in their youth, have considered positively luxurious!

As regards tipping, the compulsory 12% saves you from any serious headaches, though it is usual to give an occasional 'duro' —5 pts—to any servant who has been helpful. That costs you 1s., but is worth 2s. 6d. to him.

Naturally, shoes that you wish cleaned must *not* be left outside your bedroom door, or the assumption may be that you want them thrown away. Shoe-cleaning is a job for which you call the maid or valet and give the appropriate instructions —though 90% of the shoe cleaning in Spain is done by professional 'limpiabotas', who infest every café or bar in the country and make a very good job of it for 2 or 3 pts.

Laundry in Spain is not the problem that it has become in Britain and, if you just give your soiled stuff to the maid, it will come back excellently done within forty-eight hours. If you want something in a hurry you will be charged a very small 'suplemento' and can have it back in twenty-four hours, or even in twelve.

While on the subject of hotels some special mention must be

made of the State-run Paradores and Albergues, which are uniformly excellent.

The Paradores are usually in an out-of-the-way beauty spot, and part of some old castle or monastery. In these a traveller may stay as long as he pleases. In the smaller modern Albergues, however, there is a rule that you should not stay for more than three nights, as their purpose is to be of assistance to touring motorists rather than as places in which to spend a holiday.

The number of these State-run inns has been steadily increasing during the last seven years, and I have known people to make a comprehensive tour of all Spain without using any other form of accommodation, since there are now twenty-seven of them, and they have been strategically placed by the former Director General of Turismo, Don Luis Bolín, who happened to be something of a genius in such matters.

Since they play such an important rôle in the accommodation of any tourist to Spain, I think it worth listing some of them briefly.

Gredos. Over 5,000 feet above sea-level, and cool at nights, even in the height of summer. A good base for winter sports, from December until March; for hunting during October and November—especially the ibex; and for trout-fishing on the River Tormes in the spring.

Oropesa. Just under 100 miles south-west of Madrid. Situated in the beautiful fifteenth-century palace of the Dukes of Frias.

Merida. A modern building in the city possessing the most perfect Roman remains of any in Spain.

Ubeda. Sixteenth-century castle of great beauty.

Ciudad Rodrigo. Sixty-one miles beyond Salamanca and only some 20 miles from the Portuguese frontier at Fuentes de Oñoro. One of the least-known and most attractive of the Paradores, built within the fourteenth-century castle of King Henry II. It was here that the Duke of Wellington fought one of the decisive battles of the Peninsular Campaign against Napoleon's Marshal Soult, and the town itself is full of really

c

beautiful houses built by the followers of the 'conquistadores' during the sixteenth century, and still mostly inhabited by their noble, if impoverished, descendants. It is not difficult to look around inside one or two of these, and they are well worth it.

Parador de Gil Blas at *Santillana del Mar* (Santander). Also in a medieval palace, close to the Altamira Caves containing prehistoric paintings of bulls, considered by archæologists to be unique.

Granada. The Parador de San Francisco is built actually within the outer walls of the Alhambra, in a former monastery where Queen Isabella was buried until Granada Cathedral was completed. This is the Turismo's show-piece, but has very few bedrooms.

Parador of the Virgen de la Cabeza, near to the famous shrine in the Sierra Morena. Completely out-of-the-world mountain scenery, and a good centre for hunting wild boar—or writing a book!

Parador de Paular. Fifty miles north of Madrid, in a fifteenth-century monastery situated in the former Royal hunting reserve of the Valley of Lozoya. It is 4,000 feet above sea-level, and has a trout stream which is excellent in May and June. More is written about this Parador in Chapter VIII, but it has now been handed back to the Benedictine Order for use as a monastery, although it may still be visited.

Parador de Cruz de Tejada, in the island of Grand Canary, 22 miles from Las Palmas.

Parador de Riaño. Recently opened amid matchless mountain scenery near the Picos de Europa, between Leon and Santander, and reached from Madrid via Burgos and then northwest through the real, and very little-known, 'castles-in-Spain' country.

The Albergues, or wayside inns, can be more briefly mentioned.

Antequera. In the mountains 37 miles north of Malaga.

Aranda de Duero. On the main Madrid–San Sebastian road, 100 miles north of the capital and some 180 from the French frontier.

Bailén. On the main Madrid road to Cordoba and Seville, 185 miles south of the capital and 128 from Cordoba.

La Bañeza. In the province of Leon, on the main road almost equally distant from Madrid to La Coruña (195 miles).

Benicarló. Eighty-six miles north of Valencia and 150 south of Barcelona, on the main coast road between the two cities. Famous for its grilled 'langostinos'—giant prawns. Five miles away along the coast is the mysterious fifteenth-century island city of Peñiscola, home for a time of the anti-Popes.

Manzanares. One hundred and eight miles south of Madrid and 142 north of Cordoba, and so a convenient halting place between the capital and Andalusia.

Medinaceli. Just off the main Madrid–Saragossa road, roughly 100 miles from both. A strange almost depopulated town perched on a hill.

Quintanar de la Orden. Seventy-five miles south of Madrid and 170 from Murcia, on the road to Cartagena and Alicante. Many South Americans visit it, as it is only a few miles from 'La Dulcinea', the supposed home of Don Quixote's lady-love.

Sanabria. Near the Portuguese northern frontier province of Braganza, 70 miles from Zamora and 180 from Vigo. Nearby is the beautiful Kake of Sanabria, where you may bathe.

Puerto Lumbreras. On the main road from the Levante at Alicante (102 miles) to Andalusia at Granada (130 miles).

Parador del Puerto de Pajares (Leon-Asturias). Situated at 4,500 feet, this is really a winter sports resort, and tends to be shrouded in fog from May until September. A ski funicular is being built.

Parador de Ordesa. High in the Pyrenees, within sight of Mount Aneto (11,000 ft.) and the huge National Park of Ordesa.

There are also Paradores in the Canary islands of Lanzarote and La Palina, both marvellously off the map.

One last point: during 1952 something like twenty new hotels were opened in Madrid and Barcelona *alone*, and some forty in all Spain, so that anything but the very latest list may show a place as possessing only second- or third-class hotels when in fact there is now Luxury or first-class accommodation available.

III

COMMUNICATIONS

THIS is not an easy subject because, as in every other way, Spain is a land of violent contrasts and contradictions, and conditions vary not only seasonally but locally.

Firstly, it must be remembered that the area of Spain is more than twice that of Great Britain, and secondly that, after Switzerland, it is the most mountainous country in Europe. Inevitably, therefore, the creation and maintenance of communications is far more difficult in Spain than in most other countries and also, owing to political differences, Spain has been unable to buy railway rolling-stock and commercial road vehicles abroad, since most of her supply of both was smashed to pieces in the Civil War of 1936–9.

However, do not assume from this that communications are bad. In fact, within strictly defined limits, they are extremely good, but if you wander outside those limits you may find yourself stranded somewhere in the eighteenth century—a circumstance which you may, or may not, know how to appreciate!

To be specific: stick to the main lines or roads, unless you are prepared to rough it. Casual travelling is for the adventurous, and although adventures can occasionally be amusing, they are far more usually hot, dusty, and uncomfortable. Plan your journey from one place to another in advance, therefore, and do not assume that you can always 'catch the next train'. You may well discover that the next train does not leave for a couple of days. But if you stick to your prearranged plan you will be comfortable enough, except perhaps in the height of summer.

Since distances are so great, trains between main cities in Spain tend to leave in the evening and reach their destination the following morning. First- and second-class wagons-lits are to be had, alone in the first class, for about 350 pts, and shared in the second class, with someone who may or may not snore, for about 250 pts. There is a dining-car with the usual indifferent food supplied upon trains of all nationalities, but you will probably not find a breakfast-car for the following morning— as no one in Spain (except myself) seems to require breakfast.

Bookings for 'sleepers' tend to become difficult if you are travelling to some seasonally obvious place, such as from Madrid to Seville in April or from Madrid to the sea-side, either at San Sebastian or Barcelona, in July or August. In that case your choice is between booking two or three weeks in advance, or of paying your hotel hall porter 100 pts or so extra to obtain what you want by fair means or foul—which will, of course, be the latter.

The typical extremes of transport are probably best exemplified by the Anna Karenina type of third-class travel and the Spanish-invented stream-lined, air-conditioned, 100-m.p.h. Diesel train that links the French frontier at Irun–San Sebastian with Madrid. This last is known as 'Talgo' (the word being made up from the initial letters of the inventor, sponsor, and of the invention's special characteristics), and its equal cannot be found anywhere on this side of the Atlantic. So, as so often happens in Spain in other respects, your rail communications may vary in style from 1860 to 1960!

In any case, if you plan to do a great deal of travel by rail in Spain I advise you to investigate (through the Spanish Tourist Bureau) the possibilities of the special tickets known as 'kilometricos'. They become progressively cheaper as they provide for more and more distance and, since they can be shared among a party or family, you will find that a 10,000-kilometre kilometrico, shared among four or five persons, works out to be the cheapest railway travel anywhere in the world.

So much for railway travel. In writing of the air I know that I am up against certain prejudices. The first of these is induced by the fact that we live in a small and relatively flat island where the railway communications are good, and the second is based on the patriotic, but quite misguided, belief that the pilots of all except British, American, and perhaps Scandinavian airlines are determined to commit 'hara-kiri'. There is the additional feeling that internal air travel is unnecessary and expensive. In fact it is neither. A plane from Madrid to Barcelona, for example, costs less than a first-class sleeper and takes two hours instead of thirteen. The safety record of Iberia Airways—the official Spanish line—is as high as that of Imperial Airways, and higher than that of Air France. There are daily, twice, or thrice daily services between such cities as Madrid, Barcelona, Seville, Bilbao, Valencia, and Palma de Mallorca, and my advice to anyone who has not come by car is to use Iberia whenever possible. By doing so he will save time, energy, and money.

But my comments upon both rail and air travel assume that you know just where you are going. There are others who want to look around for themselves, and unless you are one of those strange beings, from whom I occasionally receive letters, who are determined to 'do' Spain on foot, by bicycle, or by canoe, then your best method of travel is by bus.

The whole of Spain is knit together in an intricate system of local bus services, which vary with the season, the weather, the driver's health, the price of tyres, his mother-in-law's temper, and the prospects of the local team winning the Association Football (or should I say Futbol?) Cup Tie. Such services are permanent and cheap, but I am not so rash as to advise anyone to count upon them until he is himself on the spot to investigate the current time-table.

However, realizing that there were time-ridden foreigners who insisted upon being at a given place at a given time, a new firm was launched in 1950 which provided the would-be road traveller with luxurious Diesel buses for inclusive, or package, tours lasting for anything from sixteen days to a single day.

This firm is known as ATESA—which stands for Auto-transporte Turistico Español S.A. (the S.A. stands for the Spanish equivalent of '& Co.') with offices at José Antonio 59, in Madrid, and they have got all the answers to the traveller who likes to be 'personally conducted'. Their main tour is of sixteen days, starts at the French frontier at Irun every Friday, and runs through San Sebastian, Vitoria, Burgos, Madrid,

Cordoba, Seville, Jerez de la Frontera, Cadiz, Algeciras, Malaga, Granada, Alicante, Valencia, and Tarragona to Barcelona. Another bus leaves Barcelona every Tuesday on the reverse of the same route.

The price of £97—or $272—is really inclusive, not only of transport, but also of hotels, meals, tips, and sight-seeing. They also run an inclusive six-day tour of Andalusia, which leaves Seville every Wednesday, costs £36 10s. or $102, and visits Jerez de la Frontera, Cadiz, Algeciras, Malaga, Granada, and Cordoba, before returning again to Seville. Now I am perfectly aware that these prices may be beyond the limit of the present British Foreign Travel allowance, but—and it is a big but—these services can be used, if so desired, *for transport only*, leaving the economical traveller to find his or her own less luxurious, but still adequate, hotel and restaurant accommodation. In this way the entire fifteen days of road travel, covering 1,655 miles, can be accomplished for 2,735 pts, £26 10s., or $71.25, and the six-day Andalusian Circuit of 561 miles for a mere 975 pts, £9, or $25.40.

The same firm runs a millionaire car service—19 U.S. cents a kilometre for a 1951 Ford and $0.203 a kilometre for a 1952 Mercury. Both include petrol and an English-speaking chauffeur.

IV

SPANISH FOOD AND WINE

ALL the books on Spain that I have so far seen were based upon experience of conditions prior to the summer of 1951—and these are as out of date, as far as food is concerned, as one of the famous Mrs. Beeton's Victorian recipes would be in present-day Britain. The reason why a major food change has taken place in Spain in the last two years is simple—it has rained.

The country has had to endure a long series of drought years, and by November 1950 the hydro-electric reserve was down to 8% of capacity. Street-lighting was reduced to a glimmer, shop-window lighting and neon advertising were forbidden, cinemas and theatres not permitted to light up in the interval, and whole urban areas deprived of light and current for several days in the week.

This was gloomy enough in itself, but the lack of rain also meant poor crops, which, since Spain possessed little foreign exchange with which to buy food abroad, meant hunger, shortages, rationing, and black-market speculation. The Government was active in taking measures to prevent anything like it ever happening again in the future, opening no fewer than thirteen new hydro-electric dams of the thirty-two under construction. But a hydro-electric dam is of little but ornamental use to anyone until it can be filled with water.

Then in December 1951 it began to rain, or snow, all over Spain, and it repeated the process during the winter of 1951–2. The immediate result was the suspension of the numerous lighting restrictions, the less immediate but far more important result being two bumper harvests, the ending of all food rationing on June 1st, 1952, and, with the return of plenty at low prices, the almost total disappearance of the black-market, with a consequent drop in prices. You, as a foreigner, could eat and drink well in Spain before 1952, but you can do so a great deal better since then—and it will cost you less. Both British and Americans tend to be very conservative about their food—the former suspecting anything that does not taste of cotton-wool and the latter anything that does not come out of either the deep freezer or a tin. French cooking at its best is probably unbeatable, but to be at its best it has either to be expensive or you must be very lucky. Within certain limits it is not necessary to be either rich or lucky in order to eat extremely well in Spain—*if* you are prepared to forget your prejudices and to try anything once.

I adopted the principle of 'try anything at least once' at an early age, and it has been responsible for much contentment and interest that would otherwise have been denied to me. True, my principles have occasionally been severely tested—as, for example, when in camp in the wilds of West Africa twenty years ago, I was informed that the delicious stew that I had just finished was primarily composed of the chief of a neighbouring tribe with whom there had been a cattle-raiding dispute —but such occasions have been rare!

Many Americans from the Middle West are revolted at the idea of eating lobsters, prawns, and other crustacea, presumably because they live so far from both the Atlantic and Pacific coasts that they are largely unfamiliar with them. Similarly, one has but to mention garlic to the average Englishman to send him stampeding for home.

I think that both are missing a great deal through ignorance —your Middle Westerner may decide that he does not like 'langostinos' or fresh-water crayfish (cangrejos), but his decision should be made after, and not before, he has tried them. As for garlic, I can assure you that I have suffered from its excessive employment as much as anyone, but, used in moderation—say in wiping round the salad bowl, or in rubbing over a spring chicken before it is roasted—both Spaniards and French alike agree that it is one of the essentials of good eating.

In this book I shall always mention outstandingly good restaurants in each town that we visit, so that the purpose of this chapter is more for general guidance.

As a rule fish is better in Spain than meat. By this I do not mean that you cannot obtain a matchless 'chateaubriand' of beef (solomillo de buey) in Spain, but the Spaniards themselves, like the French, have a weakness for veal (ternera). One of the principal reasons for this is that such large areas of Spain are arid that it is uneconomical to keep a calf for more than a few months after it is weaned, as its food has to be specially grown (there being no natural pasturage of grass), and this costs a great deal more than the extra weight as meat between a calf and a full-grown animal.

This shortage of pasture does not apply to the provinces of Asturias and Galicia, the Basque provinces, or the Pyrenees, but it is sufficiently general to have produced a national taste for veal. This is so marked that if you ask just for 'meat' (carne) you will automatically be given veal, and you must specify any other kind of meat, such as 'lomo de cerdo' (pork), 'cordero' (mutton), 'corderito' (lamb), &c. Do not be fooled into thinking that 'bifstek' on the menu is a beefsteak (though the waiter will assure you it is), as it will be veal. The other disadvantage of meat in Spain is that it tends to be tough, not owing to the quality so much as because the hot climate discourages the Spaniards from 'hanging' their meat for a few days, as we used to do in England; and alternatively, if kept in the ice-box, they cannot be persuaded to let it melt out gradually by exposure to the air temperature before beginning to cook it. Consequently, coming straight from the ice-box to the table it cannot be tender, however good the quality may be.

The use of oil instead of lard, margarine, or butter as the staple form of cooking fat is the subject of many Anglo-Saxon complaints. In fact, good oil is far superior to anything except butter—and butter is a little-known foreign luxury in Spain, again because of the lack of pasturage already mentioned. You can get excellent butter in all first-class restaurants, but you must ask for it specially, and you can, on request, always have your food cooked in butter if you prefer it. There is no shortage; it is just that quite half the population of Spain have never eaten (and never wanted to eat) butter, and the

other half are hopelessly puzzled that you should prefer to use
it when there is good olive oil to be had. I recently saw an
indignant letter in a provincial paper from an English school
teacher, in which she complained eloquently of the fact that
'butter and tea are unknown to the poor Spaniards, and many
of them are reduced to eating raw ham and dry bread, upon
which, if they can, they will sometimes pour oil'. She added
'It seems that they have nothing to drink but a pale yellow liquid
out of a bottle, which I take it was brandy'.

I wrote to the good lady and pointed out that, offered the free
gift of a pound of butter or a litre of oil, nine out of ten
Spaniards would select the oil; that tea in Spain was regarded
as a medicine, for use when your stomach was upset, and that
being deprived of it meant much the same to the Spaniard
as it would mean to the British housewife if she were suddenly
and brutally deprived of her shark's-fin soup. I added that the
'raw' ham she referred to is, in fact, smoked and not raw,
and tastes rather like smoked salmon, while the pale yellow
liquid was white wine with a little water, which would cost 6d.
a bottle in Spain and 12s. 6d. in Britain. However, the good
lady never replied, and I have a nasty suspicion that she regards
me as just another fascist beast! Because of the meat's tendency
to be tough (and I assure you this is not universal), the Spaniards
themselves favour stews (cocidos), but, lest you should have
visions of the tasteless horror designated as stew in Britain, let
me hasten to assure you that your stew in Spain will have a
flavour of wine, red peppers, garlic, and various savoury green
herbs. The cocido of Galicia, Spain's north-westernmost
province, is particularly good.

There is no shortage of game for the table in Spain, especially
partridge. There is also venison, all forms of wild geese and
duck (from the magnificent shooting near Valencia), hare,
pigeon, &c., all in season, and you will see chickens and,
around Christmas, turkeys turning on a spit before the open-
air grills that burn on street-corners outside many popular
restaurants in the bigger cities.

A really memorable Spanish meat dish is roast suckling pig

(cochinillo), which is particular to Castile, and so tender that it can be carved with the blunt edge of a plate in such restaurants as El Botin in Madrid (where you can try roast kid if the cochinillo is finished), Casa Candido in Segovia, and El Castellano in Burgos.

Eggs, of course, are unrationed in Spain like everything else, and the traditional Spanish omelet, containing squares of fried potato and onions, is a noble picnic dish, while a plain French omelet makes a good breakfast in a country where no one can boil an egg properly because they cannot be bothered to look at the clock for three whole minutes for a matter of so little culinary satisfaction.

Cheeses are fair only, though some of the goat cheeses are excellent, and the Basques produce a few that will stand comparison with a ripe Stilton or blue Cheshire of pre-war days.

The Catalan town of Vich, in the foothills of the Pyrenees, where grazing is better than anywhere except in Asturias, is famous for its numerous varieties of sausage—salami, chorizo (pork with a great deal of red pepper), and many others. From this part, too, come some of the really superb smoked hams which, if the lean only is sliced wafer thin, is one of the most appetizing accompaniments to a drink yet devised by man. The best I have ever eaten is in a small and not at all elegant-looking bar called after its owner Xatet ('snub-nose' in Catalan) which is to be found in the little sea-side town of Sitges near Barcelona. Xatet himself tells me that he keeps some of his mountain pig hams for over seven years before eating them.

Incidentally, do not forget that if you ask simply for ham ('jamon', pronounced 'hamon') you will get smoked ham, known more fully as 'jamon serrano'. If you want the ordinary kind of York ham (which will also probably come from Vich) it will be out of a tin—though excellent in quality—and you must ask for 'jamon en dulce' (sweet ham).

Fruit, of course, is one of the marvels of Spanish food, and it is really easier to specify the fruits that are *not* good rather than those that are.

In my opinion, you will never get a Spanish apple, pear, apricot, or peach to compare with the best in Britain. The Spaniards claim that the apples of Asturias are the best, and they certainly produce an admirable cider from them, while the hard mountain pears of the Pyrenees town of Puigcerdá have a distinctive flavour. Distinctive, too, are the flat peaches of Madrid—yes, really flat—the like of which I have met only in Ankara.

For the rest, fruit is superb all the year round, from the first wild strawberries served in kirsh in March to the ordinary strawberries, raspberries, cherries, fresh figs, various types of melon, plums, and grapes—black, red, rose, green, and muscatel. And you must try the exotic cactus fruit known as a 'chirimoya'. As the Canary Islands are Spanish it is unnecessary to be over seventy, under sixteen, or pregnant in order to eat all the bananas you may fancy for a penny apiece. To talk of Spain is to talk of oranges, and a tumbler full of fresh orange-juice can be had for a song any time between November and May.

Vegetables are more varied than in Britain, with the aubergine (translated, for some mysterious reason, as 'egg-plant' in English, and known in Spain as the 'berenjena') lending itself to various interesting blends, with minced meat and tomatoes.

Notable among the local dishes is the 'paella valenciana'. This has a foundation of rice (turned yellowish-brown with saffron) and is cooked for twenty minutes in an iron dish that will contain the hearts of artichokes, red peppers, chicken, rabbit, olives, tiny shell-fish, prawns, and various spiced herbs and delicacies, according to the inspiration of the individual cook. This is served at the table in the original iron dish in which it has been cooked.

But for the gastronome it is the fish that he will eat during his holiday in Spain that will provide him with one of his pleasantest memories. I am often asked, 'But isn't fish a bit dangerous in such a warm climate?' The answer is that fish, if it is not fresh, is dangerous anywhere, and that in a hot climate the chances of it going bad are obviously greater than

in a cold one. But you do not have to speak Spanish to recognize fish that is not fresh, and there is no scientific reason to
suppose that Spaniards are less susceptible to ptomaine
poisoning than we are.

Although there are special daily refrigerated fish-trains to
Madrid which assure that the capital is well and freshly
supplied, care is obviously necessary in summer in any city
which is some 350 miles by rail from the Bay of Biscay and
300 miles from the nearest Mediterranean port. However, anywhere in Spain less remote from the sea than Madrid, and even
there for nine months of the year, you need have no more
anxiety about eating fish than you would at home.

Vizcaya is one of the three Spanish Basque provinces, and the
British paid them the compliment of naming this particular
limit of the Atlantic the Bay of Biscay ('Biscay' apparently
being as near as any reasonable Englishman can get to 'Vizcaya').
The Basques themselves always refer to their northern coast as
the Cantabrican Sea, and for this reason you will find countless
restaurants all over Spain called 'Cantabrico', since it is in that
colder northern sea that the best fish are caught.

Small but finely flavoured oysters come from here, costing
about 5s., or 70 cents, a dozen. You will have some difficulty in
persuading the locals to give you tobasco, Worcester sauce, or
red pepper, as they consider that anything except lemon des-
troys the flavour. From this area, too, comes one of the really
great specialities of the Spanish cuisine, 'angulas a la bilbaina'.
Here we are up against the conservatives, who will demand
what they are, and will turn pale when told that they are baby
eels, caught in a fine net at the point where a river becomes
tidal—though why baby eels should be more disgusting than,
for example, unborn sturgeon's eggs—i.e. caviar—I cannot
see! They are caught and eaten at the mouth of the River
Severn under the name of 'elvas'.

Anyway, take my word for it that you will do well to try
angulas at least once. They are cooked in boiling oil with
an unbroken clove of garlic and a red pepper, and served in
the same little earthenware dish, with the oil still boiling. You

eat them with a wooden fork direct from the dish, under no circumstances touching them with metal.

Dressed crab (centollos), mussels, and clams (almejas) are all very plentiful and cheap along the Basque coast, and they are presented in a variety of different forms and flavours. Of course, there are also the more ordinary sole (lenguado), hake (merluza), and a dozen others everywhere available. But Spain's fishy speciality is the crustacea, crayfish (langosta), lobster, giant prawns (langostinos), prawns (gambas), Dublin Bay prawns (cigalas) and shrimps (quisquillas—meaning 'tickles'). Incidentally, I notice that my American friends mistakenly tend to call all these last four by the single, inadequate, name of shrimps. It would be equally misleading to refer to the felines to be found in Bengal as 'cats', when they are more commonly known as 'tigers'!

The crustacea come from both the Cantabrican Sea and also from the Mediterranean, 'langostinos'—perhaps the finest flavoured of them all when fresh grilled—being particularly excellent on the coast of the province of Castellon, just north of Valencia.

For better or for worse you cannot be long in Spain without becoming aware of the squid—though he may be hiding under such diverse names as 'pulpos', 'pulpitos', 'calamares', and 'chipirones'.

To my taste pulpos and calamares tend to be rubbery, however well they are cooked. 'Chipirones en su tinta' are much appreciated, when cooked in the ink which is common to all the octopus family, though I myself gave up ink as being suitable for nourishment at the age of five. Certainly the best squid dish is 'pulpitos salteados', where the tiny creatures, barely an inch and a half across, are stewed in fine oil with a touch of garlic and fresh tomato sauce.

The Catalans produce a fishy mixed grill which they call 'zarzuela de pescado'—'a musical comedy of fish'—in which five or six varieties are fried rather dry and then anointed with butter, green herbs, and chopped-onion sauce. However, all along the coast you will find the 'fritura de pescado'—'mixed fish fry'—and it is particularly pleasant when the weather is too hot for meat. In similar weather the Andaluz speciality is the cold soup known as 'gazpacho'—clear, strongly flavoured with raw chopped vegetables, and very refreshing.

For colder weather is the 'bouillabaisse', to be had in the Barcelona restaurant Caracoles (snails). Previously I had thought that the bouillabaisse to be found in the restaurants around the Old Port in Marseilles was the last word in fish soup, but I can assure you that according to Catalan standards the Marseilles variety is next door to starvation. However, be warned by me not to order anything else heavy to eat after it, as, although officially soup, each portion seems to contain about 1 lb. of lobster, mussels, prawns, &c., and alone constitutes a full meal for my austerity-stomached compatriots.

Fresh-water fish is in smaller supply, of course, but the spotted trout I caught myself 50 miles north of Madrid last June would have satisfied the most exacting gourmet, and the 18-lb. salmon I shared with my good friend Max Borrell, beside the swift River Narcea on the borders of Asturias and Galicia, is still devoutly remembered by us both.

Small fresh-water crayfish (cangrejos), a speciality of Burgos, should not be forgotten if you happen to be in Castile in June or July, and you may buy them in bars in Madrid at that time of the year to accompany your sun-downer drink.

For the young members of your party I should perhaps mention that there is no kind of shortage or restrictions upon chocolate or any form of 'candy' in Spain, and that there are several Spanish specialities—such as the sweet almond paste of Gijona—which they should certainly try.

So much for food; but, before turning to wine and other drinks, I should like to draw attention to the way in which one blends with the other in Spain owing to the admirable habit of the 'tapa'.

In Spain, when you order a drink in a bar or café, you will always be given, free of charge, something to eat, or at least to nibble. With your sixpenny brandy-and-soda or a bottle of beer, your twopenny glass of sherry, or even your penny glass of white or red wine, you will be presented with a tapa. This may consist of some fresh prawns, a chunk of 'cortesa' (pork crackling), a couple of fat olives transfixed with a tooth-pick and draped with an anchovy, a sliver of smoked ham, or any other of a hundred small inducements to thirst, depending upon the season and the place. Doctors say that it is an excellent practice to eat something with any alcoholic drink but, excellent or not, it is an extremely agreeable one.

Spain is a land of wine—Scotch whisky is madly expensive, almost as expensive as in Scotland—and gin is indifferent, though beer, of the light German type, is quite good. But, unless you really dislike them, try to make the most of the Spanish wines during your stay.

Wine is grown in every Spanish province, and in your travels you may always discover a local 'corriente' (vin ordinaire) that is outstanding, but which, either because it is produced in small quantities or, more probably, because it will not travel without deterioration, is unknown out of the area in which it is grown.

Apart from such accidents, it is safe to say that Spain's best table wines, both red and white, are those from Rioja, grown in the area surrounding the town of Logroño, about half-way between Burgos and Pamplona.

Well-known makes, selling both red and white wines of the claret and light burgundy type, are Marques de Murrieta and Marques de Riscal.

For sweet wines Malaga is the centre, though Sitges produces a sweet 'malvasia' thought so good by Queen Isabella the Catholic in 1496 that she reserved the whole supply for her personal use.

Brandy is good and cheap everywhere in Spain. All the large producers, such as Gonzalez Byass, Domecq, Bobadilla, and Osborne, have their establishments in or near the town of Jerez de la Frontera. The 'corriente' cognac sells at about 28 pts—say 5s. or 70 cents—a bottle, and makes an excellent drink, with soda-water, for the occasions when normally you would fancy a whisky-and-soda.

D

Of the liqueur kinds, Bobadilla Gran Reserva, costing about 35s. or $4.50 (not Bobadilla '103', which is a 'corriente' brandy), and Gonzalez Byass' Lepanto, which markets around £3 a bottle, are both fine liqueurs. It should be realized at once that they are not attempting to be imitations of French brandy but are something belonging to the country.

There is a general tendency to believe that the only good wines come from France. I would agree that France produces the best wines in the world, but how many would-be connoisseurs know that the biggest individual buyer of Spanish wine is—France!

The explanation is that the alcoholic content of the French wines tends to be too low, often as little as 8%, whereas the Spanish wines, in a dry year, will contain as much as 15% and are usually around 12% or 13%. The French wine traders therefore like to give some of their own delicate but weak wines an injection of the Spanish, to raise the alcoholic content to 10% or 11%.

So when your worldly-wise clubman puts down his glass and, with a sigh of satisfaction, says, 'There is nothing like a good French wine', he is unaware that the source of his satisfaction, though of course irreproachably labelled 'Château Parbleu de Diable 1908', was, in part at least, grown in Spain around 1948. I have no wish to spoil his illusions, and I only mention the fact so that you will have no prejudices against Spanish wines just because you happen to admire French ones.

Since the fitting end to a good meal is a good cigar to accompany your coffee and liqueur brandy, I may mention that owing to some special commercial agreement between Spain and her former colony, real Havana cigars are plentiful and, judged by British prices, very cheap.

Most of the best-known brands, Romeo and Julietta, Henry Clay, Bolivar, &c., are available, and a normal full-sized one will cost you about 3s. 6d. or 75 cents.

American cigarettes are on sale in every café and tobacconist's and cost about 2s. 2d. or 30 cents for twenty. English cigarettes are virtually unobtainable except near Gibraltar, and the local ones, from tobacco grown in the Canary Islands, are mild but gritty.

To descend from the sublime to what is, if not the ridiculous, at least the humdrum: a word on the subject of water.

As already mentioned, all the guide or travel books on Spain that I have seen relate to pre-1951 conditions, when the Great Drought was still unbroken. Obviously the tap-water at the end of that period was unreliable, and there were a few cases of typhoid reported from Malaga and the Levante. However, there were many more unreported cases of colitis which, although not serious if dealt with by rigid diet and keeping quiet for a couple of days, were yet sufficiently disagreeable at least partly to spoil the sufferer's holiday.

To-day, after three rainy winters, the tap-water is safe enough in most places (it always was safe, of course, all along the north coast), but I personally would advise travellers when they get a little off the map, especially when inland from the Mediterranean coast, to avoid tap-water in Spain. If you do not want wine and water (which is what most Spanish mothers give their children as soon as they are off milk), and do not like beer or the sickly sweet, coloured 'gaseosas', nor even milk or cider, then there are numerous kinds of excellent mineral waters to be had. Among those most universally on sale is the dead flat 'Solares', the slightly fizzy 'Vichy Catalan' or 'Imperial', and the very fizzy 'Borines'. They are not cheap, costing anything from 6 to 12 pts for a litre bottle—but they still work out cheaper than colitis!

Many Americans seem to suffer from the illusion that by putting a lot of ice in the water they thereby make it safe. Far from making the water safe, it is the ice—which may have been sitting for hours on the street pavement until the owner was ready to collect it—that very often infects the otherwise pure water.

This is not a major problem, only one of those little things, ignorance of which might possibly spoil for a few days your enjoyment of your holiday.

Now in all this talk of food and drink we have made no

serious mention of sherry—the wine that is grown only in
Spain. This was deliberate, because sherry deserves a chapter
to itself and we have been invited to spend a whole day as the
guest of Don Carlos Gonzalez in the famous sherry bodegas
of Gonzalez Byass, in the very heart of Jerez de la Frontera
(see page 139).

V

SPANISH ART

THIS is a tremendous subject, so tremendous that it cannot be wholly ignored, even by the casual tourist, without grievous loss.

There are many people who come to Spain primarily because of the country's great artistic heritage, and there are several excellent books available which will take them upon an almost picture-by-picture journey round the peninsula lasting for several months. They are, however, the exception and for most visitors it is sufficient to know where they can spend an occasional half-hour or hour, seeing nothing but the very best that the country has to offer, but without attempting to make an exhaustive study of the subject.

There are also a large number of visitors who would not dream of going into an art gallery in any circumstances, and they can safely skip this short chapter. For the normally art-conscious remainder at least some slight knowledge of the masterpieces that may be seen in Spain will add a great deal to the pleasure they may obtain from their visit.

Italy holds an unrivalled place in the world of art, if only for the tremendous flowering known to us as the Renaissance, but the Anglo-Saxons became conscious of it largely from the artistic writers of the nineteenth century. If Byron, the Brownings, and above all Ruskin (to mention only three of a dozen august names) had not made Italy into something like a religious cult, it is doubtful whether her treasures would have been so generally regarded as approaching the sum total of artistic achievement.

While not for a moment attempting to suggest that Spanish art could ever have successfully rivalled that of Italy, I think it is worth considering the reasons which prevented her from doing so.

The first is the physical fact that all Spain's intellectual forces were dedicated to a vast crusade until the expulsion of the Moors was achieved in 1492, and she accordingly turned to the development of her artistic talents a century later than Italy.

The second must be laid as a charge against the Church in Spain, which forbade the painting of nudes at a time when the same Church in Italy freely permitted it. This retarded the representation of the human form, which was the principal subject of the Italian Masters, and confined the Spaniards to endless repetitions of sacred subjects which, however inspiring, severely limited the scope of artistic development. This prudish attitude was not confined to the fifteenth, sixteenth, and seventeenth centuries, but flared up anew as late as the reign of Charles III in 1777, when priceless canvases representing nude figures by Titian, Botticelli, Rubens, and Tintoretto had to be hidden in dark cellars for fear that the priest-incited crowd would burn them in the public squares as 'indecent'.

Despite these restrictions, the art of El Greco, Velazquez, Ribera, Murillo, and Goya alone is sufficient to prove how much greater would have been Spain's and the world's artistic heritage if those handicaps had not been there.

Nearly every provincial capital in Spain has its own art gallery, and some contain canvases that are without equal—notably those of Valencia, Bilbao, Barcelona, Seville, and Cadiz for Zurbarán. But, by and large, the best of every artist has, since 1816, been assembled in the Prado Museum in the centre of Madrid, where to-day there are well over 1,000 canvases on exhibition—these 1,000 being the pick of the 3,000 actually in its possession.

Among the 1,000 on view there are works by Van der Weyden, Fra Angelico, Bellini, Botticelli, Brueghel, Canaletto, Gerard David, Dürer, Greuze, Jordaens, Mantegna, Memling, Quentin Metsys, Poussin, Raphael, Rembrandt, Reynolds, Romney, Rubens, Teniers, Tiepolo, Tintoretto, Titian, Van Dyck, Van Orley, Veronese, and Watteau—none of them Spanish, but when added to the unrivalled collection of work by Spanish Masters, entitling the Prado to claim the position of the third best art gallery in the world. The best of these are concentrated upon the first floor—a fact worth noting. While it is only third in the world as a complete collection, it is unquestionably first in the world in its collection of Spanish artists, and it is this aspect of the Prado upon which I wish to concentrate.

The early Spanish artists, prior that is to the year 1400, are well represented, but for most students of Spanish art the first arresting figure is that of El Greco, whose real name was Domenikos Theotokopoulos. He was born in Crete in 1541 and studied in Venice, so that at first glance it may seem strange to speak of him as a Spanish artist, but before he was 30 he was established in Spain, where he evolved a strongly personal and mystic style of unmistakably Spanish inspiration, which he employed until his death in Toledo, in 1614, at the age of 73.

Some of his best works can be seen in his carefully preserved house in Toledo, and the most famous of all, his 'Burial of the Count of Orgaz', is also in a church there, to which reference is made in Chapter VIII. Despite these exceptions, however, the Prado's collection of thirty-two of his canvases is sufficiently representative for a visitor to obtain a full impression of every phase of his work. These are to be seen in Hall 30, on the first floor.

Greco's reputation to-day stands as high as that of any artist the world has ever seen, but it is only within living memory that this has occurred. Quite late in the nineteenth century eminent critics were describing him as 'insane' and his paintings as 'revolting caricatures', and, if they are viewed as attempts to reproduce visual facts, such descriptions are sometimes not difficult to understand. Put quite simply, Greco sought to paint a man's soul, spirit, character, or whatever you choose to call it, and not—or only incidentally—his body. He was a kind of psychoanalyst, struggling to render things of the spirit in terms of the body, and such a task demands perception on the part of the beholder as well as on that of the artist. His vision in painting his saints was of their spirits drawn upwards from their frail bodies by a force that, to him, seemed to distort and elongate the flesh that held them.

Greco is an acquired taste, but the tremendous power of his work can be appreciated by a very simple test. This consists of leaving a ten-minute study of Greco and going direct to those of another acknowledged Master such as, for example, Murillo. The effect is of drinking grocer's port after Imperial Tokay!

Greco's influence upon Spanish art was immediate and far-reaching, and opened the way to such purely Spanish artists as Claudio Coello (Halls 29, 74, 90, and 91), Francisco Herrera (Hall 29), del Mazo (Halls 11, 12, 29, and 88), Murillo (Halls 28, 90, and 91), Ribalta (Halls 26 and 89), Ribera (Halls 26, 90, and 91), Zurbarán (Hall 26), and even to the great Velazquez himself.

The seventeenth century—so disastrous for her politically—was Spain's artistic Golden Age, and the peak of that age was epitomized by the work of Diego Rodriguez de Silva Velazquez, born in Seville fifteen years before the death of El Greco and dying at the age of 61 in 1660. His great patron was the unfortunate, dissolute, but culturally intelligent King Philip IV, whose infant and almost idiot son Charles, born to his old age, was to end the once great line of Hapsburg rulers of Spain.

To admire Velazquez you do not require the artistic perception that is necessary to appreciate Greco: he was concerned with the outward aspect of his subjects, though he laid upon much of his work a special kind of enchantment. This is difficult to explain but easy to recognize by looking at the most famous of all his paintings, known as 'Las Meninas'—'The Maids of Honour'—which is in a small room quite by itself numbered Hall 15. There is some quality of light and shade here that puts me in mind of the old German legend of how a powerful magician could freeze into a mirror the reflection of a certain moment in time. The illusion is strengthened by the fact that 'Las Meninas' is placed opposite to a mirror, in which certain qualities can be perceived which escape you when looking at the picture itself. One day, perhaps, the magician will say the word that froze to stillness that particular moment in the Court of Philip IV, and the figures of nearly 300 years ago will move again to complete the actions in which they were magically caught and held.

Though 'Las Meninas', with the exquisite figure of the ugly little Princess in the centre, is considered Velazquez's supreme masterpiece, many people prefer 'The Spinners'; and there are no fewer than fifty canvases in the Prado from his brush—a greater number than is possessed by any other gallery in the world.

Velazquez's immediate successor was Bartolomé Esteban Murillo, who survived him by twenty-two years. His idealization of women and children (personally, I long to kick his impossibly angelic little boys), appeals unalterably to the Spanish passion for children. There are fifteen of Murillo's canvases in Hall 28, sixteen in Hall 90, and four more in Hall 91.

The years of the Golden Century of Spanish art were now running out. As Murillo is a step down from Greco or Velazquez, so too is Claudio Coello a further step down from Murillo —but it was still just the Golden Century when he died in 1693, and you may find his seven pictures in Halls 29, 74, 90, and 91 of interest, even if only in order to trace the outlines of the artistically bleak three-quarters of a century that were to follow.

From this long period of decadence there exploded the gigantic personality of Francisco Goya, born in 1746 but achieving fame and real maturity only in the last quarter of the eighteenth century and the first quarter of the nineteenth. The same reasons that cause the Spaniards to admire Murillo automatically ensure their dislike, or grudging admission of the greatness of Goya. While Murillo idealizes and observes all the most obvious conventions, Goya debunks and defies the whole established order of things. Velazquez captured a golden age by magic; Murillo saw a decadent age through rose-tinted spectacles; and Goya painted a dying age with a brush dipped in vitriol and blood.

The stages of his development are clearly marked. The

young Goya painted angels in the likeness of the less reputable ladies of his considerable acquaintance, and left his native Saragossa in a hurry when the Inquisition started making inquiries into his private life.

The middle-aged Goya was Court painter to that peculiar 'ménage à trois' that consisted of King Charles IV, his Italian wife Maria Luisa, and her peasant-born lover (and actual ruler of Spain) Godoy, Prince of the Peace. Looking at the vicious monkey, nymphomaniac character of the Queen, exposed with a clarity so brutal as to be almost frightening in every one of Goya's portraits of her, I have always wondered how he survived without being shot for high treason! Belonging to the same period is the masterly portrait of his painter brother-in-law, Francisco Bayeu (Hall 34), whose more or less permanent disapproval of him he has so miraculously captured, and the world-famous 'majas'—the naked and the clothed—supposedly of the Duchess of Alba, whom the romantic like to believe was one of his many mistresses.

The third period is the elderly Goya, stone deaf, mourning his dead wife, brushed by the wings of insanity, and yet inspired in one final flare-up of tremendous rage against the Napoleonic invasion to produce the most terrible indictment of war ever recorded, of which his 'Executions of Moncloa' is perhaps the best known (Hall 35).

The 'show' Goyas are to be found in Halls 32, 33, 34, 35, and 36, and again in Hall 95. His designs for the Royal Tapestry Works are in Halls 55, 56, and 57, but if you are a real Goya enthusiast (as I must admit that I am), then find your way to the obscure corner dignified by the title of Hall 36 where the Spaniards rather uneasily hide away the violent, tortured, terrifying outpourings of the deaf giant's immense genius which are referred to as the 'black paintings'.

These were saved by Baron Emil d'Erlanger in 1873 from the decaying walls of Goya's house, upon which they were painted between the years 1819 and 1823, when the place was locally known and shunned as 'Deaf Man's Folly'. Psychologically and artistically these revelations of the septuagenarian mind are unforgettable, particularly those known as the 'Witches' Sabbath'.

I quote an eminent Spanish art critic on the subject: 'It is difficult to believe that such rude strokes of the brush as are displayed in the "black paintings" could have been made by the same hand as performed the delicate, silvery touches of Goya's portrait of Bayeu'. In short, if I may be permitted to quote a now happily defunct maiden aunt, Goya was, on occasions, 'not quate nace'—but I think the 'black paintings' are, after Velazquez's 'Las Meninas', the best thing in the whole of the Prado.

At the end of the excellent film 'That Hamilton Woman', a character who has been told of the events ending in the death of Admiral Nelson asks 'What happened after that'? The reply was, 'After that—nothing happened.' As to Spanish art I would say the same: 'After Goya—nothing happened', though in this I may be doing less than justice to the polite portraitists of the late nineteenth and early twentieth centuries, who are as good or bad as any that have emerged elsewhere during the same period.

As a final word of advice, do not attempt to 'do' the Prado in a single visit. Take a half-hour a day for a particular artist, and make straight to and from the Halls where his pictures are to be found; and do not risk the critical exhaustion of wading along through vast areas of underdone meat (which may, or may not, represent Rubens' idea of feminine beauty) on your way to or from the artist whose work you wish to see. After a certain time, varying with the individual, one's perceptions become dulled by surfeit, and capacity for enjoyment, or even appreciation, is temporarily exhausted. You best appreciate a fine wine by slowly savouring its bouquet. It would be a pity to 'bolt' your visit to the Prado.

VI

ADVENTURES IN SHOPPING

IT is always exciting to find that you can buy luxuries abroad for a small part of the price you would have to pay for them at home, assuming that they can be bought there at all.

Spain is a particularly happy hunting ground in this respect, and my object now is to indicate those things which are a particularly 'good buy'. I have not, however, attempted to work out the Customs Duty that you will have to pay upon introducing them into Britain or the United States (Americans can, of course, take back $500-worth of foreign purchases from anywhere in Europe), since there are too many unknown elements involved in any such calculations. I have always found the British Customs extremely tolerant in their attitude towards the introduction of articles bought abroad if these are obviously for your own personal use and not suitable for re-sale. Thus it may be a bargain to buy in Spain a limited number of any of the things I mention, but would be quite the reverse if you bought them in large quantities. All I have done is to list the things which can be bought in Spain of a superior quality and inferior price to anything of the same kind that you can buy at home.

Clothes. A man's suit, at a really first-class tailor, made of English or best Catalan cloth (for light-weight suits the latter is as good as the former) to-day will cost—in Madrid or Barcelona—2,200 pts, or about £20 or $55. The normal time for making it is a fortnight, but for an extra 200 pts you can obtain it in as little as three days.

For women's clothes such houses as Pedro Rodriguez sell 'models' for about one-third of their price in Paris. The best 'buy' for women, however, is the ready-made summer frock, or 'between-season' coat and skirt, for £8 or £10, which are exquisite. Silk or artificial silk hand-embroidered 'lingerie' is a Spanish specialty, at correspondingly low prices.

Shoes have always been a Spanish speciality, though they are built for a less severe climate than the British. Men's antelope shoes ready made cost about £3 10s. a pair and, made to order, £5.

Ties. Artificial silk or wool, from 5s. to 10s. Pure silk from 15s. to £1.

Leather Work. The extreme beauty of hand-made Spanish leather goods of all kinds—suit-cases, note-cases, toilet-cases, cushions, &c.—is a continuation of the Moorish tradition introduced into Europe through Cordoba in the Middle Ages. It is not particularly cheap, but is of a quality not to be found anywhere else in the world. Women's handbags, men's wallets, and above everything *gloves* are superb. For these last try the little shop almost opposite the Palace Hotel in Madrid—known as 'El Guante Verde'.

Linen. If you want to buy some hope chest sheets, you will save the cost of your trip to Spain on the difference in price between half a dozen pairs of sheets compared with what you would have to pay for them at home.

Hand-embroidered table-cloths with six napkins cost £2 10s.

Lace. All over Spain the ancient female relatives are set to making lace—and the clicking noise of the bobbins as they are manipulated at incredible speed is one of those small and unmistakable noises that will subsequently always recall the country to your memory. (Another is the click of lace fans being opened and shut during mass in the dim interior of the churches.) Often in remote villages in Catalonia each old woman has her own private pattern (which she hands on to her eldest daughter), and she will sell you as much as you want, exquisitely done, for a few shillings a yard.

Glass. The pale green glass of Majorca is already known to collectors as rivalling that of Venice. The price in Spain of ordinary, everyday tumblers and wine-glasses is about a fifth of the cost of similar articles in London.

Curtain Materials and Tapestry. Granada produces some most attractive heavy woollen curtains with a 'motiv' that a visitor pointed out to me was of Mexican design, with the stylized birds and flowers of Central American native embroideries. I did not bother to point out that the Mexicans got it from the Spaniards in the sixteenth century. It is most rich and original in appearance, and sells for about 30s. a yard.

You will find pieces of old embroidery on velvet, heavy with real gold and silver thread, in every antique shop in Spain. A piece worked perhaps in the form of a coat-of-arms makes a most attractive wall-hanging.

Gaily coloured plaited mats of all sizes made of palm leaves are decorative, clean, and very cheap everywhere in Spain, as also is raffia work for shopping bags, baskets, or hampers.

Copper Pots and Pans—highly burnished and made by hand—together with wrought-iron lamps, brackets, &c., are the speciality of the Andalusian town of Ronda, but can be bought almost anywhere.

Glazed earthenware, with coloured designs, is particularly lovely in Spain, and I have found it a very welcome and inexpensive present. I gave a large salad bowl recently to some London friends, who told me that the same thing would cost them £1 to 30s. I had paid 2s. 6d.!

There is an infinite variety of pots, jugs, vases, bowls, basins, dishes, platters, &c., from which to choose—most of them made in Talavera de la Reina, Lucena, Alcora, and Triana.

However, a word is necessary on the subject of the locality in which you go shopping.

As a safe general rule you may take it that everything costs 25% more in Catalonia than in the rest of Spain, though against that must be balanced the fact that the Barcelona shops have a greater variety, and probably better taste, than anywhere else, even including Madrid. Barcelona has always been more expensive than any other town in Spain ever since I first went there twenty years ago, and the only explanation I have ever heard is that the inhabitants of the Catalan capital have more money to spend. Whether or not this is true I cannot say, but the fact that prices there are considerably higher is undeniable.

As a gift for children it is worth remembering that the

variety and ingenuity of toys and their relatively low cost are just another manifestation of the Spaniards' idolatrous worship of their young, to which I have referred elsewhere. Chocolates and sweets generally are also excellent—in fact exactly the same as they were in Britain before the war. However, here a strange change of taste has taken place, of which the British themselves are usually unaware. Through the compulsion of long years of sugar rationing and real shortage, the British have become accustomed to going without sweet things, and the children who started eating sweets before 1939 are already sixteen or seventeen years old. There is, therefore, an entire new generation of candy-chewers whose taste has been formed to meet the national shortage of sugar. To them Spanish chocolate and 'candy' seem far too sweet—as would have seemed those of their own country as sold fifteen years or more ago.

I have attempted only to indicate the broad lines along which to direct your bargain-hunting while in Spain. Without knowing individual tastes it is pointless to attempt to do more.

In Madrid the street known as the Gran Via or the Avenida José Antonio, and in Barcelona that called the Paseo de Gracia, contain the finest shops, but since their position ensures sales, their prices are higher than elsewhere. In Madrid I would advise such near-by streets as Peligros, Clavel, Carmen, or the Calle de Cedaceros, and in Barcelona the Ramblas or, still cheaper, that which leads from the Ramblas to the Ayuntamiento (Town Hall).

I myself have never experienced a holiday at the end of which I had money to spend on buying bargains, but no doubt there are many provident people who arrange their finances better.

In Spain they should be able to reap the reward of their wisdom and return home with some attractive and valuable souvenir for a fraction of what they would have had to pay for it in their own country—or would have had to pay, always assuming that its equivalent could be found, which is by no means certain.

PART II

THE LAND OF SPAIN

VII

MADRID

IT is really only during the last few years that Madrid has become the capital of Spain in fact as well as in name. The Franco régime has forced it to grow up and take its place as the intellectual, as well as the administrative, heart of the nation, thus completing the idea first conceived by Philip II.

Spain is composed of such completely dissimilar elements—the Basques and the Catalans, each with a separate language; the Andalusians and Valencians, more Moorish than European in blood and character—that regionalism has always been very strong. Under the Republic of 1931–6 this tendency towards decentralization was encouraged and, to ensure support against Franco, something like independent Basque and Catalan governments were set up in Bilbao and Barcelona. Franco is opposed to regionalism, and history would seem to justify his belief that Spain can only be an economic unit if separatist tendencies are suppressed. We in Britain adopted the same attitude towards Wales and Scotland, and the American Civil War was fought, primarily, with the same motive.

Since the end of the Spanish Civil War in 1939, therefore, every effort has been made to concentrate the limelight upon Madrid, and the result is immediately apparent to anyone who, like myself, is able to compare the city of the nineteen-thirties with that of to-day.

There was quite a struggle in order to coax the population of Madrid to surpass that of Barcelona, which, when I first knew Spain, was at least 200,000 more than that of the capital, but, partly by including suburban villages in the metropolis and partly by a gigantic building scheme, it is now officially 1,400,000 to Barcelona's 1,300,000. This building scheme is one of the first things that will strike you. Madrid was right in the firing line for over two years, and whole districts were reduced to rubble, so that there was no difficulty in finding building sites, and huge blocks of apartment houses and flats have been shooting up like mushrooms ever since. One is familiar with boom towns, and also with ancient cities, but Madrid is a rare combination of both.

While it has only become the capital in fact during the last few years, it has also only been the capital in name for a time which, for a country of such ancient institutions, is relatively short. The Moors had a fortress there, and Philip II in 1561 decided that its almost mathematically central position made it a desirable seat of Government. His son disagreed with him and removed to Valladolid in 1601, and it was only in 1607 that its title as Spain's capital was finally settled.

Apart from its central position (the little monastery-crowned hill, known as the navel of Spain, can be seen from the south-eastern suburbs), it is difficult to understand why King Philip should have selected a place 2,000 feet above sea-level, blasted by temperatures of over 100° F. in summer, and swept by icy gales from the Guadarrama snow mountains in winter. The local definition of Madrid's climate is 'nine months of winter, and three months of hell' and, although unkind, it is a fair description. Madrileños defend it by saying that it is dry, though I cannot see that being either cooked or frozen is any more agreeable on that account.

However, since it is a great city, climate is not all-important, and in its nearly three and a half centuries as the capital it has become a tourist centre of world importance, though my personal advice is to avoid it during July, August, January, and February. The best months there are April, May, June, October, and November.

Madrid possesses some 150 listed hotels, from such luxury establishments as the older Ritz and Palace and the 1953 Plaza, Wellington and Hilton, to modest little pensiones where you can sleep and eat for 60 pts a day. For a stay of a month or more the little Mayorazgo Hotel, in a back street 100 yards from the main shopping, night-club, restaurant, cinema, theatre street, currently called the Avenida José Antonio and generally known as the Gran Via, is to be recommended. There you can get a double bedroom, private bathroom, and telephone, small sitting-room *and* a tiny kitchenette, with a gas-ring, all for 150 pts a day—and the gas-ring will save you a lot of money on breakfasts and suppers if you need to economize. There are other 'residencias' besides the Mayorazgo, and you may like the idea in that, by taking the rooms without food, you can better afford to try the city's innumerable restaurants.

The huge building known as the Telefónica in the Gran Via is an obvious landmark, though it is no longer (as the guide-books inform you) the tallest building in Spain, having been surpassed by the monster in the Plaza de España which, among other things, houses the Hotel Plaza and its private swimming-pool.

A little farther along you will not, I hope, pass Chicote's famous bar. Chicote's museum of rare bottles is now included on the itinerary of all enquiring visitors.

Continuing along the Gran Via, you cannot miss its inter-section with the street known as Alcalá. A few hundred yards farther on will bring you to a fountain surmounted by a statue of a powerfully built lady driving a chariot drawn by lions. Shying nervously to the left, you will be in the Castellana and, if the weather is kind, you will do well to sit under the trees at one of the avenue's countless cafés, between 9 p.m. and 2 a.m., and take a look at the inhabitants.

For the most they are a good-looking lot and, when they are ugly, they are usually interestingly so. Looking at the ugly ones, you will realize how miraculously Goya captured the deeply lined, half-humorous, half-animal faces that he saw around him a century and a half ago, and how little the type has changed. But one type of face which afflicts me among the Nordic races you will not see, and that is the lineless, empty, vacant, fried-fillet-of-plaice face, that always makes me feel that its designer abandoned his job when only half-completed.

Although you can pass your holiday in Madrid without ever being aware of the fact that it is anything but a twentieth-century boom town, you have only to turn a few corners to drop back into the seventeenth or eighteenth century, with crooked, dark, unevenly paved streets, humming with vital yet half-secret life.

Three minutes' walk from the Puerta del Sol—Madrid's Piccadilly Circus—brings you to the huge Palacio de Santa Cruz. Now it is the Ministry for Foreign Affairs, but not so very long ago it was the headquarters of the dreaded Inquisition. Almost beside it is the Plaza Mayor, built at the opening of the seventeenth century and barely altered since Philip IV, from a balcony, watched his courtiers acting as bull-fighters. From the same balcony his almost idiot son, Charles II, later watched the 'autos de fé', where the prisoners of the Inquisition were 'released to the secular arm'—the pious formula of the day for the process of being burned alive for the good of your soul! Under the arcades of the Plaza Mayor bands of urchins fought with naked knives for leadership—and the shops selling these deadly, slightly curved, blades are still in business.

Within one of the walls of the Plaza is the restaurant Las Cuevas, once the hide-out of a famous highwayman to whose memory there is a delightful little poem painted on the wall describing his crimes, amours, and final execution. The last verse gently reflects that if only he had lived to-day he would not have been thus cruelly executed, but would instead have been made a Cabinet Minister!

Almost next door is the superb little restaurant known as Botin, where you will find roast suckling pig that will melt in your mouth, and where the next table may be occupied by a famous 'matador de toros'. Forget your insular prejudices and try that 'cochinillo'—it is one of the really great dishes of Castile.

If you are determinedly unadventurous about your food, you can pay five times as much in order to eat imitation French cooking at such magnificently elegant places as the Jockey (pronounced Hockey), where the smoked salmon is justly famous, or at Horcher, or Recoletos (with a 'frontón' attached, where you can watch the incredibly fast and exciting Basque game of 'pelota' being played, and lose your shirt betting), or at Chipén, which is particularly good for oysters. For good and

plentiful cheap food try La Hoja de la Selva in the Calle Mora-
tín, not far from the Palace Hotel. There you will find most of
the French Embassy staff, with a sprinkling of other diplomats,
silently eating large and underdone châteaubriand beefsteaks,
preceded by 'lobster americaine', hot, with cheese sauce. I
have found the presence of the local French Embassy staff a
sure indication of good, inexpensive food, everywhere from
Bucharest to Baghdad—and you are not obliged to eat as much
as they do!

A little serious sight-seeing is essential, and in the chapter
on Spanish Art I have attempted to indicate the incomparable
riches that await the picture-lover in the Prado Museum. A
good second to the Prado is the huge Royal Palace, which stands
on the edge of the bluff that, for two and a half years, marked
the front line of battle for the contending forces in the Civil
War but which, despite a few ugly scars, was respected by
both.

The principal building of Madrid has always stood on this
site, and when Philip II decided to make the city his capital he
rebuilt the existing Moorish Alcazar and filled it with art
treasures amassed during the century of avid and intelligent
collecting, which was such a marked characteristic of all the
Spanish Hapsburgs. Some of these were destroyed when the
old Alcazar Palace was burned down in 1734, though the
majority were saved, or not damaged beyond repair. The
present vast building was not completed until 1764, but it
contains that peculiar mixture of masterpieces and china orna-
ments marked 'A Present from Brighton 1907' which seems
typical of all unoccupied Royal Palaces that I have ever visited—
the former being the heritage from earlier monarchs and the
latter, apparently, indicating the personal taste of the last
occupants.

Although Spain is still officially a monarchy (a fact which
very few visitors seem to realize), the Palace has, of course, been
unoccupied since the flight of Alfonso XIII and his still living
English-born Queen in April 1931, but it has not quite the
abandoned aspect that might be expected, as General Franco

uses it for the reception of foreign ambassadors or ministers and their staffs. These are escorted to the Palace by the incredibly colourful Moorish Guard, dressed in blue and silver or crimson and gold, and magnificently mounted upon horses whose hoofs have been painted gold or silver and whose harness glitters blindingly in the sun. I was present at the reception of the British Ambassador, Sir John Balfour, early in 1951, which, however, was not held in the vast Throne Room, with its splendid Tiepolo ceiling. This is used only once a year—on October 1st—when Franco receives the heads of foreign diplomatic missions and all the high officials of his own Government, an occasion which marks the return to the capital of the administration, which leaves at the end of every July for the cool of San Sebastian. On this occasion Franco stands in front of the throne, but despite both the physical advantage and political significance that might be obtained thereby, has never yet sat down upon it.

There is a collection of pictures, second only to that contained in the Prado, but I have never seen any guide-book yet that mentioned the two most beautiful things that may be seen there. One is a triptych or three-panelled painting upon wood, similar to the ikons of the Greek Orthodox Church, which belonged to Queen Isabella the First, and the other a circular table inlaid with exquisite naked figures painted on ivory.

The Palace contains 2,500 lengths of wall tapestry, some of it fifteenth-century Flemish and some from designs by Van Dyck and Van der Weyden, and the carpets from the Royal factory of Santa Barbara (which employed Goya and his brother-in-law, Bayeu) cover no less than 5 miles of floor and passage!

The Royal Library contains some 150,000 volumes and administrative documents dating back to 1479, besides many beautifully illustrated eleventh-century missals. A certain consolation for having been born in the dreary twentieth century may be obtained by a brief glance at the Royal Pharmacia, where sinister-looking phials and mis-shapen retorts look more like the paraphernalia of witchcraft than the last word in seventeenth-century ideas on scientific healing!

The Royal Palace is open to visitors except when it is being prepared or used for some official ceremony. As these occasions are fairly frequent, it would be wise to consult the 'Turismo' or your Hall Porter before going round there. Such visits are very tiring, and if you prefer something smaller, yet in its way more perfect, then ask the Tourist Bureau to obtain a pass for you to visit the private collection of the Duke of Alba. The small Liria Palace was badly smashed up by the Republicans, and the late Duke built a modern five-story house almost next door. He lived, when in Madrid, in the upper two, and the first floor is devoted exclusively to housing his collection of pictures, armour, and the fine library, until repairs to the Palace are completed. It is open, free of charge, to any visitor who can obtain a card of recommendation. Although free, it is usual to tip 10 or 15 pts to the servant who shows you round, though he will probably refuse to accept it unless you insist.

Since this is a private collection, it seems somehow less tiring than a public art gallery such as the Prado, and you can see canvases by Greco, Velazquez, Reynolds, Titian, Rubens, Van Loo, Kneller, Goya, Winterhalter, and many others of the greatest masters, that are the equal of any in the world.

As the historically minded will remember, the Great Duke of Alba was responsible for an attempt to stamp out the Protestant rebellion in the Low Countries and, since our historians are all Protestant, his Governorship is part of the Black Legend against Catholic Spain that even to-day still colours the relations between the two countries—just as disapproval of King George III still directly affects American relations with Britain.

Reading both English and Spanish history in the original serves only to emphasize the guilt of historians who will insist upon labelling events as a 'good thing' or a 'bad thing', instead of confining themselves to recording the facts.

Spain, and the Great Duke of Alba, sincerely believed Catholicism to be the sole true manifestation of Christianity, and that Protestantism was wholly evil. They therefore fought it with all the means at their disposal. To-day we may, rightly, disapprove of persecuting people for their religious convictions, but we were not backward ourselves in persecuting Catholics, as the countless secret Priest Holes in old British country houses amply testify. Contemplation of the axiom about stones and glass houses would appear to be in order before we are too emphatic about the activities of the Great Duke of Alba.

Anyway, there is a room devoted to him by his present-day descendant, with two portraits of him by Rubens and Titian, one of them showing him as a grim-visaged man of early middle age, and the other in old age, with the grimness slightly softened by time. His armour, and some fine Flemish tapestry, complete the furnishings of this small room.

The family of the Duke of Alba were firm supporters of the British Catholic Royal House of Stuart, from whom they received the additional title of Dukes of Berwick, and there is another room containing portraits of Mary Queen of Scots, Kings Charles II and James II (James I and Charles I are omitted as backsliding Protestants), and also of both the Old Pretender and Bonny Prince Charlie.

Still another room is dedicated to Napoleon III's beautiful wife, the Empress Eugénie, who lived to be nearly 100 and only died between the two World Wars. She was born the Countess de Montijo and so was the present Duke's grand-mother's sister. In the same room as that containing the Winter-halter portrait of the Empress Eugénie there is also one of Napoleon the Little (as Victor Hugo named him in distinction from his great uncle—if, as seems by no means certain, his father was the great Napoleon's brother Louis, and not one of Queen Hortense's numerous amours). A third reveals the weak features of the Prince Imperial, sole fruit of the marriage of Napoleon III and Eugénie. He was speared to death when his stirrup snapped as he sought to jump on his horse to flee from a sudden enemy attack during the British Zulu War.

The late Duke of Alba was General Franco's Ambassador in London and, although it was a difficult period in the relations between the two countries, he made very many personal friends there. He left no son but, under Spanish law, his daughter's son has succeeded him, so the ancient name is in no immediate danger of extinction.

Before leaving the subject for lighter topics I must mention very briefly two other sightseeing 'musts'—the Church of San Francisco el Grande, and the Hermitage of San Antonio de la Florida. The former contains among many other things the exquisite walnut-wood choir-stalls, taken from the ruined monastery of Santa Maria de El Paular (of which more is said in the next chapter). The monastery has now been turned into a Goya memorial museum, and contains the matchless fresco known as 'St. Anthony preaching to the Crowd', in which the artist included devastating portraits of Court dignitaries hob-nobbing with well-known ladies of easy virtue as part of the crowd. If you are interested in antique furniture, tapestry, damasks, miniatures, armour, and old, eggshell-thin porcelain, then I advise a visit to the Museum de Cerralbo.

Only 9 miles outside Madrid is the Royal Palace of El Pardo, which is never open to the public, but which I had an opportunity of examining when I was granted a journalistic interview with General Franco in November 1951. It has been the site of a Palace since the Middle Ages, but the present structure was the work, some 180 years ago, of King Charles III, who used it for the hunting trips which, apart from building, were the sole passion of his life.

The neighbouring park, although so near to a great city, still abounds in wild boar and deer, apart from the thousands of partridges, which Franco enjoys both shooting and eating. The Palace is particularly rich in carpets and tapestries from the Royal Santa Barbara carpet factory, and includes several of Goya's best designs.

Not far from the Palacio del Pardo is Madrid's super-smart golf-club, known as the Puerta de Hierro, where it is pleasant to dine in the open when Madrid itself is like an oven. There are a few members who even play golf, but the Club is mainly social and the game unlikely ever to be very popular in Spain. The essential qualities of golf being humility, patience, and self-control, and all these qualities being heartily despised by ninety-nine out of a hundred Spaniards, the reason for its lack of success with all but the international smart set is fairly obvious.

Madrid possesses one of Europe's largest and loveliest parks —the Retiro. Created by the artistic, pleasure-loving but tragic King Philip IV for the open-air theatrical performances that he particularly enjoyed, it still retains the formal beauty of the seventeenth century, with classical statues of vaguely improbable Visigothic Kings, a large artificial lake, and deeply shaded empty avenues. It is beautifully kept, and the small circular rose-garden is rich with bloom from April until Christmas, and in early May is an extraordinary riot of colour and perfume.

There is an open-air restaurant and night-club that disturbs the midsummer peace of one corner of the old park—but only one corner.

Two casual amusements offered by Madrid are the bargain-hunter's paradise known as the Rastro, and the Sunday morning cock-fights.

The Rastro—flea market, Caledonian Market, thieves' kitchen—consists of open-air stalls on either side of the street and, if you have the time, temperament, and essential knowledge of values, you can find some really astounding bargains there. Even if you make no purchases you will have a good cross-sectional view of Spanish low life.

In this connexion I have seen a few indignant letters from tourists complaining that 'gold' watches, pencils, or pens, and 'platinum' and 'diamond' rings, bought from persuasive youths wearing broken-down shoes and two days' beard, have been subsequently found to be valueless. I feel no sympathy with the victims. Anyone who is such an incredible 'sucker' as to expect anything else ought to stay safely in Clacton for their holidays.

Cock-fighting was outlawed in Britain nearly a century and a half ago as being a cruel sport, in my opinion rightly so, and it is officially illegal in Spain to-day, but it is a law that is not very rigorously enforced.

I had seen it before in Bali, in January 1942, in what were then still called the Dutch East Indies, and the frantic betting which it produced had interested me more than had the fighting itself.

I am not one of those people who think that other centuries are necessarily more interesting than that in which I happen to have been born, but I have always tried to understand how peoples of other times lived and amused themselves. The Englishman of 150 years ago got a great thrill out of cock-fighting, and to go to a cock-fight in Madrid was rather like taking a trip into rural England of the Regency period. Spain is not really the place for people who want to see the things of the twentieth century, which, surely, can be better seen in the United States. Spain's charm lies in the fact that it presents limitless opportunities for the intelligent tourist to glimpse the past, without the discomfort of having to live in a period when it was considered eccentric to take more than one bath a year.

Here in Madrid the twentieth and seventeenth centuries rub shoulders, mingle, and become part of the same living design that was begun some three centuries ago, and which still remains unfinished.

You will feel this yourself when you return home to your twentieth-century flat or hotel at three or four in the morning. You will find the door locked, and you probably will not have a key. Then, by loudly clapping your hands so that the sound echoes sharply down the silent, cliff-like streets, you must conjure up the eighteenth century to your assistance. From some invisible tavern or shadowed corner a grotesque, gnome-like figure, straight from a Goya print, will materialize and shamble rapidly towards you, answering your signal with the counter-sign, which consists of stumping his lead-loaded cane so that it resounds from the pavements.

'Voy, voy, señorito', it will cry, while it fumbles with keys and flutters its many-caped, ankle-length overcoat, and finally opens the door for you to step back into the twentieth century. Its parting glance is at the sky, and its last words a reassurance about the next day's weather.

It is not a far cry from the Madrid 'sereno' of to-day and the comfortable cry of the night-watchman of Georgian London that must so often have caused our great-great-grandfathers to waken briefly from between two dreams: 'Four o'clock on a fine summer morning—and all's well'!

VIII

MADRID'S SURROUNDINGS

Toledo—Avila—El Escorial—Segovia—El Paular—Aranjuez—Alcalá
de Henares—Valladolid—Salamanca and Burgos.

MADRID undoubtedly possesses a certain charm of its own, but
it is a charm that becomes apparent only after you have spent
long enough there to see behind the rather aggressive, boom-
town façade, and casual visitors cannot always be expected to
possess the necessary patience to do so. Even so, Madrid is the
essential hub from which to visit the circle of historic Castilian
towns which together constitute—with the exception of Andalusia—the greatest sight-seeing attraction that the country
has to offer.

Of the ten places I have listed at the head of this chapter, the
first eight can be visited from Madrid in a single day by car or
bus, though it is quite impossible to obtain anything like a complete idea of Toledo during one such visit. The last two, it may
be pointed out, are not in the surroundings of Madrid, Salamanca and Burgos both being some 150 miles from the capital,
and in order to visit them as they deserve at least one night has
to be spent in each. My reason for including them is that visitors
to either of them are, almost necessarily, on their way to or
from Madrid, owing to the nature of the road and rail communications, since they lie respectively athwart the main rail
link between the capital and the north-west, and the principal
road and rail link with San Sebastian and Paris.

If unkind circumstances should limit a visitor to a single
excursion from the city, I think that the choice would have to
be Toledo.

It is easy to reach by the regular Pullman bus service, known
as Continental Auto, and the 42 miles of almost flat road is in
excellent condition.

The whole town of Toledo is a kind of living museum and,
after three days and nights there, I was still discovering places

which, anywhere else, would alone constitute a sufficient reason for going there. Accordingly, it is one of those places where only the real student can make anything like an exhaustive tour, and he will require at least a week, assisted by Baedeker, in order to achieve it. For others the problem becomes a question of what *not* to see rather than the reverse and, after some misgivings, I now advise the single-day visitors to confine themselves to the Cathedral, which, with Burgos, Leon and Seville, is the finest in Spain; the house of the Duchess of Lerma (referred to, if at all, in the guide-books as the Hospital of St. John the Baptist); the perfectly preserved house where El Greco spent the last ten years of his life; and the small twelfth-century church known as the Hermitage of Christ of the Light (Hermitage de Cristo de la Luz). In addition, any picture-lover would rightly never forgive himself if he failed to see Greco's 'Burial of the Count of Orgaz' in the otherwise uninteresting little Church of San Tomé, since it is fairly generally regarded as being the artist's supreme masterpiece. Also there is the Arms Factory, where the finest sword-blades in Christendom have been forged since Roman times, and where the gold inlay 'Toledo work', or damascening, introduced by the Moors, is still practised. If this seems a rather formidable list I can only say that my omissions are so numerous and, on artistic grounds, so indefensible, that they are enough to make the late lamented Herr Baedeker not merely turn, but positively spin, in his grave.

Probably the most beautiful thing to be seen on your visit to Toledo is simply Toledo itself, viewed from the opposite side of the gorge along which the River Tagus flows. The river is crossed by the fortified thirteenth-century Bridge of St. Martin, and forms a moat round three-quarters of this natural fortress. The city rises, proud and golden, against the steel-blue sky of Castile. Materially unchanged since Greco lived and painted it three and a half centuries ago, it is wholly Moorish in form and character even though it has been the spiritual capital of Christian Spain since 1095.

In the centuries between its liberation from the Moors in that year and the compulsory conversion or expulsion of the Jews nearly 400 years later, the Jewish community of Toledo was both rich and powerful, and some of the finest buildings of the present-day city were originally built as synagogues. Perhaps the best of these is the thirteenth-century building restored and transformed into the Church of Santa Maria la Blanca in 1405, from the pulpit of which St. Vicente Ferrer delivered the sermons that fired the people to complete the final expulsion of the Moors. It is decorated with typically Moorish tiles, known as 'azulejos', which are still produced and used for interior decoration in twentieth-century Spain.

The treasure supposed to have been buried by Samuel Levi, the Jewish Treasurer of King Pedro the Cruel, is still the object of periodic searches in the huge, underground, cavern-like conduits that provided the city's water supply from Roman times up to the last century.

Toledo was Tolentum to the Romans, and served as the capital of Spain for the Visigoths, Moors, and Christians when Madrid was little more than a village. In a country where fabulously beautiful cathedrals abound I have promised else-where to write of them in detail only in four cases—Seville, Burgos, Leon, and Toledo—so I am not inconsistent if I urge you to begin your sight-seeing with the Cathedral, See of Spain's Cardinal Primate, and a Bishopric since the days of St. Eugenio in the sixth century.

As is so often the case, Toledo Cathedral is too closely surrounded by houses for it to be possible to get a good view of it from the distance that is essential for an adequate impression of the building as a whole. But from the door opposite the Town Hall (this last designed by El Greco's illegitimate son, who was a notable architect), some idea of its stately proportions can be obtained. Dry facts and figures sometimes help to frame a tremendous artistic conception, and for this reason I give some now. The building is roughly 364 feet long by 182 wide, and the tower containing the $17\frac{1}{2}$-ton bell 'La Gorda'—'the Fat One'—is 293 feet high. There are 22 separate chapels, 88 pillars, and 750 stained-glass windows, the best, in the central aisle, being of fifteenth-century workmanship.

F

There was a Christian Visigothic Chapel on the same site in the year 587 which was enlarged into a mosque by the Moors. The existing cathedral was begun by the Saint King Ferdinand III in 1227, but not finished until 1493.

So much for hard facts: after that you must just go in and get bewildered for yourself among a collection of artistic treasures that defy description! It is sufficient to say that there is a wealth of pictures by Titian, Velazquez, Raphael, Van Dyck, Rubens, El Greco, and Goya, and the Sala de las Ropas contains priceless tapestries and jewelled Church vestments going back for 400 years. The giant 'custodia' or monstrance, for the carriage in procession of the Host, is usually kept in the Treasury of the Cathedral, though I last saw it, with the Papal Legate Cardinal Tedeschini kneeling before it, being drawn through the streets of Barcelona at the Eucharistic Congress of May 1952. It is of gold, silver, and platinum, is nearly 7 feet high, and weighs some 450 lb.

So much wealth in a country where poverty is so acute rouses many Protestants of my acquaintance to fury. 'Sell all and give to the poor' may have been the teaching of Christ, but He also said, 'For the poor you have always with you', and, even if the artistic contents of every church in Spain were sold, it would only solve the problem of poverty for a day or a week, after which the poor would again be as poor as ever, and the whole world would be the poorer for the disappearance of many things of irreplaceable beauty. There is poverty in Britain to-day, but I have heard no suggestion, as yet, that the entire contents of the National Gallery should be sold to America for much-needed dollars, so I suspect that the origin of my Protestant friends' humanitarian anger lies, at least partly, in their Protestantism.

In a place so crowded with artistic masterpieces only a few can possibly stay permanently in your memory. They may include the portraits of all the Bishops of Toledo for the last 1,400 years (though obviously the earlier ones are mythical likenesses), or the delightfully naïve painting of Hell over the door of the same room, or the matchless sixteenth-century choir-stalls by Berruguete; but, whatever they may be, your mind will retain something of abiding beauty from your visit to Toledo Cathedral.

If you find sight-seeing as tiring as I do you will probably feel in need of repairs after an hour or so in the cathedral and, if so, try the restaurant called Venta de Aires, where, if it is the season, they do something very special with partridges cooked in a thick wine sauce. An alternative is the newly opened Hotel Carlos Quinto. If not, then on to the Toledo's second 'must'—the House of El Greco.

This was the small palace of the Marquis de Villena when the great painter lived there, but it has been kept almost unchanged since his death in 1614, and contains the complete series of the Twelve Apostles, considered to be among his finest works. Greco frequently copied his own work two or three times, and most of this series have at least one authentic duplicate.

The first impression of those harsh lurid colours is almost one of shock, but no one can look at the weeping St. Peter and ever again doubt the artist's supreme genius.

There are a few canvases belonging to Greco's earlier period, showing him as a more or less conventional portrait-painter, before he finally adopted the intensely individualistic, almost psychic, style for which to-day he is principally known.

In the garden is the well down which Samuel Levi is supposed to have hidden his ill-gotten treasure and where, over five and a half centuries later, part of the cathedral treasure was also hidden when, in 1936, it seemed certain that the ancient city must soon fall wholly to the Republican troops. In this modern variation on the fourteenth-century theme some of the treasure was recovered, but not all, so that the existing legend of buried wealth has now been reinforced by a further £100,000 or so! The small Hermitage of Cristo de la Luz is the oldest in Toledo, and it was here that the Thanksgiving Mass for the liberation of the city was said in 1095. In the tenth century it was a mosque, and in the twelfth was restored in the form of the pre-Moorish Visigothic chapel. Its strange name—the Church of Christ of the Light—comes from the fact that below the Mosque the Christians buried a particularly venerated image of Christ before which, without their conqueror's knowledge, the Spaniards maintained a light continually burning throughout 373 years of Moorish occupation.

On your way out to the Palace of the Duchess of Lerma you may notice the iron chains decorating the outside wall of the fifteenth-century monastery of San Juan de los Reyes. These were taken from the Christian prisoners released from the dungeons of Granada when the last Moorish stronghold fell to Ferdinand and Isabella in 1492.

The Hospital de San Juan Bautista is another example of the architectural work of Greco's son, and has been called a miniature of the vast monastery-palace at El Escorial. Its charm for me lies in the fact that it is a perfect example of a sixteenth-century nobleman's house which is still a private home and not a museum—though its days as such are now numbered. The Duchess of Lerma still lives there, and her suite of rooms may be visited if she is not in residence; but at her death it will become an orphanage for children whose parents were killed in the Civil War, and already a large part of the building is employed in this way. The Duchess's husband and only son were killed by the Republicans during the Civil War, and, remembering this, I feel that it fairly reveals her sincerity that she made it a condition of the gift that orphans of Republican parents are equally welcome with those whose parents died fighting for Franco.

The palace contains pictures by Titian, Greco, Tintoretto, and Rubens, besides many others. Of deeply moving appeal is the only Greco portrait of a woman that I have ever seen, though there are a few others. She was the woman he loved but never married, and whose death broke his heart.

Singularly unbeautiful is the strange seventeenth-century portrait of an hermaphrodite—heavily bearded and suckling a baby—which is usually kept discreetly veiled unless the visitors are, unlike the subject of the portrait, all of the same sex.

The famous Posada de la Sangre—Inn of Blood—where Cervantes stayed while writing part of *Don Quixote*, was totally destroyed during the bitter fighting of the autumn of 1936, when a small garrison under Colonel Moscardó held out against the Republicans, through incredible sufferings, within the stout walls of the sixteenth-century fortress known as the Alcazar. Leaving political considerations entirely on one side, the defenders of the Alcazar of Toledo, both men and women, revealed the same iron courage that nearly 2,000 years earlier had produced fear and mutiny, even in the matchless legions of ancient Rome.

The story is old, but I tell it again because it is so essentially Spanish. Moscardó's only son was captured by the Republicans and ordered to telephone to his father, telling him that his life would be spared only if the fortress was surrendered. Moscardó answered immediately, 'Well, my son, you are a soldier too, so I do not need to tell you my reply. Good-bye, my boy, and God bless you!'

The defence of the Alcazar had so captured the popular imagination that Franco's No. 2, General Mola, ordered General Varela to turn aside from his march upon Madrid to relieve it. This delayed him a week, and in that time reinforcements of the International Brigade were rushed into the capital. If Mola had marched straight on, leaving Moscardó and the garrison to die, the capital would have fallen and the Civil War have lasted six months instead of thirty-two. So an act of heroism and an act of humanity led directly to three-quarters of a million needless deaths. The hero is now a lonely and ageing man, and the humanitarian Mola died in an air-crash. The moral of the story, if any, you must discover for yourself.

Days, even weeks, could be spent in visiting places of real interest and beauty in Toledo without even going to the few I have mentioned here. They are merely my personal choice from among an 'embarras de richesse'.

Most people's second choice, after Toledo, is El Escorial, though it would certainly not be my own. Still, the monstrous monastery-palace-morgue, known as St. Lorenzo del Escorial, has been called the eighth wonder of the world, and I may be unreasonable in my dislike of this grey granite record of a mind clouded with inherited religious mania. It is precisely its incredible size that makes it of interest, and which at the same time makes it for me both overwhelming and sinister. Philip II was particularly attracted to Saints who died in demonstratively painful ways, and San Lorenzo, having been grilled (like a pre-war rump-steak), was an obvious favourite. So as to keep the fascinating idea well to the fore, Philip II built this vast place in the form of a grill, with lines, or wings, crossing the main square of the outer walls. Once again I must resort briefly to facts and figures, because only by the use of them can the repetitious use of such adjectives as vast, huge, and monster be avoided. The building is 676 feet long by 527 feet wide, contains 16 interior courts, 15 cloisters, 300 rooms, 86 staircases, 88 fountains, 3 chapels, 2,763 windows, and 7,512 holy relics, mostly bones of saints! This gigantic task was begun in 1557, immediately after Philip had taken over the throne from his father the Emperor Charles V (who had retired into the monastery of Yuste for the purpose of attending his own funeral service disguised as a monk), and finished in 1584, fourteen years before Philip's own death. The setting chosen by King Philip is magnificent, 3,000 feet above sea-level on the fringe of the Guadarrama Mountains, only 31 miles west of Madrid, and it has lately become a popular summer week-end resort. From the terrace of the luxurious Hotel Felipe Segundo you can obtain a better general view of the monastery than from anywhere else.

Philip II's intention was to build a harsh, spartan residence, far from the traditional luxurious temptations of royal courts (to which he had shown himself highly susceptible in his youth), and the rooms where he died, unchanged for over three and a half centuries, are moving in their silent tale of suffering, disillusionment, and masochistic repentance. Grisly representations of the seven deadly sins decorate the walls of the small, bare, unnaturally chilly room, and although his love and real appreciation for great pictures led to the inclusion of canvases by Titian, Holbein, and Dürer, he selected only those depicting the gloomiest possible subjects. A small window by his bedside opens directly upon the high altar of a chapel, so that he could be present at mass even when too ill to be carried in the special chair, also to be seen there, with its rest for his gout-racked legs.

But while Hapsburg Philip II planned the Escorial as a place in which to prepare for death, his Bourbon successors of 150 years later turned it into one of the most sumptuous of all Spain's many royal palaces, though they had the grace to leave Philip's own rooms as he had wished. Latterly there has been something of a return to Philip's original purpose, since some of the best of the pictures have been removed to the Prado Museum in Madrid, and the only State occasion upon which the building is used is in connexion with its rôle as the Royal Pantheon. All the Spanish kings, beginning with Philip's father, are buried here, with the three exceptions of Philip IV (1621–65), Ferdinand VI (1740–59), and the last King, Alfonso XIII, who died in Rome during World War II. Franco and all his Cabinet always attend a great Memorial Mass on the anniversary of Alfonso XIII's death. Incidentally, he was best man by proxy at Franco's wedding so as to impress the latter's in-laws to be, who were uncertain whether a hard-up young Colonel was a good enough match for their beautiful daughter!

Even though the best of the Escorial's pictures have been removed to the Prado, there still remains an incredible wealth of canvases by Veronese, Tintoretto, Titian, Guido Reni, El Greco, Zurbaran, Goya, Giordano, Rubens, and Teniers, not to mention 338 Flemish and Spanish tapestries, some designed by Goya and Bayeu, while the library of 40,000 volumes contains some unique treasures, notably the 5-foot-high books of religious chants, and the eleventh-century Codici Aureo, in the illumination of which 17 lb. of pure gold were employed!

I myself was attracted to the thirty-seven illustrations of Bible stories painted on ivory and ebony, and the Sèvres china clocks, with designs by Rubens and Teniers, in the Ambassador's Hall; the oddly pathetic little harmonium upon which the dying Emperor Charles V helped to pass his agonizing hours in the remote Monastery of Yuste; the incredible 150-foot-long sweep of the Hall of Battles; and the old porcelain in the eighteenth-century Casita del Principe.

Even nearer to Madrid is the little town of Alcalá de Henares, birthplace of Cervantes and seat of the famous University set up by Ferdinand and Isabella's greatest counsellor, and one-time Regent, Cardinal Cisneros, at the beginning of the six-teenth century. The great university buildings were abandoned during the Napoleonic invasion, but there is a charming inn called the Hosteria del Estudiante which is authentically sixteenth-century, and possesses a fine central courtyard. There your wine is drawn from huge animal skins, black with age, and you will eat extremely well. Since Alcalá de Henares is barely 20 miles from Madrid, it can be visited simply as a lunch outing if your time is limited.

Another half-day excursion is 30 miles due south from Madrid, on the main road to Andalusia, to the sleepy little town of Aranjuez, famous in spring for its particularly delicious wild strawberries and asparagus.

Here the River Tagus winds slow and green under leafy trees as un-Spanishly as the Thames at Oxford, and the con-trast to the near-desert wastes immediately surrounding Madrid made it an obvious choice for a royal residence. Accordingly Ferdinand and Isabella took over the old house belonging to the Grand Master of the medieval Order of San-tiago, which was destroyed by fire immediately afterwards with a promptitude that insurance companies would to-day have considered suspicious. Philip II—that indefatigable builder—started work on the same site, but the result of his labours was also consumed by fire. Then Philip V tried his luck in 1739, and yet again the palace went up in flames, this time in 1747. As the Royal Palace in Madrid had also been destroyed by fire in 1734, it is difficult not to suspect either deliberate arson or an almost unbelievable degree of courtly carelessness at this period! The present, mid-seventeenth-century building, in which are incorporated sections of its numerous predecessors, is looking a little run down and neglected to-day. It contains a few fine pictures, a room of which the walls are entirely covered by porcelain from the Royal Factory, and a quite ghastly, bogus Moorish room, the perpetration of which fully justifies the expulsion of Queen Isabella II in 1868! Our own Queen Victoria could scarcely have imagined anything worse—and even she might have hesitated before accepting Isabella's assumption that the dear Arabs habitually decorated the Alhambra with potted palms!

The real interests of Aranjuez are the small Casa del Labrador, built over a mile from the Palace by Charles IV while still Heir Apparent, and the justly famous Palace Gardens. The Casa del Labrador epitomizes the strange passion which afflicted most European monarchs while slipping down the steep slope that led inexorably towards the day when Samson lifted the severed head of Louis XVI for the delectation of the Paris mob, and their graceful, useless way of life ended for ever. But these plump and futile gentlemen—and none was plumper or more futile than Charles IV of Spain—had excellent taste whenever they could be persuaded not to build 'Roman' ruins, and the Casa del Labrador captures the period more completely even than does the Petit Trianon with its phoney milkmaids. Here there is the same tidy rusticity (the pigs being washed and perfumed before being allowed to take part in the proceedings), combined with glass work valued at £200,000 and an entire room decorated in platinum!

The elaborate gardens of Aranjuez were inspired by the grandson of Louis XIV of France, Philip V, whose home-sickness for Versailles is revealed both here and in the La Granja Palace Gardens, just outside Segovia. They were begun in 1727 and finished in 1746, after his death.

However, his son Ferdinand VI was even more enthusiastic about Aranjuez than his father had been, and had a special weakness for organizing naval battles on the Tagus (battles which I have no doubt he always won). It was during his reign that the two most beautiful of these formal gardens, complete with classical statuary, corinthian columns, and illuminated waterfalls, were completed. These are known as the Island Garden and the Queen's Garden.

Although the Palace itself is falling into decay, the Gardens are beautifully kept and, on the high days and holidays when all the waterfalls and fountains play, they almost justify the millions that were spent upon them.

So far all our excursions from Madrid have been south (except for Alcalá de Henares, which is due east), but the spokes of the wheel also radiate north-west to Avila and Salamanca, and north to Segovia, El Paular, and Burgos.

Avila is a strange city, completely ringed by its stout eleventh-century walls, nearly 4,000 feet above sea-level in desolate, rock-strewn country, where on still winter nights the wolves can be clearly heard hungrily howling at the moon. It is 70 miles from Madrid, with unusually good rail and road communications, and its mile-and-a-half-long circle of walls, surmounted by eighty semi-circular towers, make it unique. Those of Carcassonne are more famous, but they are largely the work of nineteenth-century restorers, whereas these have suffered only the slightest of repairs in their near millennium of life.

The oldest part of the thirteenth- to fourteenth-century Gothic cathedral, begun in the eleventh century, actually forms part of the defensive walls—for those were still the days when bishops occasionally left their churches to help crack Moorish skulls with spiked iron mace or heavy sword.

But Avila's greatest claim to fame is as the birthplace, in 1515, of St. Teresa, whose story clearly reveals her indomitable if slightly unsympathetic personality. If she had been born some three and a half centuries later she would have been a militant suffragette, and all the tales told of her reveal not only her genuine piety and greatness of mind and spirit, but also the slightly belligerent determination that seems to develop so markedly in all elderly maiden ladies with a mission in life. Without irreverence I must quote one of her 'straight talks to God' to illustrate my point. Once, when St. Teresa was being carried in a litter, she was abruptly tipped out into a river, and the litter itself was found to be immovably stuck to the earth. Clearly perceiving the Hand of the Almighty, St. Teresa asked, with pardonable asperity:

'Why did You do that to me?'

To this God is reported to have replied, in effect:

'I do what I please to my friends.'

Nothing daunted (and apparently by no means pacified), St. Teresa rejoined:

'Now I understand why You have so few friends!'

Although Avila itself is set in bleak country, the road north-west to Salamanca, 63 miles away, skirts extremely beautiful mountain scenery, rich in trout streams and dominated by the Gredos mountains, where there is a State-run Parador over 5,000 feet above sea-level. If you are prepared to travel slowly over bad mountain roads (and your tyres are new), the secondary road from Avila south-west to Plasencia through Barco de Avila is wildly beautiful and, in summer, delightfully cool. In winter it is usually made impassable by snow, since it rises to over 3,700 feet, with surrounding peaks reaching nearly 8,500. Your first glimpse of Salamanca is of golden-brown walls on the opposite bank of the River Tormes, behind which there is an exciting jumble of towers and spires piled against the sky. Perhaps it is this too rich promise that, to me at least, has always made Salamanca as it really is a little disappointing, but I know many people who consider it one of the most interesting of all Spanish cities.

Although its origins are pre-Christian, it suffered so terribly in the ebb and flow of the reconquest that when it was finally liberated in 1085—ten years before Toledo—it was a dead city and had to be repopulated. Yet, less than a century and a half later, its university ranked in importance with those of Oxford and Bologna. Alfonso the Wise presented its library with 100,000 volumes, and the city's importance reached its peak during the sixteenth century. As a result, perhaps its greatest beauty is to be found in the mansions constructed by various nobles during the reigns of Charles V and Philip II, of which that still used by the Duke of Alba is perhaps the finest. The original fortress-

palace of the Alba family, now in ruins, is only some 14 miles
from Salamanca, near the village of Alba de Tormes. Salamanca has two cathedrals for its 100,000 inhabitants, the 'Old'
with 10-foot-thick fortress walls having been begun when the
newly ejected Moors might still be expected to strike back, and
the 'New' (or new for Spain) sixteenth- to eighteenth-century
one, near the seminary for Irish priests. The New Cathedral is
described as of the Plateresque style, a word which puzzles
many Anglo-Saxons (among them myself), and for which my
dictionary merely supplies the alternative of 'decadent Gothic',
which somehow sounds slightly insulting.

Salamanca is one of the two greatest centres for the breeding
of fighting bulls, and the great annual 'fiesta' from September
8th until the 22nd always attracts the leading matadores from
all over the country, though the population is highly critical.

The monastery set on a peak known as Peña de Francia, 52
miles south of Salamanca, makes an attractive excursion in summer (Salamanca can be excessively hot), as it is nearly 6,000 feet
above sea-level. It contains an interesting old Dominican
monastery and a tremendous view across the tawny-coloured
plateau of Extremadura, birthplace of Cortes, Pizarro, and most
of the other supermen whose missionary intentions and piratical
actions (similar, though mortally opposed, to those of the con-
temporary British Elizabethan sea-captains) carried Spain's
power and riches to unimaginable heights.

The city of Valladolid, 127 miles from Madrid and 78 from
Salamanca, was a gift from Alfonso VI to the Count of Ansurez
in the eleventh century, and only returned to the Kingdom of
Castile in time for the historically important marriage there of
Ferdinand and Isabella when, by the unification of both their
territories, Spain began to emerge from the Middle Ages.
Valladolid, like Toledo and Segovia, has been Spain's capital
more than once, the last occasion being under Philip III early
in the seventeenth century. This indecisiveness as to where to
fix the capital is largely explained by the fact that Ferdinand
and Isabella not only had no time for a Court, but barely
enough for a home. They lived in camp, permanently at war,

permanently on the move, and usually under conditions of discomfort that would horrify a modern farm labourer. Charles V had first to resist the long and dangerous revolt of the 'Comuneros' and then, after his election as Holy Roman Emperor, was wholly engaged in European power politics, with the mercurial French King Francis as his principal adversary. It is not surprising, therefore, that it was not until Philip II's time that the Kings of Spain got around to the task of establishing a permanent administrative headquarters.

Valladolid's chief claim to fame is literary—though it was the place of birth of Philip II, and also of the death of the embittered, half-mad Christopher Columbus, still fighting for the fulfilment of an agreement that had accidentally made him ruler and part owner of two continents, instead of a province.

Firstly, it was the home of Cervantes—and his house may be visited—and then of José Zorrilla, who was born there in 1811.

Zorrilla is largely unknown outside Spain, but his morality play, *Don Juan Tenorio*, forms an integral part of Spanish education and, for the foreigner, probably provides a more effective revelation of Spanish character than is afforded even by Cervantes' *Don Quixote*. Zorrilla's work is presented for a season every autumn simultaneously in three or four of the largest theatres in Madrid, and plays to packed and emotional audiences. Participation in the production has tremendous prestige value, and the performances of the greatest Spanish actors in the part are eagerly compared. In short, where in Britain or America the highbrows in speaking of an actor will ask, 'But did you see his Hamlet?', in Spain their opposite numbers will ask, 'But did you see his Don Juan Tenorio?' The importance given to the play can be judged from the fact that Salvador Dalí preferred decorating the 1950 presentation of *Don Juan* to accepting an infinitely more profitable contract in America. Whereas it is a matter of opinion whether or not Dalí is a really great artist, I have never yet heard anyone accuse him of being unbusiness-like!

The play itself hinges upon the idea that the great lover, Don Juan, returning from a night with someone else's wife, meets a funeral and, upon gazing at the face in the coffin, discovers it to be his own. This brings about his somewhat tardy repentance and renunciation of the woman whom he really loves. It contains all the elements dear to the Spanish heart—the man who is irresistible to women; the macabre preoccupation not only with death but also with physical corruption; the redeeming influence of a beautiful woman; and a repentance which, despite its lateness and the irreparable harm already done to others, is, nevertheless, acceptable to God.

Almost equally revelatory of character is the sixteenth-century Virgin of the Knives and Seven Sufferings, by Juan de Juanes, to be found in Valladolid's Church of Las Angustias, or the figures carried in religious processions, known as 'pasos', representing the Passion of Christ, which may be seen in the fifteenth-century Colegio de St. Gregory, now a museum. The same building contains a wonderful collection of polychrome religious sculpture.

An interesting alternative road back to Madrid from Valladolid is through Tordesillas (19 miles), where the Spanish Borgia Pope Alexander VI divided the New World into two spheres, one Spanish, the other Portuguese. Farther on (15 miles) is Medina del Campo. Here you may glance at the grim Castillo de la Mota, where Queen Isabel died in 1504 (sternly forbidding her ladies immodestly to uncover her feet); and here her daughter Joan the Mad lived on, grieving for her handsome, profligate Philip (whose body she kept with her for months after his death), long after most of the principal actors in her tragedy were dead.

Burgos is 150 miles north of Madrid but, since it is on the main Madrid–Paris road, via San Sebastian and Biarritz, most visitors to the Spanish capital pass through it. The road is excellent, though the scenery, as it climbs to the 4,000-foot Somosierra Pass, is wild and desolate in the extreme. Just 100 miles from Madrid there is a State-run Albergue at Aranda de Duero which is worth visiting since it is the only possible stopping place for a meal.

Burgos is at nearly 3,000 feet above sea-level and is reputedly

one of the coldest places in Spain, even in summer. The Hotel
Condestable is good without being pretentious, and the city's
restaurants are famous for the Castilian delicacy of roast suckling pig.

This is the spiritual home of Spain's greatest hero, El Cid
Campeador, a kind of combination of Robin Hood, Hereward
the Wake, St. George, and Tarzan! His name was Rodrigo
Diaz de Vivar, and his importance lies in the fact that he was
the inspiration of the Spanish switch-over from the defensive to
the offensive against the Moors. The Battle of Covadonga halted
the Moorish advance in the eighth century, but in the next three,
though the invaders had been pushed back in Galicia and Leon,
the sum total of the unending war had been defeats and re-
prisals that would have broken the morale of a less fanatically
courageous people. Then, in the eleventh century, the first
great wave of reconquest liberated half the Peninsula, and
although some of the Cid's conquests, such as Valencia, were
lost to the twelfth-century reaction by the Moors, the stage
was set for the second great wave under the Saint King Fernando
during the thirteenth which finally paved the way for the final
blow at the end of the fifteenth.

A popular story of El Cid is how he raised a loan for one of
his expeditions by giving a large locked chest as security to the
Jewish money-lenders. He informed them that it contained
gold, though in fact it was filled with sand, but his word was
accepted. When he returned victorious and rich he went to
repay the loan and to confess the deception. However, when the
chest was opened it was found to be full of gold, even as El Cid
had said! This was a miracle any way you may care to look at
it, though whether a divine one or only a miracle of tact on the
part of the money-lender (who thereafter enjoyed the protection
of the national hero), is one of those questions that you must
decide for yourself. The chest itself is on view in the Cathedral.

While there is much of interest to see in Burgos, there are
two sight-seeing 'musts'—the Cathedral, and the fifteenth-
century Carthusian monastery of Miraflores, 2 miles outside the
city.

To my mind Burgos Cathedral is architecturally the finest in Spain (though that of Leon runs it very close), while interiorly Toledo and Seville are its only superiors. This impression is no doubt partly due to the fact that there are various places from which it can be seen from a reasonable distance. All too often elsewhere in Spain—Barcelona being a typical example—surrounding slums make it impossible to see more than a wall or a porch at a time, with occasional neck-breaking cranings at over-close towers and flying buttresses. It is only due to the efforts of Adolf Hitler that twentieth-century Londoners have been given the necessary space to enable them to appreciate seventeenth-century St. Paul's, and in most places the problem remains unsolved. Burgos Cathedral was built between the thirteenth and fifteenth centuries, when Gothic architecture was at its purest in Spain, and there is something almost unearthly about the vast grey, intricately carved mountain of ancient stone that, despite its bulk, always looks as though, to the rending blare of celestial trumpets, it may one day detach itself from its moorings in the harsh, noisy town and drift away into the tawny emptiness of the Castilian plateau. If this should happen would it not provide a fitting epilogue for the almost legendary Cid, whose body it contains?

You can lose yourself among the countless side chapels, and the later impression left upon your mind is of little but quiet shadows shot through with the gleam of candle-light upon gold-leaf, and of softer colours from the stained-glass windows forming strangely patterned carpets for your feet upon the grey stone.

Sooner or later you will come across the crucified figure salvaged by fishermen centuries ago as it drifted past them, far from sight of land. The substance covering it appears to be of human skin, and it certainly gives to pressure upon it by finger and thumb in the way that only flesh can do. Its miraculous appearance, and equally miraculous incorruptibility, led to the belief that it was modelled by Nicodemus directly after witnessing the Crucifixion and had been rendered indestructible by the Will of God so that the world should possess a true likeness of His dead Son. Though its origins lie in the realms of legend, the whole town was witness of the fact that, when the figure was at last brought into the Cathedral, all the bells pealed in rejoicing, even though no man's hand had touched the bell-ropes.

It is only 2 miles to the Carthusian monastery known as La Cartuja de Miraflores, which is perched on a low hill away to the right of the main road as it leaves Burgos en route for San Sebastian. Founded in 1441, it contains the tombs of King Juan II and Queen Isabella of Portugal carved by Spain's greatest sculptor Gil de Siloe, but its real interest lies in its 500 years of uninterrupted employment as a house of prayer, and of total withdrawal from the world. The Order is a strict one, with fasts, mortification of the flesh, prohibition of speech among the monks, except upon special occasions, and a particular emphasis upon solitude.

I visited a temporarily disused cell when last I was there in June 1952. It was not more than 12 feet by 8, and the bare floor was of earth. The only furnishings were a narrow, hard bed without sheets but with a single coarse blanket, a small wooden table and chair, and a wooden prie-dieu before a crucifix on the wall. Across the prie-dieu was the knotted string contraption, with holes for the four fingers, with which it is possible conveniently to beat one's own shoulders. The heavy wooden door contained a hatch, through which the daily ration of bread, fish, water, and a little wine could be thrust, without the disturbance caused by the entry of anyone else into the cell. However, the room was saved from complete grimness by the other door, which led into a high-walled garden about four times as large as the cell itself, in which I saw that my predecessor had grown a few rather pathetic-looking flowers with which to beautify his physically narrow world.

The life chosen by these men is so remote from present-day ideas that there is a tendency to condemn it without any attempt to understand it. Obviously, it is only for the very few who feel a genuine vocation for such a life but, from my

G

personal knowledge of those few, there is no possibility of denying that they had all found a degree of spiritual peace which amounted to definite, active happiness, of a kind which could not possibly be counterfeited for my, or anyone else's, benefit. The common cry is that, while such a life may be all right from their own point of view, it is selfish in that it contributes nothing that can benefit the rest of mankind. The answer to that unfortunately must be on the spiritual rather than the material plane but, even so, it demands no great effort to comprehend.

Burgos is the starting point for exploring the little-known 'castles in Spain' region that lies to the city's west and north-west, and also around Palencia. But this is not the country for those who are bound to their own day and age by the iron fetters of physical custom and habit of thought. Their memory of it will be of a bare countryside, poverty-stricken ruins, and extremely bad roads. It is those bad roads, when you get off the beaten track in Spain, that make it still possible for a few escapists to slip away occasionally from the Brave New World of scientific mass murder, and temporarily join the Cid, who was barbarous enough to kill for God instead of for Oil Wells.

For the few, therefore, remember the secondary road that runs west from Burgos to Osorno, and then the forbidding-looking track to Carrion de los Condes and Sahagun, which then turns, through the emptiness of 1,000 years, to Cistierna and the remote but comfortable Parador at Riaño, on the fringe of the 8,000-foot Picos de Europa Mountains. It will take you a day if you are to appreciate it—and have any respect for your car—but do not consider attempting it except in summer. If you must return to the Middle Ages you must also accept the fact that the people of those days did not travel, if they could possibly avoid it, after the autumn rains had broken. If you do risk this most untouristic road, do not miss the tenth-century carving on the portico of the Convent of San Zoilo, showing the annual tribute of Christian Virgins demanded by the Moorish Emir Miramolin.

But this is to stray too far from Madrid for the purpose of

this chapter, and there are two more spokes to the great wheel, whose hub is the modern capital, of which I have still said nothing.

The first is the ancient city of Segovia, 55 miles north of Madrid and 3,300 feet above sea-level, where the first-class little Hotel Las Sirenas was opened in the spring of 1952. It is reached through the Guadarrama Pass by road or electric railway, and stands second only to Toledo in historic and artistic interest.

I must confess that Roman ruins leave me lamentably unmoved, and it is perhaps the fact that Segovia's Roman aqueduct is not a ruin that accounts for my interest in it. Begun in the time of Augustus, but not finished until that of the Spanish-born Emperor Trajan, it was still the main source of water supply to the town within the memory of many of the inhabitants, and still transports pure water from the mountains 10 miles away. I do not think that age necessarily adds to the beauty of a building, and it is the size of Segovia's aqueduct that makes it fascinating to me.

If you lunch on roast suckling pig at the famous Restaurant Casa Cándido—and I hope that you will—you gaze directly up at the highest of its 118 arches, towering nearly 100 feet above your head.

The sixteenth-century cathedral is also monumental, even for Spain, and its giant tiled 200-foot-high cupola is visible above the surrounding hills for many miles before you catch your first glimpse of the city itself. It contains works by El Greco and Goya, but probably the most unusual treasure is the tapestry in the Chapter House, designed by Rubens, and showing the story of Queen Zenobia of Palmyra.

The show-piece of Segovia is the pure fairy-tale castle, perched on a 260-foot bluff above the confluence of two mountain streams, and known as the Alcazar. Approached through the main gate, it is far less striking than when seen from below, and I advise you to go to the thirteenth-century octagonal Church of the Knights Templar (called Vera Cruz), from which it looks like some fantastic ship, eternally sailing through time

as well as through the limitless spaces of the empty Castilian
sky.

It was from the Alcazar that Isabella rode out to be crowned
Queen, and her Aragonese husband swore forever to respect
Castile's special privileges. Although the building is now used
to store the archives of the Spanish War Office, some of Isabella's rooms have been preserved unchanged. Outside one of
them is a balcony, still without a protecting rail, from which a
fifteenth century nursemaid allowed her princely charge to fall
into the valley nearly 300 feet below and then, when she realized
what had happened, leapt to her own death after the child.

Most visitors to Segovia find their way the 7 miles to La
Granja and the Palace of San Ildefonso, around which King
Philip V built another of his nostalgic imitations of the gardens
of his grandfather's Palace of Versailles. I personally prefer
the gardens at Aranjuez, but the grouping of the statuary for the
fountains and waterfall, known as 'Diana's Bath', is exquisite,
and I cannot help being impressed when I am told that 'La
Fama' shoots a jet of water no less than 154 feet into the air.
If I am tempted (like the elderly Colonel, who was told that
the whole of Britain could be placed within the State of Texas)
to reply, 'No doubt, but with what object?', then I suppress
the urge, lest I spoil the innocent pleasure of those who enjoy
such things.

Last on my list is my own private choice, and in writing of it
I may do myself the same disservice that I committed when I
told my friends of the Costa Brava in 1946 and of Ibiza in
1951. Alas, they told *their* friends as well—and now there is no
room left for me in either place! Only 40 miles from Madrid
is a small but popular summer resort, with the agreeable name
of Miraflores de la Sierra ('Look at the Mountain Flowers'),
where people possessing cars park their wives and families,
drive to their city offices each day, and return to sleep in the
relatively cool air. Behind this little town the road climbs and
twists to the Morcuera Pass, 5,000 feet above sea-level, and
usually closed by snow for four months of the year. Few
people climb to the head of the pass, and still fewer explore

1 The mountain monastery of El Paular between Madrid and Segovia

2 Philip II's palace-monastery-museum-pantheon of El Escorial

beyond it. If they did so they would wind their way down for 1,000 feet to the Valley of Lozoya, a royal hunting preserve 600 years ago, and one of the most enchantingly beautiful stretches of mountain, forest, and rich, park-like grazing land that I have seen anywhere.

Remote still in 1953, it must have been infinitely more so when, in 1390, King John II began to carry out the instructions left in his father's will to build a monastery here, and it was not until the time of his own son Henry III that the work was completed in 1440 and a number of Carthusian monks installed. When the monastery of Santa Maria del Paular was being built the final expulsion of the Moors from Spain was still nearly a century in the future, and Moorish architects were freely employed, in this case the famous Abderraman of Segovia.

During Spain's Golden Age the monastery waxed rich and influential, and history records that, at any specially critical moment in battle, the Emperor Charles V was wont to exclaim, 'I hope my monks at El Paular are at their prayers!'

Later it passed into the possession of the Benedictine Order, and fine stone bridges, fish tanks, stately avenues of oak and walnut trees for miles around still testify to their industry. By the beginning of the eighteenth century over 1,000 monks helped to produce one of the supreme examples of Spanish baroque decoration. But Spain's wealth and greatness declined with her people's Faith, and by 1835 the thirty remaining monks abandoned their overwhelming heritage, and went elsewhere. A few of the greatest treasures were removed, such as the matchless walnut choir-stalls, relating the life of David and the Last Judgement, which can to-day be seen in the Madrid church and museum of San Francisco el Grande. The remainder was left to rot, as similar places of irreplaceable beauty were simultaneously rotting all over bankrupt, eternally warring Spain. For the greater part of a century the place was totally abandoned. Storms blew in the windows, damp stained the vast alabaster reredos begun by Francisco Hurtado in 1719, and, the first time I saw it, pigeons, flying in and out of a 5-foot hole in the roof, had nested upon the gold-leaf-covered altar.

On the same occasion I climbed up the very shaky, empty bell-tower and found the floor an inch deep with the tiny bones of animals devoured here by the huge family of owls now in sole possession.

Obviously there were plenty of people who after 1835 knew that the monastery, or what might remain of it, was still there but, being off the beaten track and protected both by mountains and incredibly bad roads, the only recorded visit during this period was by a party of three Englishmen who sought to reach Segovia on horseback one December day in 1895. Caught in a snowstorm with the light failing, the ruined bulk of the monastery loomed into view with a promise at least of shelter. Riding into the square inner courtyard, with its strange pavement mosaic made of cattle bones, they beat upon the great wooden door, and were relieved when it was opened by a monk. Explaining their plight, and the fact that they carried their own food and bedding, they were led inside, through the long refectory, where the friars were eating in the absolute silence required by their Order, and round the half-ruined Gothic cloisters, in the centre of which are buried their dead. Their guide indicated a clean but bare cell, and left them to kindle a small fire, prepare their food, and, finally, to sleep.

By morning the storm had cleared away, but heavy clouds over the high Navacerrada Pass, that they still had to traverse, made them anxious to start without delay. Failing to find their guide of the previous night, whom they suspected might be at the service, sounds of which they could hear faintly through the broken windows of the chapel, they left a polite note of thanks and rode on their way. I have that yellowed note before me as I write these words.

After a difficult journey, they met a search-party on the outskirts of Segovia on its way to look for them, as the authorities feared that they might have come to grief in the storm. The first question by the leader of the search-party was:

'Where did you pass the night?'

One of the Englishmen replied:

'The good monks of El Paular gave us shelter.'

Without surprise, the Spaniard replied:

'I thought they would,' and then added gently, 'Of course you know that there have been no monks at El Paular for over half a century.'

It was only in the nineteen-forties that the Spanish Tourist Department, inspired by my friend Luis Bolín to carry out his plan for a nation-wide string of State-run inns, took over a corner of the vast crumbling ruin and turned it into a comfortable, modern Parador.

I am writing these lines sitting in the shade of the walnut trees planted by the monks in their old walled garden. The only sound to be heard is the stirring of the leaves above my head, the distant chuckle of the hurrying trout-stream, and the soothing clank from the metal bells worn by the huge, placid oxen as they draw their wagon-loads of ancient timber. Now it is too hot to sit in the late September sun, but winter comes early here, and soon I shall be glad to sit in the corner of an evening, and watch the flames flaring upon the huge open fire-place, while I sip my almost black local wine.

This is my idea of peace, though I realize that it might not appeal to everyone. I mention it only because I have not found anything quite like it anywhere else in all my twenty long years of wandering across the world.

IX

THE BULL-FIGHT

I NEVER advise anyone to go to a bull-fight, and I never go alone to one myself. Nevertheless I have seen a hundred or so—good, bad, and indifferent—over a period of twenty years, because I have been obliged to do so by visiting British and American friends.

My reason for including a chapter on the subject is that I have noticed that the great majority of Anglo-Saxon visitors insist upon seeing at least one 'corrida'[1] during their holiday in Spain. They may hate it, disapprove of it, be—though very rarely—bored by it, or they may become wild 'aficionados',[2] but, whatever the outcome, they insist upon going.

As it is a subject on which even generally well-informed people seem to have very peculiar ideas, I shall try to clear up some popular misunderstandings before taking you with me to a typical corrida.

Firstly, bull-fighting is *not* a sport. It is, perhaps, the nearest modern equivalent to the Roman pastime of watching early Christians being eaten by the lions. If I had lived in Rome some 1,800 years ago I suppose that I should have gone along with the other chaps to see 'what was on to-day at the Colosseum', though I suspect that I should not even then have particularly enjoyed the spectacle, unless of course some of my creditors had been among the involuntary performers. Both the Roman and the Spanish holiday feasts may be called exciting, colourful, pagan spectacles, but neither can be justified on strictly moral grounds, and neither can claim to be sporting, but only to be popular amusements belonging to a certain day, age, place, and temperament.

Bull-fighting has been called an art, an amusement, a ritual sacrifice, a pagan science, and a whole lot of other things, some of them rude, but no one in his right mind calls it a sport, for

[1] Corrida: bull-fight.   [2] Aficionado: critical enthusiast.

the simple reason that (except when one is withdrawn for some physical defect) there is no element of luck, skill, or uncertainty that can influence the fate of the bulls. If they have fought bravely, their dead bodies will be enthusiastically applauded as they are dragged out, and if cowardly their exit will be booed, but either way they come in bulls and go out beef—which seems finally to establish that bull-fighting is not a sport.

Secondly, I am always receiving letters asking me to arrange for some intending visitor to see a 'good bull-fight' for such and such a date and place. Unfortunately, no one can guarantee that a given fight will be good, any more than they can guarantee in advance that a certain cricket match or baseball game will be good. One can pick a fight in which the 'matadores'[1] are of high repute, but whether or not any of them fight well on a given afternoon may depend upon such imponderables as what he had for lunch or whether or not he has just had a row with his girl-friend.

An equally important factor is the quality of the bulls. If they are brave (which means stupid) they will charge persistently and straight, which will enable the matador to exhibit his best passes with cape or 'muleta';[2] if they are cowardly they may not 'follow through' (to employ a golfing term) and at the same time may 'hook' sideways with their horns. This not only prevents the matador from showing to advantage, but is also extremely dangerous. Nine out of ten matadores who are killed in the ring are killed by cowardly, not by brave, bulls.

A windy day may also prevent a fight from being good. Everything depends upon the matador succeeding in focusing the bull's attention on the muleta. If this flaps about suddenly (despite having been specially rendered heavy with water by his watchful assistant) it may cause the bull to become more interested in the matador than in the muleta—often with un-comfortable consequences for the matador.

[1] Matador: bull-fighter.
[2] The muleta is the red cloth used by the matador in the phase immediately preceding the killing of the bull.

As to place and date, the 'cartel'[1] of a bull-fight is rarely known until a week or so before it takes place. The reason for this is that most matadores get put temporarily out of action at least once every season, and also their form varies. If a first-class matador is having a bad spell and a relatively little-known one has given a recent series of brilliant performances, the promoters may prefer at the last moment to engage the latter.

Prices for seats, also, vary enormously, depending upon the supposed quality of the performers, both human and taurine.

Thirdly, please note that a bull-fighter may be a matador, a 'novillero', an 'espada', or a 'torero', but never, outside of Bizet's opera, a 'toreador'.

Fourthly, avoid loud comment during a fight until you know what it is all about. I am not easily embarrassed, but audible female comments upon a cricket-match and a bull-fight provided two memorable occasions when I earnestly wished myself elsewhere.

The former was when I took the then lady of my choice to the Eton and Harrow Cricket Match at Lord's, where, for more than an hour, she enjoyed the pageant of smart dresses and passing notabilities. In a period of silence I saw her knit her exquisite brows in puzzlement and, pointing to the players, she then exclaimed, all too clearly:

'But do tell me, Cedric dear, what *are* those men in white doing out there, running about in all this heat?'

Similarly, a matador having just finished a magnificent 'quité' had disengaged from the bull, and was walking slowly away with his back to the animal. After a moment's reflection the bull charged again, and the matador having concluded his quité, quite properly sprinted for shelter in a 'burladero'—one of the narrow, box-like shelters in the 5-foot-high wooden ring provided for such occasions.

My companion, a hockey type of muscular build, let out a hoot of mocking laughter and shouted:

'Dirty, rotten coward! You see he runs away as soon as the

[1] Cartel: published programme.

bull doesn't want to fiddle about any more with his silly bit of red cloth!'

Fifthly, the Spanish term 'bull-fight' covers two major and one minor materially different kind of performance, apart from the supposedly comic shows which are, quite rightly, despised by your real aficionado.

The minor one is the 'rejoneo', a variation upon which is the only kind of bull-fighting permitted in Portugal, in which the bull is 'played' from horseback, and which affords a brilliant display of dangerous and skilful riding. On these occasions I have never seen the magnificent steed ridden by the 'rejoneador' even scratched by the bull's horns. After planting a dart in the fatal point between the bull's shoulder-joints, in Spain the rider descends to despatch what the newspaper reports call 'his enemy' in the usual way. One of the best rejoneadores in Spain is the Duke of Pinohermoso, who frequently performs in the public ring when the proceeds of a bull-fight are for some approved charity.

Bull-fighting proper is divided into corridas in which fully-fledged matadores are engaged, and 'novilladas', engaging apprentices, or 'novilleros', usually young men in their late teens. The procedure followed is identical, but in the former the bulls are larger, older, and stronger. While I have occasionally seen better performances in a novillada than in an afternoon of full-blown matadores, I would still advise anyone to choose the latter for a first visit. The novilleros, though as brave or braver than their seniors in their play of the bull, are rarely as efficient as they when it comes to the kill, and it is precisely a first experience of inexpert—and so messy—killing that may upset you.

I am very often asked hopefully by animal lovers, 'Is it true that football is gradually ousting bull-fighting?' The answer is 'No'—though not for quite the reasons my questioners expect.

The question is like asking whether football is ousting cricket in England, or baseball in the United States. The point is that they are not in competition with one another, since they take place at different times of the year. The bull-fight season opens as a rule on Easter Saturday and closes, except for a few 'benefit' performances, at the beginning of October. Football in Spain begins in early September and ends in May, so the two great national amusements barely overlap.

Love of the 'fiesta brava'[1] is very deeply ingrained in the Spanish character—just how deeply you will realize when you notice that urchins will often stand in the middle of a country road to 'torear' with your car, using their ragged jackets in place of a muleta. As a nation they worship physical courage, feel something of the Russians' fascination with the idea of death, and certainly possess none of the Anglo-Saxon's inhibitions about 'showing off in public'. In fact, Spanish children are fondly encouraged to show off on every possible occasion, and the bull-fight must be the world's supreme opportunity for the individual to show off—complete with the perfect setting of idolatrous crowds, appropriate music, and brilliant clothes.

The popularity of bull-fighting varies a certain amount according to the current standard of the principal performers. With the disappearance of the giants of the nineteen-twenties, such as Joselito (killed in the ring) and Juan Belmonte (to-day running a prosperous farm for raising 'toros de lidia'),[2] there was a flat spell when attendance dropped, though it revived again in the nineteen-thirties under such as Lalanda, Cagancho, Ortega, and the Mexican Arruza. Abandoned during the Civil War, the almost matchless brilliance of Manolete then blazed across Spain until his death in the ring in 1947, due to the absence of adequate means for giving him a blood transfusion. His disappearance left another gap, which has not been adequately filled by the brothers Dominguin, the brothers Vazquez, and relative new-comers such as Litri, Aparicio, Rafael Ortega, Ordoñez, and Pedrés.

Often some young boy will, for a spell, give a hint of real greatness until, inevitably one day, he gets badly gored. Then he usually loses his former dash and love of danger, and drops

[1] Fiesta brava: 'rugged feast'.   [2] Toros de lidia: fighting bulls.

3 'Rafaelillo' placing the first pair of banderillas

4 Juan Belmonte, having completed a 'faena' with the 'muleta', shows his domination of the bull before making the kill

away to become a good second-rater. The sudden access of wealth produced by their first successes, perhaps after years of bitter poverty, is also the cause of much early promise never being fulfilled.

A factor that may one day seriously undermine the popularity of the national pastime is the increasingly poor quality of the fighting bulls. When you consider that some 3,500 are killed every season, you will readily understand the growing difficulty in maintaining the necessary standard—and it is necessary, since even the best matadores can provide only an indifferent spectacle when pitted against 'un manso', a tame bull.

However, something will no doubt be done to deal with the problem, either by limiting the number of fights, or by some fresh cross-breeding between the best remaining herds.

Lastly, before we get to our bull-fight, let me try to answer the old, old question: 'Is it cruel?'

I am not evading the question when I reply, 'To us, yes. To a Spaniard, no.' Realization of cruelty depends upon the possession of a certain kind of imagination, combined with sentimental education. An affectionate baby will cheerfully stick its finger in its mother's eye, but it does so only because it has not yet developed imaginative perception of pain.

Latins in general, and Spaniards in particular, are far less imaginative than Anglo-Saxons—though this may surprise many people. The fact becomes immediately apparent if you compare the reactions to be seen in a dentist's waiting-room in, let us say, London and Madrid. The Englishman *before* the event is an obvious victim of his imagination—sweating, pale, and miserable in anticipation of the pain he is about to suffer. When actually in the torture chamber he is apprehensive but silent, except perhaps for an occasional grunt, and he finally emerges looking almost surprised that his suffering had turned out to be so moderate.

The Spaniard, while waiting his turn, is gay, talkative, and entirely unpreoccupied. He enters jauntily, and the next you hear is probably a yell like that of a banshee, as he emerges scarlet and, as often as not, indignantly exclaiming, 'That this should happen to *me*! What have I, Pedro López y García, father of a growing family, done to deserve this?'

Another example of this lack of imagination—and one intentionally encouraged by the Church—is the almost entire absence of Spanish ghost literature. When you consider the inspiration found in the occult by such writers as M. R. James and Algernon Blackwood, to mention only two among dozens, you will again realize the very special limitations in the scope of the Spanish imagination. Perhaps it is the lack of these same qualities of imagination which is responsible for the fact that while you will find good doctors and superb surgeons in Spain, you will never find even fair hospital nursing.

Secondly, the question of sentimental education. Bull-baiting, cock-fighting, and other equally cruel activities flourished in Britain until Victorian times. 'Sensibility' then became the fashion, and the capacity to swoon at the mere sight of a drop of blood was considered unmistakable proof of gentility. Simultaneously, a best-seller about a horse—*Black Beauty*—for the first time interpreted the sufferings, hopes, and fears of an animal in terms hitherto applied only to human beings, and its effects, like its sales, were enormous. Further, children were soon given Teddy Bears and other animal toys to be the objects of their earliest affections. In our own day Walt Disney has done even more to make animals understandable and lovable characters.

The Spanish child is rarely given animal toys, he is not taught that kindness to animals is one of the cardinal virtues, and he has never read *Black Beauty*. Further, the Church in Spain actively disapproves of the Anglo-Saxon tendency to endow animals with the same capacity for suffering and affection as mankind. In the lists posted inside church doors, in many parts of Spain, for the moral guidance of the people, I noticed only the other day that a revival of Walt Disney's *Bambi* was marked 'morally unsuitable'. When I asked why, I was told that it tended to divert human sympathy, and, consequently, individual charity, away from the relief of 'those made in God's own image'.

Attempts to form a Society for the Prevention of Cruelty to

Animals in Spain was opposed by the Catholic Press, and its sponsors were assailed as 'old maids who have become perverted because they have failed to bear children'. It further attacked the proposed name of the Society, saying that it was unpatriotic in its implication that any Spaniard required preventing, and the Society was finally called 'for the protection of animals and plants'—and has since reluctantly concentrated on the plants!

Before the bull-fight is the spectacle known as the 'entrar en los chiqueros',[1] leading up to the 'encierro' or shutting up of the bulls in their separate stalls ready to be released at the great moment.

It was after my first 'entrar en los chiqueros' that I had my only experience of having a bull personally dedicated to me. It was during the 'fiesta mayor'[2] in Burgos, late in June 1945, and my wife and I were on a short tour of the north as guests of the then Minister for Foreign Affairs, Don Felix Lequerica, now Spanish Ambassador to the United States.

During the fiesta mayor in Burgos, as elsewhere when the city's patron saint is being honoured, there is a bull-fight every afternoon on two, three, or four consecutive days, and we were asked by the Civil Governor both to this special preview on the day before a fight and also to share his box at the fight itself.

Inside the great outer circle of the bull-ring, but in a fairly small separate enclosure, were eight magnificent black fighting bulls of the famous Miura breed. The general public are not admitted, but there was a fairly large sprinkling of aficionados with enough local 'pull' to have secured entry, including a priest who, I was told, was a great enthusiast and had himself, at private parties, stood up to a charging bull long enough to make a few memorable passes.

We circled round the enclosure on a narrow ledge about 10 feet above the heads of the bulls, and I noticed that it was considered correct not to talk loudly, or to make any sudden

[1] Entrar en los chiqueros: preview of the fighting bulls.
[2] Fiesta mayor: principal annual holiday, which varies in date with every town or village, according to its patron saint.

noise or movement. This, I was told, was so as not to excite the animals, causing them perhaps to charge and damage their horns, or to start fighting among themselves. As they had cost about £250 each, such a possibility would be no light matter.

But although I behaved with irreproachable discretion, one 670-lb. beauty decided, without hesitation, that he did not like the look of me. I felt no resentment, as, quite often when shaving, I feel just the same about my appearance as he apparently did, but his opinion was so marked as to be a little embarrassing. Rising from the ground where, until my arrival, he had been contentedly reclining, he approached slowly and menacingly and, after regarding me balefully, snorted in an unmistakably insulting manner. (Luckily I took an excellent photograph of him at this moment.) Wherever I moved he would doggedly follow, his port-winey, bloodshot eyes fixed furiously and exclusively upon me. The other fifty or so people present there meant less than nothing to him, but he obviously felt that if only, just once, he could get me alone in the ring, then life, with all its trials and tribulations, for him would have been worth the living.

At this moment Domingo Ortega arrived, and I was introduced to this most cultured and distinguished-looking matador, who, although nearing the veteran age of 40, was then still one of bull-fighting's Big Three, though never as great as Manolete.

Ortega, whom I had seen fight in Barcelona no less than ten years earlier, had, at close quarters, a rather romantic air of tragedy about him, and I recalled that he had been married to a beautiful Spanish lady of title, whose premature death had reputedly broken his heart. I pointed out to him the really remarkable interest in myself being displayed by the bull, and he smiled and said, 'I will cure him of his discourtesy to-morrow', though I did not know just what he meant until the following afternoon.

It is the custom at bull-fights for the senior matador— seniority depending not upon age but upon the date when he took his 'alternativa' (i.e. ceased to be a novillero or apprentice)

—to take the first and fourth of a normal afternoon of six bulls; the second in seniority, in this case Pepé Luis Vazquez, taking Nos. 2 and 5, and the junior matador being assigned Nos. 3 and 6.

Ortega is rather an untypical bull-fighter in that he likes to make difficult things look easy, whereas most matadores specialize in making easy things look difficult. With Ortega, more than with anyone else, the duel between the will of the man and the will of the animal is particularly apparent, and it is extraordinary the extent to which he seems gradually to hypnotize the animal he is fighting.

If a matador has performed well the crowd will solicit a special reward for him from the President of the fight (the official in charge), usually by waving handkerchiefs. The rewards vary from the right to make a tour of the ring to one ear of the dead bull, two ears, two ears and the tail, and, on extremely rare occasions, a hoof as well! Similarly, where a matador has shown gross cowardice and inefficiency with a brave bull, he may not only have to stand up to whistling, cat-calls, shouted insults, and cushions hurled at his head, but (though I have only seen this once) be obliged to shuffle round the ring on his knees as a final sign of ignominy, and then be fined £50 into the bargain.

Ortega did well with his first bull, and was awarded an ear. Then, after the third bull had been dispatched and sand spread freshly over the bloodstains on the ring floor, there was the usual shrill of a trumpet and—you have guessed it—there was *my* bull! Incredible though it may seem, he hesitated only a moment, apparently located me, and, letting out a bellow, rushed straight up to the nearest barrier to regard me with undiminished hatred.

I saw Ortega laugh and, turning towards my seat, he dedicated the next bull to 'mi amigo, el escritor ingles' (my friend, the English writer). Even Ortega had a job to get the animal to forget me, and it was perhaps this (for him) unusual difficulty in capturing its undivided attention that made his performance below his usual standard.

H

I felt bad about the poor animal, but it was a consolation to recall that perhaps I had been indirectly responsible for speeding him on his way to his next reincarnation as something pretty superior, such as a White Elephant or an Income Tax Inspector.

When a bull is dedicated to you it is usual to send the matador a present of £5 or so, but the Civil Governor stopped me and sent one of the silver cigarette-cases supplied by the dozen to all officials for the purpose, from Madrid.

And now, fortified morally (I hope) by my advice and physically by a large and alcoholically liberal lunch, we are ready for the ordeal. It is five o'clock, and so, smoking a nobbly black cigar known as a 'faria' (costing all of threepence, but actually a great deal less lethal than you might suppose), we will mount our horse-drawn cab and roll regally through the 90 degrees in the shade of the narrow, twisting streets of this typical Andalusian city on the last Sunday in July.

The crowd thickens steadily, a noisy, excited, good-humoured crowd of all types and ages, including babes in arms, and you will marvel that our horse has not yet trampled on anyone, way being made for it at the very last instant by the peculiar clickings and long-drawn-out cries of 'C-a-a-a-a-a-b-a-a-a-ll-o-o-o' —meaning 'horse'—varied with an occasional 'Vay-ay-ay-ay-ay-a'—'keep going'.

At a corner there is a sandy open space, with a glimpse of the sea. From the centre of the dusty brown space rise pale red circular walls.

We have arrived at the 'Plaza de Toros' of Cadiz.

I have really ignored my own advice in bringing you to a novillada, but a provincial city such as Cadiz probably has only three or four big fights in a year, and the three novilleros who are fighting to-day are considered the most promising of the rising generation, and all have recently given sensational performances elsewhere.

There is a milling crowd round the ring, but our tickets are marked 'Tendido 7. Sombra', and we can circle gently until we see an entrance marked 'Tendido 7'. As we plunge into the

gloom under the tiered cement seats, there is the usual aroma of
last Sunday's fish and this Sunday's urine, but steps lead us up
to the open arena and, while waiting for the attendant to deal
with those ahead of us, we can afford to look around and get
our bearings. Below us are five rows of ring-side seats, known
as the 'barreras' and 'contra-barreras', the former being
separated from the ring only by the 7-foot-wide 'callejón',[1] in
which stand the various ring assistants, Civil Guards, and so
on. These to-day (in the shade) cost 150 pts each, but we are in
the 'tendidos', costing 75 pts—to be precise, in the eleventh
row from the ring. This I consider near enough to see everything well, and not near enough to make it difficult to look
elsewhere if things get too messy. On the sunny side the
barreras are 75 pts and the tendidos only 25 pts. The seats
farthest back cost 25 pts in the shade and 10 pts in the sun.

In Andalusia in late July it is worth paying extra not to be
in the sun, and anyway, from the remotest seats much is lost,
and the bulls appear deceptively small. Perhaps you would
have liked to make a day of it and have bought barreras, but I
have an aversion to ring-side seats ever since, in 1935, I saw an
imperfectly placed sword fly out of a bull's back, sail through
the air, and kill a spectator in the second row. The seating
accommodation is a narrow strip on a bare cement step and,
unless you are well provided by nature, it is worth the 2 pts
for a cushion, plus another 2 pts for the man who finally ejects
the determined optimists who have occupied our places in the
vain hope that we might fail to turn up and claim them. Safely
installed, and three minutes to go, you will notice the President's
box, draped with handsome hand-embroidered silk shawls. It is
he who gives the signals for each stage in the fight, and who also
makes awards of ears, tails, &c. for any deserving bull-fighter.

There is an immense buzz of quite unsuppressed excitement
which, whether or not you approve of its motive, is infectious.

The clock touches the half-hour, a bugle blows, and the
parade enters from the opposite side of the ring to that where
the President's box is situated. First comes a finely mounted

[1] Callejón : passage way.

elderly official known as an 'alguacilillo', wearing the clothes of 300 years ago, complete with white starched ruff. Behind him march the three 'espadas': Antoñete, dressed in green silk with silver embroidery, Montero in white with gold embroidery, and Pedrés in pale blue with silver. These costumes, known as 'suits of light' ('trajes de luces') and often encrusted with bullion, may cost several hundred pounds each, and can rarely be worn more than once or twice. The jackets are short, and the knee-length trousers are tight-fitting and without any adornment, so as to ensure clean wounds. All wear pale pink stockings and light, specially made soft-soled, black shoes. Each carries his ornamental cape wrapped tightly round his left arm and shoulder. They rarely smile, and indeed look pretty grim and cross themselves as they enter. So would I in their position— and anyway they have had nothing to eat for the last eighteen hours, so as not to complicate stomach wounds. Behind them march their 'cuadrilla' or assistants, who have received almost the same training as their star but have decided to hitch their wagon to him rather than to attempt to be stars themselves. They may include a specialist or two in the art of placing the 'banderillas', which is attractive to look at and not so dangerous as it appears. Espadas and picadores all wear the short pig-tail required by tradition.

Then come the two picadores, mounted on sorry nags. They wear wide-brimmed hard hats and (though you cannot see them) metal underpants, and carry under their arms the long lances topped with a guard which is supposed to prevent the metal point from penetrating the bull's hide for more than 3 inches or so. Their aged mounts have one eye blindfolded, and on the same side are protected by a thick mattress which hangs down to the ground. This innovation was introduced by Dictator Primo de Rivera about a quarter of a century ago. Prior to that at least one horse got ripped to bits for every bull, which, despite the employment of only the most ancient and economical of animals, was considered needlessly extravagant. At least the animals live longer now, and you are spared the sight of trailing bloody intestines, though whether it is more agreeable to be hit in the side by an express train or torn to pieces by sharp horns is a matter of opinion—but the opinion of animals is not considered of importance in Spain.

Last come the men in red shirts whose job it is to remove the dead bulls by harnessing their horns to a team of four gaily caparisoned horses.

The brilliant colours flash in the sun, and the President throws down the keys for the release of the bulls to the alguacilillo, who, having caught them in his plumed hat (considered a good augury), is duly applauded. After all have saluted the President, the picadores disappear to await their turn and the three novilleros and their cuadrillas take up their positions against the 5-foot-high wooden wall that encircles the sanded ring. Here they leave their ornamental capes or, occasionally, throw them up to some friend or admirer in a ring-side seat, who will proudly spread them over the ledge in order to show the world the compliment that has been paid to him.

As already explained elsewhere, the first and fourth bulls will be killed by the senior espada—in this case Antoñete—the second and fifth by Montero, and the third and sixth by Pedrés, but all three play a part in the ritual that leads to the death of all six bulls.

The big moment has arrived; there is a nerve-jarring blast from a trumpet, a short silence, and then a black monster tears into the ring at a speed that is amazing. To-day's bulls are from the farm of Don Carlos Nuñez, and this being a novillada, they are three-year-old novillos (instead of four- or five-year-olds), but they look quite large enough to me. However, in judging bulls you must wait until they have suffered the attentions of the picador before you can be sure whether or not they have the real fighting spirit. Generally, however, pawing the ground or mooing are sure indications of poor spirit.

On my right is Don Patricio, whom I have never seen in my life before, but of whose commercial, family, and health problems I have been fully informed during the preceding five minutes. Beyond him is his exceedingly pretty eighteen-year-old daughter, who twinkles at me from behind her fan. Her name is Mary Light (Maria Luz), which, with Don Patricio's Andaluz accent, becomes 'My Loo'. It may strike you as an odd name until she informs us that her sisters are called Conception, Pilar, and Africa, and her brothers Jesus and Angel! Anyway, Don Patricio is pessimistic about the quality of to-day's bulls.

Antoñete makes a few good 'naturales' (passes to the left) while he mentally 'fixes' the bull. Montero and Pedrés also do their best to show whether the animal has any special tricks that will need watching. No two bulls react in quite the same way, and all realize that an oversight now may prove fatal later.

Now there is another trumpet call, and the picadores come in on their tragically obedient mounts, who already know from previous and painful experience what is in store for them. The various passes of the cape are now designed to head the bull towards the horse: once he sights it the men efface themselves. The bull charges the horse, and the object of the picador is to transfix the bull with his lance in the slight hump, known as the 'morillo', which rises between the shoulder-blades (if bulls have shoulder-blades) on the back of every fighting bull. He pushes with all his strength, and may be able to prevent the bull from getting his horns into the mattress that protects the horse. Often his lance slides off the morillo and the bull knocks the horse flat, leaving its stomach exposed to the horns and the picador considerably agitated because he cannot get to his feet again, owing to his tin pants. On the present occasion the bull is held off and, as he thrusts again and again to get at the horse, the red blood begins to pulse down his black skin. The crowd begins to whistle and boo the picador for 'spoiling' the bull, and the President decides that one go at the horse, instead of the usual twice, will be enough.

Now is a chance for any one of the three espadas, or the members of their cuadrillas, to distinguish himself with a good quité, the object now being to lead the bull away from the horse.

The picador retires to the usual accompaniment of boos and cat-calls, plus shouts of 'Assassin', and I later learn that he has been fined 500 pts for having 'spoiled' the bull—which is certainly looking considerably the worse for wear. However, he may have been paid 1,000 pts to make a dangerous bull less dangerous. There is no reason to suppose so in the present case —but such things have been known! By and large, it is difficult to understand why anyone deliberately selects the profession of picador—everyone hates him, and the work is dangerous, inglorious, and badly paid!

The next phase is one of the most attractive—or it may just be that I feel better after the horses have gone. Now a member of Antoñete's cuadrilla detaches himself from the 'barrera' holding two yard-long coloured darts, at the end of which are short metal hooks known as 'banderillas'. His job is to place them neatly together on the same place as was attacked by the picador, the object being further to tire the bull's neck muscles so that he will charge with his head lower, and so permit the espada to thrust his sword above and between the horns into the tiny fatal point (no larger than a five-shilling piece) by which his heart can be directly pierced without hitting bone on the way.

The 'banderillero' walks slowly towards the bull with the banderillas raised above his head, while the bull, alert but with painfully heaving flanks, watches him. The man runs across the line of charge and for an instant is poised in the air, feet together, and the points of the banderillas in the bull's neck, while the other ends are still in his fully extended arms. One, two, or three differently coloured pairs may be fixed in this way, according to the state of the bull, but to-day only one pair is allowed. Judging by the way the bull tosses his head to rid himself of the barbs, they must be more painful than one would expect. In some cases the bull-fighter likes to place the banderillas himself, this being particularly the case with Arruza, Dominguin, and Bienvenida.

The stage is now set for the final act.

Antoñete raises his 'montera', or black hat, in dedication of this bull to the President, and with the crimson cloth of the muleta masking the yard-long, naked, and slightly down-curving sword with which the kill is to be made, advances alone towards the bull. Antoñete's style is neat, and he keeps his feet still while making a pass (which is a good thing), but he lacks the great bull-fighter's ability to bring the bull to him, and has to chase it round the ring to secure its attention for each 'faena', or group of passes.

Each kind of pass has its own name, usually that of its inventor—such as 'chicuelinas' (after Chicuelo) or 'manoletinas' (after Manolete)—apart from the routine 'naturales', and 'derechas' (rights) which are the ABC of the business.

The bull, having lost a great deal of blood since the picador left, is poor-spirited and, failing to get him to charge, Antoñete suddenly kicks him in the nose. The crowd applauds and the music plays—always a sign that a bull-fighter is doing well!

Now is 'the moment of truth', when Antoñete must go in over those still-wicked horns and find that alarmingly small fatal spot, in a single thrust carrying behind it all the weight of his undefended body. The first time he hits bone, but the second attempt sends the sword in up to the hilt. The bull stands quite still, gasping, but even so, at every move his head still faces his enemy.

Suddenly blood pours from the bull's mouth in convulsive spasms, his knees crumple, and an assistant quickly severs the spinal cord with a short dagger. His quarter of an hour of agony is ended, though he is booed and whistled as his body is dragged away.

The crowd flutters handkerchiefs in petition for a reward, and the President grants Antoñete an ear.

That is the ritual followed six times, though with infinite variations.

With No. 4 Antoñete does fairly well and kills with his first attempt. The crowd asks for an ear, and his assistant cuts one for him without the President's permission, for which he is subsequently fined 250 pts.

Montero is poor with No. 2, and to complete the kill has to pursue the bull round and round the ring for five minutes—the bull just wanting to be left alone to die in peace, and the bull-fighter taking countless ineffectual jabs at it because it will not

stay still and die like an officer and a gentleman. (Don Patricio
remarks that the only logical conclusion to my dislike for pro-
longed animal suffering is to become a vegetarian. I think he
may have something there but, anyway, for the moment I
much prefer looking at Maria Luz—or My Loo—rather than
at the bull.)

Pedrés has the most pleasing style of the three. He plays
No. 3 bull so close that his nice blue silk suit is badly stained
with blood, which shows how near he is—correct, of course,
though presumably unpopular with his insurance company—if
he has one, which I doubt. Montero gets what was coming to
him with No. 5, being hooked by a horn in the crutch, and in
this case it is his own blood instead of the bull's that stains his
suit. He carries on, and is caught again in the base of the neck.
He faints for a moment against the barrier, but recovers to kill
badly before being removed to the infirmary.

No. 6 bull is upset by the sudden appearance of an 'espon-
taneo', an enthusiastic amateur who evades the police and
jumps into the ring, pulls a strip of red cloth from under his
coat, and takes a couple of the bull's charges before Pedrés'
assistants can catch him and hand him over to the police. He
will spend the night in prison, unless he has impressed some
rich spectator enough to pay the fine of 1,000 pts. Quite often
young men who cannot get into the bull-fighting business take
this method of showing what they can do, and the rich patron
who pays the fine later secures them a job. More often they
get stopped before they can show their talent, or else make a
mess of it, and the adventure ends with the night in jail.
Recently there was the first case of an 'espontanea'—a girl
belonging to a well-to-do Madrid family.

Whatever may be the feelings of the espontaneos, there is no
doubt whatever of the feelings of the professionals towards
them, and it is true that such a sudden intrusion may place the
matador in real danger by breaking his control of the bull's
attention. Perhaps for this reason, Pedrés gets caught, but only
with the bull's head, not with his horns, and he wisely lies
absolutely still while the animal takes a sniff and slowly decides

whether or not to kill him. Within a few seconds the cuadrilla have 'led' the bull away with their capes, and Pedrés goes on to kill, apparently unhurt. He later attributes his escape to the ten silver medals of the Virgin of the Pilar which he happened to be wearing at the time.

The bull-fight is over, and the time is 7.15 p.m. We both feel surprisingly tired, and go in search of a drink.

This post-bull-fight tiredness is a well-known and universal reaction, and there are lots of stories in Spanish about the jealous wife who could always tell from his appearance when her husband had been unfaithful to her, until he demonstrated to her that he looked exactly the same after attending a bull-fight. After that he confined his infidelities to the days when there was a bull-fight in the neighbourhood—and they both lived happily ever after!

This bull-fight that we have attended was below the average standard, principally owing to the poor quality of the bulls. I have not attempted to portray the pure poetry of motion that constitutes a good series of passes, since this afternoon there have been very few such moments. However, you may have seen enough, notably during Antoñete's first and Pedrés' first bulls (Nos. 1 and 3), to have caught a faint suggestion of what bull-fighting at its best can be. Whether or not it is worth going to a number of indifferent shows in order to capture one of those supremely colourful, passionately exciting moments, is a problem which every individual must decide for himself.

I have purposely not gilded the lily, and tried only to tell you roughly what to expect. As they used to say on large posters before dangerous traffic corners in the days of my youth: 'You have been warned'. But warnings, after all, are only for the unadventurous!

X

ATLANTIC ANDALUSIA

Gibraltar—Algeciras—Cadiz—Puerto de Santa Maria—Sanlucar de Barrameda—Huelva.

TO begin a tour of Spain's southernmost and most colourful province of Andalusia from the British fortress of Gibraltar may seem strange, but there are good reasons for the choice.

Firstly, there is the question of communications. Andalusia being the area of Spain farthest from the United Kingdom, British tourists, suffering from currency restrictions, can only visit it in anything like comfort if they can pay their return fares in London. British European Airways provides a direct link by air, and there are also a certain number of passenger ships calling at Gibraltar.

Certainly it requires the best part of a week to reach Andalusia by car from Britain, and it means at least two nights in a 'sleeper' from Paris to Seville by train.

For visiting Americans who prefer not to travel by air, the selection of Gibraltar is also defensible as, even if they do not first land there, they do so at Tangier and, once tired of that modern Sodom and Gomorrah (a title that may be disputed by Casablanca), they cross the Straits by ferry-boat to Algeciras, which is just across the Bay from 'the Rock'. Alternatively, most of the ships of the American Export Line touch at Gibraltar, or else at Cadiz, only some 80 miles north-west of the fortress and itself our first objective on this tour.

The second major reason for picking Gibraltar is that the Spanish Government now permit all foreign visitors to bring with them into the country up to 10,000 pts in Spanish currency (though they may not take out more than 2,000 pts)—this quite apart from any foreign currency, which must be declared on entry and accounted for (as having been legally changed at a bank or hotel) on departure. Most tourists, both British and American, are aware that this permitted 10,000 pts can be purchased more cheaply in Gibraltar or Tangier than at the official tourist rate of exchange in Spain. Many feel that this is taking an unfair advantage of the Spanish authorities, who have already provided them with the cheapest holiday in Europe, but many more, since at present it is perfectly legal, prefer to profit from the situation.

Unkind critics have said that in Gibraltar it always feels as though it were Sunday afternoon. If that is so, then it would be only fair to add that in the Spanish border town of La Linea it is permanently Saturday night. Gibraltar has been in British hands for two and a half centuries, and until quite recently it was of vital importance in keeping open Britain's trade communications with India via the Suez Canal. The aeroplane has greatly reduced its strategic value and, despite all efforts during World War II to build one across the narrow base of the peninsula, the Crown Colony's air-strip is still too short for the fast-landing fighter planes, so essential to its defence, unless the wind is in the right quarter.

Military experts agree that the fortress as it is depends upon a friendly or at least upon a not hostile Spain and, in the fortunately unimaginable event of hostilities between the two countries, it could only be defended by thrusting out a perimeter 20 miles or so deep into the surrounding country.

Most people like to see the famous Gibraltar monkeys—Barbary apes, to be exact—whose disappearance, superstition says, will mark the end of British rule, but few know that during the last war they very nearly died out owing to all the young being born males. Winston Churchill, although at the time somewhat busy with Messrs. Hitler and Mussolini, arranged for a number of female Barbary apes to be rushed to 'the Rock', and the population subsequently increased. Now, however, the same tendency has again developed—namely, a growing shortage of females—and the non-simian inhabitants of Gibraltar are beginning again anxiously to shake their heads.

The British possession of Gibraltar has always been an irritant to Spanish public opinion—understandably so, as we should hardly appreciate a Spanish naval base occupying, let us say, the Isle of Wight or Rhode Island. However, the popular sentiment is not shared either by the Gibraltarians or the Spaniards of La Linea and Algeciras. The Gibraltarians at present pay virtually no taxes, and the population of La Linea and Algeciras live extremely well under the shadow of the fortress, chiefly by smuggling.

Every single day thousands of Spaniards enter Gibraltar to work, principally as domestic servants to the large military garrison or as dockers, and every night they troop back again into Spain. This almost total reliance upon 'foreign' labour is, in my opinion, dangerous. I saw the chaos that was produced in Burma and Singapore when the Burmese, Malay, and Chinese household servants and dock labourers walked out on their British employers at the approach of the Japanese in 1942, and the same thing might have occurred in Gibraltar if Franco had not firmly refused Hitler's attractive offer of assistance to capture the fortress in 1940.

No doubt actuated by what are called strategical considerations, the Spaniards have never built any kind of railway communication with Gibraltar, and the rail-head is at Algeciras 5 miles away. Even this links up only with an extremely poor service, which carefully avoids going directly to anywhere that you are at all likely to wish to visit—such as Cadiz, Seville, or Malaga. Instead, it climbs inland to Ronda and Antequera, which are both well worth seeing, before turning north to Cordoba and east to Granada. It is not a journey that I recommend, even though Algeciras is our first call in Andalusia. It is reached either by the 15 miles of road from Gibraltar or—and far more agreeably—by ferry-boat direct across the Bay. Customs, exchange, and passport formalities are not very arduous—they rarely are anywhere if you are reasonably patient, unflustered, and co-operative. Even as early on as this you may notice that hectoring and bullying will get you nowhere (except perhaps into trouble) while you are in Spain, while ordinary politeness will work miracles. If you have, accidentally or intentionally, broken some red-tape regulation, remember that there is one infallible charm with a Spanish official. If you first say you are sorry, and then ask him, 'What do you advise me to do?', he will take immense pains to work out some system whereby you can get away with it, not only now but also for all future occasions! If he is helpful, offer him some cigarettes; but he will be mortally offended if you try to give him money.

To most tourists Andalusia is the 'most Spanish' of Spain's provinces. Its character is, in fact, wholly African, upon which has been imposed a Spanish overlay. Moorish blood is clearly apparent in the people, and there are nearby mountain villages where even the everyday clothes are unchanged since the Reconquest. African, too, are the date-palms, the pale-coloured, untidy, jumbled, dusty buildings, indifferently combining any number of conflicting architectural styles, and African the beggars, who elsewhere in Spain have been largely abolished by the Franco régime. As in Africa, the numerous flea-bitten cats are all either in an advanced state of pregnancy or else vociferously announcing their intention of becoming so within the minimum possible period of time.

Founded by the Romans, Algeciras is to-day chiefly noted for a Moorish aqueduct and a large hotel. The latter is much frequented by the wives of garrison officers from Gibraltar, and is set amid orange trees and fine gardens.

Although Seville is the first objective of most visitors to Andalusia, there are various good reasons for making the great Atlantic port of Cadiz our first call.

Firstly, as already explained, the railway communications with Seville are bad; secondly, the road from Algeciras to Cadiz is very beautiful; and, thirdly, there is the question of temperature.

Most of us wage-slaves have to take our holidays in the summer, and Andalusia between June and October can produce maximum shade temperatures of over 110° F. Cadiz is the exception and, although in its narrow, twisting streets it also can be hot during the early afternoon, the Atlantic Ocean has only to sigh in its sleep for cool breezes to stir the palms and rustle the dry petals of the purple bougainvillæa that cascades everywhere over its whitewashed walls.

The fashionable time to visit Andalusia is in April and May (when you can be sure that it will rain), and the best time is in October and November. But if you decide to visit it in the summer, then give consideration to my idea of making Cadiz your base.

There are various daily bus services from Algeciras to Cadiz but, if you can make your departure from there at 3 p.m. on any Sunday or Monday, you can make use of the really luxurious new service run by an organization called ATESA (whose activities I have described in more detail in Chapter III). If your objective should be Malaga, they also have a service leaving Algeciras at 9.30 a.m. every Sunday.

Only a few miles from Algeciras, in the little town of Puerto del Cabrito nearly 1,000 feet above sea-level, there is an unforgettable view of the Atlas Mountains on the African side of the Straits—cloudy, dark and mysterious, as when the Pillars of Hercules were the western limits of the known world.

Then comes Tarifa, the southernmost town in Spain, from which the defeated Moors four and a half centuries ago made their final departure. In 1492 the still-standing 7-foot-thick walls, protected by twenty-six towers, withstood a memorable siege, but to-day it seems to live only on its memories and on the proceeds of the thousands of huge tunny-fish brought in by its fishermen.

The road runs along by sand-dunes across the River Salado, beside which grave-looking storks and an occasional white egret are usually to be seen, until it reaches the dead-white gipsy village of Chiclana de la Frontera. Three miles away is the magnificent sand bathing-beach of La Barrosa, where the little restaurant set among umbrella pines will serve you delicious fresh lobster, and not far from which are the ruins of a temple of Hercules.

Then comes San Fernando and the long, circuitous road into Cadiz.

Cadiz at first glance looks distinctly battered—and with reason. Although it is known to have been a port town for nearly 4,000 years, you will find very few complete buildings that date from before the seventeenth century A.D. Its history is stormy, even for Spain, the city having been the object of particularly persistent naval attacks by the British and Dutch and, as the Spanish chroniclers say, 'other pirates', who destroyed the thirteenth-century cathedral in 1596, while the 1755 earthquake, which entirely destroyed Lisbon, also did great damage here.

It is perhaps worth mentioning that you will find quite a number of Plazas de Trafalgar in Spain, commemorating a naval battle fought within sound of this same road between Algeciras and Cadiz, which I was brought up to believe was won by the British Admiral Nelson against the French fleet, the latter being assisted by some Spanish vessels. Not at all! The Spanish history books assure us that while their side was technically defeated (owing entirely to the incredible inefficiency of the French supreme command), they, individually, did far better than anyone else!

Anyway, they can fairly take the credit for having inflicted upon Nelson the only real defeat he ever suffered—namely, that off the Canary Islands, where he lost his arm as well as the battle.

Cadiz does not claim to be a first-class sea-side resort, though during July and August it is a favoured point for escape from the heat of the interior. Its life is as a port, for here come tourist ships from Scandinavia, the United States, and South America, while there is a regular service to and from the Canary Islands.

However, the setting of the Hotel Atlantico, on the extreme tip of the long, narrow strand of land upon which Cadiz is built, and the magnificent sand bathing-beach known as the Playa de la Victoria, 3 miles away, are being developed.

Its greatest charm, however, is its climate in summer, and the small excursions for which it is such a good centre.

The town itself is a rabbit-warren of incredibly narrow and confusing streets, occasionally opening out into a plaza containing a baroque church; but, in a country that is so overwhelmingly rich in ecclesiastic architecture, there is little here that demands sightseeing attention. We may, however, pay our respects to the famous Murillo 'Purisima' in the oratory of the little church of San Felipe Neri. It is an odd church, tucked away in a back street, and the interior looks like a University Debating Club. A kindly priest abandoned his confessional box to lead me to the 'Purisima' over the main altar, switching on the special lighting for my benefit. Try as I would, it still looked altogether too much like a Christmas card to signify anything to me, but I murmured enthusiastic nothings, so as not to hurt my guide's feelings.

As we walked towards the door he told me something I had not known—that the church had in fact been of a kind of Debating Society, as it was precisely here that, as victory at last approached in 1812, the abandoned people of Spain worked out their new Liberal Constitution, which incidentally was summarily withdrawn as soon as that most lamentable of monarchs, Ferdinand VII, believed himself to be firmly enthroned.

Murillo (1617–82) is to-day rather out of fashion as an artist, but it is said of him that he will never be outmoded with the women of Spain, to whom his slightly sickening idealization of children and maternity irresistibly appeals. This extreme idealization of their young by all Spaniards will strike you forcibly before you have been in the country for very long, and I think that Spain is the only country in the world where you will see frail old ladies—and men too—giving up their seats in the Metro to strapping young males of 10, 12, or even 14 years of age. Nor will the said youths say 'Thank you' as they sprawl in comfort, for such tribute from their elders is their unquestioned right.

All over the world, of course, there has been a reaction against the excessive child discipline of the Victorian age, which, the psychoanalysts assure us, later produced all sorts of nasty inhibitions. However, the entire absence of any kind of discipline for Spanish children might well produce undesirable complexes in the visiting adult, such as, for example, a craving for a new Massacre of the Innocents. You will tend to find excessive freedom granted to the weakest elements in any

I

community in which life is abnormally difficult. The shortage of women in America during its colonist days is directly responsible for the old joke that the life of the modern American male is divided into three stages—when he is a slave to his mother, a slave to his wife, and a slave to his daughter. Similarly, in Spain infant mortality was appallingly high until well into the present century, and the absence of any kind of parental discipline for Spanish children probably stems, at least partly, from this recent memory.

In fact, Spain to-day—thanks to the Church's opposition to birth-control plus the universal custom of the after-lunch siesta —has a population which is increasing at the rate of over 100,000 a year. So, perhaps before long, the present attitude towards child discipline will be modified.

The Hotel Atlantico in Cadiz is rather remote from the city if you have no car, but quite near it there is a charming square, open on its fourth side to the sea, known as Alameda de Apodaca. Here itinerant musicians confine themselves to the soothing and pleasant thrumming of a couple of deep-toned guitars, which produce a not too intrusive music for either thought or conversation. Recalling how many diverting conversations, over dishes of 'scampi', had been ruined for me in Italy by the high neighing of Neapolitan tenors, the contrast epitomizes the subtle but profound difference between a holiday in Spain and a holiday in Italy.

Here in the Alameda there is a shady flower-garden, with such old friends as hollyhocks rubbing petals with exotic-looking poinsettias, banana plants, deep red oleanders and, of course, the ubiquitous bougainvillæa, presided over by a single giant magnolia tree. Few places could be pleasanter for you to sit and sip your 'manzanilla' (very dry sherry) and get your fingers messy eating delicious 'cigalas' (Dublin Bay prawns) or 'gambas' (ordinary prawns).

As the sun goes down and the myriad swifts wheel and scream overhead in pursuit of their supper, you will probably find the sky before you, out across the Atlantic, burning with immense smoky fires that look unquenchable. Sunsets, of course, are not what they were, ever since Technicolor so markedly improved upon the Almighty's handiwork, but in Cadiz you may occasionally have your doubts. As the last light fades, the murmuring of lovers under the flowering trees becomes more intense but, if you value your illusions, never risk eavesdropping. If you do you will hear the 'corniest' love-making imaginable, bearing out the theory that no Spanish woman is in the least interested in what a man *says*, except inso-far as it indicates what he is going to *do*. Being witty or pro-found to a physically attractive Latin woman is less likely to achieve the desired result than reciting the multiplication tables in a voice choked with passion.

If you doubt this, watch the antics of a Spanish professional 'masher'. As the object of his admiration approaches, he will halt in his tracks, open wide his mouth, raise his clutching claw-like hands level with his shoulders, roll his eyes, and grimace hideously. His general appearance suggests that he is suffering from the opening pangs of a sharp attack of dysentery—but it works like a charm, because it is taken as an evidence of his uncontrollable intentions, and not of what he may think or say.

The men and women of Andalusia are not among Spain's handsomest, the Moorish characteristics being unmistakably marked. The men seem too lightly built, fine boned, and fragile, and the women, with Nature's usual tendency to compen-sate against extremes, assiduously cultivate the hour-glass figure.

The tendency to judge the beauty of women primarily in terms of weight is, of course, purely Oriental, and is particularly marked in the parts of Spain where Moorish influence is strongest—namely, in Andalusia and the Mediterranean Levante—but it is perceptible, in a less pronounced degree, all over the country. Spain is, in fact, one of the last countries in Europe where women dress to please men—as distinct from the Anglo-Saxon women, whose clothes are designed with the sole idea of making other women jealous.

If you have by now consumed enough manzanilla and cigalas, we can stroll across to take our dinner on the pavement of either of the two first-class restaurants there. In El Telescopio, if there had been an R in the month, Don Mariano Gonzalez would have produced his speciality of fried oysters; however, as it is summer, there is always 'langosta' (crayfish) or the still finer flavoured 'langostinos' (giant prawns, four or five inches long), or a dish of mussels cooked in a sauce in which a delicious trace of garlic may just be detected.

On the following morning I suggest that we catch the little ferry-boat that leaves the harbour at 11.30 bound for Puerto de Santa Maria just across the Bay. This one-boat service heads its printed time-table with the representation of a three-funnelled Transatlantic blue-riband luxury liner doing 30 knots an hour, but in fact the antique tug is provided with what appeared to me to be a one-candle-power motor-bicycle engine, and the 3 miles takes us forty-five minutes. But it is cool in the shade and the sea breeze, and the charge is only 8d. or 10 cents!

I mention Puerto de Santa Maria (home, incidentally, of two famous marks of Spanish brandy) because it is typical of how, by taking trouble to get a little off the beaten track, all this hot and uncomfortable rushing about in third-class trains, recommended by some of the current guide-books on Spain as 'adventurous', is wholly unnecessary, even for the tourist of strictly limited means.

Until after sunset it is a sleepy little town whose prosperity suffered when, with the coming of the railway to Cadiz, it ceased to be the port from which all the sherry-growers sent their wines abroad. However, the strangely shaped yellow boats, each relying on sail but carrying an auxiliary motor, that come from Puerto de Santa Maria are often met with as far afield as the Canary Islands in search of the fish by which the town, since Greek times, has gained its surest living, independently of the wine-growers.

The fine palm-tree 'paseo' leads to an excellent sand bathing-beach just beyond the mouth of the river up which our ferry vibrates its unconvincing way to the little landing-stage.

Sight-seeing can be limited to a glance at the impressive, crumbling Gothic church with its baroque portico. Inside it is dark and cool, and the carved oak choir-stalls are littered with ragged music-books for the singing of High Mass. I opened one at random and read, 'Office of the Mass. Printed by Montserrat Cancella in Barcelona on February 10th, 1686, by favour of His Most Catholic Majesty King Carlos II.' In Spain they still use and live with ancient things, instead of putting them away in a museum.

The remnants of a Moorish castle 100 yards away bears a tablet 'in honour of Juan de la Cosa and Pedro de Villa, neighbours of this city, who accompanied Cristobal Colon[1] on his great voyage of discovery'. This is no place for holiday-makers who require ready-made amusements—though there was a cinema showing a twenty-year-old Marx Brothers film—but only for those who want sun, peace, excellent sea-bathing, and the best sherry in the world at twopence a glass—and that, of course, includes olives or fresh prawns as a 'tapa'.

I spent one night in the Hotel Loretto, sleeping far better than usual in a clean, eighteenth-century wooden bed between hand-embroidered lace sheets. The floor was of cool black-and-white stone blocks, and my window opened out upon grass-grown, yellowish-brown roof-tiles, where two storks were raising a promising family. The charge for the room alone was 15 pts a night—roughly 2s. 9d. or 37 cents. For the room with all meals—and *what* meals—of a six variety hors-d'œuvres, a fried mixed grill of eight different sorts of fish, followed by a huge veal cutlet and two vegetables (this last served, as always in small places in Spain, as a separate course before the meat) and a mountain of fruit, including cherries, fresh figs, bananas, and plums—the charge was 45 pts a day, or roughly 8s. or $1.15.

Even a travel allowance of £50 will last a long time at 8s. or 10s. a day, including drinks and general self-indulgence.

Farther up the coast is the similar but slightly larger port of Sanlucar de Barrameda, at the mouth of the River Guadalquivir, though the only road to it from Cadiz is through Jerez de la Frontera.

It is only about 50 road-miles from Cadiz, but you may find

[1] Christopher Columbus is an Anglo-Saxon invention. He called himself Cristobal Colon.

some difficulty in making the return journey in a single day by bus, for the same reason as applies generally in out-of-the-way parts of Spain—namely, that the bus services are designed to bring the country-folk into the big city for the day, and not for the benefit of the townsman who wishes to spend a day in the country. Buses therefore leave the villages early in the morning, and the cities late in the evening, for the return journey.

Sanlucar is famous for two things: it is the home of 'manzanilla', known, if at all, to the outside world incorrectly as 'dry sherry', and it was the port from which Columbus sailed on his third voyage to America in 1498.

The last Spanish province before the Portuguese frontier begins on the opposite side of the River Guadalquivir from Sanlucar, but there is no direct communication except on horseback across the 50 miles of sand dune, pine, and marsh that separates it from La Rabida and Huelva.

It is from Sanlucar that one of the three cavalcades of horsemen and women sets out two days before Whit Sunday every year on the most famous and picturesque of all Spain's 'romerias'[1]—the 'Romeria de El Rocio'. They cross an area of some 65,000 acres in which there is no single human habitation except the little 'palacio' or hunting lodge, built 300 years ago by Philip IV in the centre of this tremendous royal game preserve. The pilgrims spend most of the night round campfires, singing and making love to the sound of their guitars, and at dawn are on the last lap of their journey to pay their respects to the miraculous Virgin of El Rocio, not far from Almonte.

There is a saying among the local peasantry: 'She is so ugly that even the Romeria de El Rocio could not get her a husband'.

This huge uninhabited area of land is still a hunting preserve, owned by a combine of three rich families, though the State Tourist Department is thinking of taking it over for dollar-bearing foreign sportsmen. Red and fallow deer, wild boar, sand-grouse, duck, geese, partridge, lynx, and various other kinds of large and small game abound.

[1] A romeria is a kind of picnic excursion to a shrine, usually on horseback or in ox-wagons.

5 The Romeria de El Rocio

6 The Romeria de El Rocio leaving Sanlucar de Barrameda

The whole of this coast from Cadiz to the Portuguese frontier has associations with Columbus and the discovery of the New World.

The first towns we come to, after crossing the endless empty sands of the Playa de Castella, as this stretch of coast is named, are La Rabida and Palos de Moguer. It was from Palos that Columbus and the Pinzon brothers set out on the first and greatest voyage that discovered America, and it was in the Franciscan monastery of La Rabida that the former took shelter with his son when utterly discouraged by his failure to find the necessary financial backing for his project. The accident that the abbot, Friar Perez de Marchena, as a former confessor to Queen Isabel, was able to interest her in his plans finally secured him his long-awaited opportunity.

Forty miles farther west the ancient Phœnician trading town of Ayamonte, with its crumbling yellow stone turrets and fortifications, marks the frontier with Portugal and the limit of Atlantic Andalusia.

XI

SEVILLE AND CORDOBA

BY whatever route you come to Andalusia, whether by road, rail, or plane, whether from Gibraltar, Cadiz, Madrid, or Malaga, you will most surely find your own way ultimately to Seville.

This is the Spain of the tourist agent's coloured posters—of lithe gipsy 'flamenco'-dancers with carnations in their sleek black hair, and the slender loveliness of the Giralda Tower, flung against a blazing sky and circled by white pigeons; of free sherry and proud-stepping bull-fighters in their 'suits of light'; of serenades and romance, and hooded black figures walking barefoot in candle-lit processions.

Just like that paragraph, Seville during a fiesta always leaves me a little breathless until I get over the first emotional impact of the place!

Here everything is 'laid on' for the perfect Technicolor holiday, but I have never been helped to enjoy myself by being told that something is going to be 'terrific', whether it is a play, a film, a book, or a place, and during the Semana Santa and the Fair in Seville it is hard work convincing everyone you meet that there never was such a party, such flamenco, such a bull-fight, such a brunette, such a procession, as this one, particularly when you and they know perfectly well there was, just a year ago, and that there will be at the same date next year.

This may be just the personal prejudice of an incurable introvert, but I am sure that the best moments 'happen' and are not arranged annually on a given date. Perhaps for that reason, I found the Easter Week processions in Granada far more moving than those in Seville, and heard the best flamenco of my life in a gipsy encampment under a broken railway arch in Catalonia.

Although Seville is visited by tourists all the year round, I find that all British and most American visitors agree with me that from June until mid-October it is too hot for sight-seeing, and the fashionable season is in the spring, with Easter week, followed a few weeks later by the Annual Fair, as the season's culminating point. Spring comes early in Andalusia, and although the seasonal heavy rains may spoil an occasional day, there is a pagan excitement carried on the orange-blossom and acacia-perfumed air that is lacking at other times of the year. But since my object all along must be to try to tell you just what to expect, I must say a warning word about hotel accommodation and prices during the spring in Seville.

Firstly, every hotel or 'pension' not only in Seville but everywhere else within 100 miles, at Jerez or Cadiz, is booked up solid three or more months in advance, and there are many firm bookings made, and paid for in advance, from one Easter to the next. There are very few occasions indeed in Spain when you cannot just stroll in at the last moment and find a room waiting for you, but this is one of them. Others are at San Sebastian from July 20th until September 30th, Pamplona for the Fiesta de San Fermin (when the bulls are coursed through the streets on July 7th–11th), Palma de Mallorca and the Costa Brava during July and August, Madrid during the celebrations of San Isidro, beginning on May 15th, and Santiago de Compostela around August 15th. On all these relatively few dates and occasions you must either book well in advance, and confirm your booking again two or three weeks before the date of arrival, or else choose some other date for your visit.

I was telephoned during Easter Week in Seville in 1952 by an American novelist and his wife, who had arrived there on impulse. I asked him how they were fixed, and he replied that they were in an hotel which was apparently more accustomed to hiring the rooms by the hour than by the day or week, and that they were so depressed sitting in their grim little room, with a stone wall opposite as the only view, that he was reduced to dropping little pencilled notes out of the window in the hope that some kind passer-by would pick them up and then come and rescue them! I am glad to say that I was able to play the rôle of rescuer, but the incident may serve as a warning to casual travellers that this is an occasion when, for once, they *must* plan in advance.

Secondly, although hotel prices are very rigidly controlled in Spain by the Tourist Department, special concessions have been granted in Seville for Holy Week and the Fair whereby the hotel-keepers may legally charge double their normal rates, and these rates are fixed to include full pension, whether or not you eat in the hotel. Additionally, rooms are charged for by the week—that is, from the Monday before Easter until the Monday after—regardless of whether you stay for one night or seven nights. This means that a double room ordinarily costing 250 pts with full pension for two people now requires a minimum payment of 3,500 pts, or around £32, or $88.

I think enough has been written elsewhere about Seville's Holy Week ceremonies and processions and the great annual Fair for it to be unnecessary for me here to describe them in detail. The days commemorating Christ's Passion and Death are days of deep and, in a way, surprisingly sincere mourning for Spaniards of every class and condition. As a people they are, like the Russians, fascinated by the idea of suffering and death—not as a rule morbidly so, but as a theme which makes them even more intensely aware of their own aliveness, and of the imperative need to enjoy life to the full—a characteristic which is also unmistakably revealed by the bull-fight.

On Thursday and Friday theatres and cinemas are closed, or open only for religious plays or films, and between noon of Thursday and midnight on Friday private cars are not supposed to circulate, and even public services, such as trams and buses, are reduced to a minimum, while many people wear only black. All figures, images, and pictures, except some of the 'Dolores'—the sorrowing Mother of God—are shrouded or covered in black cloth. Churches are not only filled, but you will find queues of many hundreds waiting silently to enter; and this is true not only of Seville but of the whole country.

Then, on the evening of Good Friday, the greatest of the processions sets out, carrying the beautiful jewelled image of the Virgin Mary known as 'La Macarena', and various life-sized

7 The twelfth-century Giralda Tower of Seville's sixteenth-century
Cathedral. It was originally part of a mosque

groups representing scenes from the last days before the Crucifixion. Some of them are beautifully wrought by famous artists of the fifteenth, sixteenth, and seventeenth centuries, and nearly all bring home the idea of intense human suffering in a way which may shock some Nordic susceptibilities. It must be remembered, however, that their only object was, and up to a point still is, to move the emotions of simple people who cannot be made to feel intensely except through the senses. The various 'pasos', as they are called, are carried on the shoulders of barefooted penitents, who each hold a lighted candle in their free hand. The strange atmosphere is intensified by their long pointed black or white hoods, which completely cover their faces except for the slits through which their eyes gleam in the wavering light of the candles. The town is blacked out, and the only sound is the occasional tolling of the church bells as for the dead, and the nerve-tightening beat of a single hand drum, which sets the slow pace for these hooded figures, moving stiffly in unison, as though part of some fantastic nightmare. If one of the famous flamenco singers chooses the moment to cut through the heavy silence with the sudden wild and desolate cry of an impromptu lament, the pricking of the hair on your scalp may perhaps make you realize that the uncanny drama of the scene has gripped you far more deeply than even you yourself had suspected.

Then on Saturday occurs one of those inexplicable things that could happen only in Spain. Mourning is over and done, and bull-fights, theatres, cabarets, and celebrations in general are the order of the day. Now, I have no wish to labour the point, but, although the exact hour of the Resurrection is a matter of uncertainty, all authorities are agreed both that Jesus of Nazareth died during the course of Friday and 'on the *third* day rose again'. In conformity with this, the Pope himself waits until after midnight on Saturday before he announces 'Christ is risen'—and Spain is a devoted follower of the doctrine of Papal Infallibility. Yet everywhere in Spain, Easter Saturday —Sabado de Gloria—is a day of rejoicing, and I can never get a Spaniard to explain to me how, if Christ's death took place on

Friday, they can start celebrating his Resurrection 'on the third day' considerably less than twenty-four hours after His removal from the Cross.

I think the explanation must be partly, at least, in the Spanish tendency to celebrate the eve of any kind of anniversary rather than the anniversary itself. We have the same tendency in seeing in the New Year, and no one would deny that the night of December 31st is much more of an occasion than January 1st. This is particularly noticeable in the case of a Spanish Easter, where it apparently brings national custom so directly into conflict with the teachings of the Church.

The annual Fair, which usually opens at the end of April, is a week-long carnival, with no religious background to it. If you go, you had better be prepared to get an average of from three to four hours' sleep a night; but if you have friends who know their way around, it can be tremendous fun—if you can 'take' it. The beautiful fair-grounds are dazzlingly lit each night, and in countless little booths—'casetas'—families invite all and sundry to take a glass or two of wine, discuss the afternoon's bull-fight, and throw handfuls of flowers at the endless cavalcade of beautifully mounted men and women. The best gipsy flamenco dancers and singers are employed by those who can afford it, and the quick hand-clapping, followed by the guitar and castanets, can be heard as one or other spring to their feet, stamp, and break into the passionate and exciting rhythm for which they are famous.

But Seville is not all fiestas, and there is much to see there that it would be a pity to miss. I promised to limit my comments on cathedrals to half a dozen or so because, in a land of such incredible architectural riches, it is essential not to set myself the impossible task of trying to compete with Baedeker. But Seville Cathedral is the largest in Spain, and one of the few that really must not be overlooked.

The building of Santa Maria de la Sede was begun in 1402 and finished in 1519, but it incorporated in itself the lovely twelfth-century minaret of the former mosque, known as the

Giralda Tower, and there are other traces of the Moorish building to be seen in the orange patio.

When you first step inside and the heavy leather curtains have fallen back over the blazing sun and the noisy street, the immensity of this dim-lit cathedral is almost intimidating and, when your eyes become accustomed to the rich soft tones and the pale gleam of gold and silver, you will probably find the stones at your feet are patterned with rich reds and blues from the sixteenth-century stained-glass windows.

The Spaniards claim that the body of Christopher Columbus —Cristobal Colon—was brought to Seville at the time of the American conquest of Cuba in 1898, and that the impressive tomb in the south transept contains his remains, but this is denied by certain of the South American Republics. Quite recently, in pursuit of her policy of 'hispanidad', Spain offered the remains for interment in South America, but although the combined result would almost certainly have added up to at least one complete Columbus, the offer was refused, on the basis that they could not very well bury two men under one name.

'Hispanidad' is rather badly translated as 'Spanishness', but it corresponds to the British idea of culturally binding together the English-speaking nations through their common language.

But whether or not the tomb in Seville Cathedral contains the true remains of Christopher Columbus, it is full of beautiful things concerning the authenticity of which there can be no doubt. In the Chapel Royal there is a particularly fine 'reja', or wrought-iron grille, guarding the tombs of King Alfonso the Wise and his mother, Beatrice of Swabia, and the altar contains the remains of the thirteenth-century Saint-King Ferdinand in a silver coffin, together with the miraculous 'Virgin of the Kings', patron of Seville, which was a gift to Ferdinand from the French Saint-King Louis. Near by are the tombs of Pedro the Cruel, and the tiny ivory 'Virgin of Battles' that always accompanied Saint Fernando when he mounted his charger to lead his troops against those of Islam. Four times every year the body of the Spanish Saint-King is exposed to the faithful at a special service.

The cathedral is rich in Old Masters—a 'Dolorosa' by Murillo, and fine works by Valdes Leal, Alonso Cano, Goya, and Zurbaran of the Spanish school, and others by Titian, Van Dyck, and Van der Weyden. Since the best work to be seen in Spain of all these artists is the subject of a separate chapter[1] I need only recommend you to visit the sacristy (Sacristia Mayor), where most of them are to be seen, together with many magnificent gold and silver church vessels.

While the Christians made use of the Moorish Giralda Tower, the Moors, in building it, had made use of many early Christian and Roman buildings, and it is a little-known fact that near the base of the tower there are stones to be seen bearing Latin inscriptions of the fourth century.

The ascent of the Giralda Tower was designed in a gradual winding slope so that armed men could reach the top on horseback, but although this may no longer be possible, the view over the city from the top is worth the climb. Crowning the tower is the 13-foot-high bronze sixteenth-century wind-vane that 'girars', or turns, and is responsible for its name.

The Lion Gate of the Moorish Alcazar is only a few yards from the cathedral, across the square. It was for many years the Palace of the Moorish emirs, but the building as it stands to-day was mostly the work of Pedro the Cruel in the fourteenth century. He employed the best Moorish artisans for the tiling and interior carving and decorations, which are as good of their kind as any in Spain, with the sole exception of Granada.

The offices of the Spanish Tourist Bureau are just inside the Lion Gate and, if you want an English-speaking guide to show you the white marble Patio de las Doncellas, the Calif's Bedchamber, and the Ambassador's Reception Hall, they will provide you with one. It is probable, however, that he will not think it worth while to draw your attention to the magnificent wall tapestries depicting various of the battles of the Emperor Charles V, which I found to be full of fascinating and amusing detail.

The gardens are extremely beautiful, with their marble

---

[1] See pages 41 to 47.

fountains, Moorish tiling, and fine date-palms and orange trees.

The near-by Archives of the Indies, which contain all the documents relating to the government of the New World for the first three centuries after its discovery, are still a happy hunting ground for historians, and there was an elderly American lady (she had been working there for over thirty years) who was responsible for some sensational discoveries regarding the lives of the men who accompanied Columbus in 1492. Seville is so full of strange or historic buildings that any kind of a list here would be tedious and necessarily incomplete. To visit them all requires a stay of several weeks.

For those who are interested in pictures it should be mentioned that the Museo de Pintura contains works by the Sevillian Masters that are superior to those on view in the Prado in Madrid, where, as a rule, the best from all the Spanish Schools have been assembled under a single roof.

But Seville is too large and varied to yield up all its treasures to you during any single visit, and my advice is to go there at some other time than during the Semana Santa or the Fair for your more serious sight-seeing.

It was only on my last, and tenth, visit that I seemed to find time to go out through the famous gipsy quarter of Triana to the small village of Camas, and to see something of the Roman town of Italica, founded in 200 B.C. and birthplace of the Emperor Trajan. I have no doubt that my eleventh will still reveal something equally new to me.

The day will come, however, when you must continue on your way, and the road should be either north to Cordoba and Madrid or east to Granada and the Mediterranean. On my present journey I chose the former, for, whichever of the two most famous cities of Andalusia you decide to visit, Cordoba will always be my personal choice.

From Seville to Cordoba is only 86 miles by road, and the surface is excellent. It leads through the Moorish fortress town of Karmuna, now called Carmona, which towers dramatically from the crest of a sudden hill, and here I paused for a glance

at the Roman-built, but Moorish-reinforced, Seville Gate in
the town's old walls. Despite a huge fifteenth-century church
built by the same architect as Seville Cathedral upon the site of
the earlier mosque, Carmona to-day struck me as one of the
few places where I have been made aware of Andalusia's traditional poverty.

Here the sun is not man's friend but his most remorseless
enemy. It does not caress the earth and its fruits, but blasts and
scorches them into sterility. Many arm-chair reformers will tell
you that the reason for the poverty of the Andalusian peasant is
that so much of the province is held by a relatively few large
landowners. 'Break up the big estates and give every peasant
his own three acres and a cow' is one of those invaluable parrot
cries that can be relied upon to earn any aspiring politician the
reputation for being an enlightened democrat, but which, in
fact, only reveals his dangerous ignorance of local conditions.

If the large estates in Andalusia were parcelled out in lots
of three acres and a cow or, for that matter, thirty acres and
ten cows, only one in ten of these areas of land would have an
adequate supply of water, either to raise a profitable crop or to
supply their cows with enough pasturage to keep them alive.
Water is so scarce that ownership and administration must be
based upon the centres that have an adequate supply, and not
upon such idealistic considerations as equality. Experience has
shown that one of the few profitable agricultural enterprises
that the heat and scarcity of water permit in Andalusia is the
production of olives for oil, and everywhere in the province you
will see the dark green foliage of carefully spaced lines of olive-
groves—the width of the spacing depending upon the volume of
the local water supply. With the nearest water 5 or 10 miles
away, what would happen to your peasant with his three acres
and a cow? It seems that Nature requires that Andalusia should
be held by a few large landowners, who have the financial
resources to sink wells and compensate the loss from poor land
against profits from richer areas. This is nothing to do with
politics, and where the water supply is no real problem, as in
Asturias, Galicia, the Basque country, and the Catalan Pyrenees,

the peasants do own their land, and the large estates have been broken up.

The solution in Andalusia is for the Government to exercise pressure upon the large landowners to increase production by improved fertilizers and moderate mechanization and, from their larger profits, to pay a higher minimum wage to the agricultural workers. I say 'moderate mechanization' since Spain, as a poor country, could not afford to produce large areas of 'dead' land such as exist in the United States as the result of only a few years of intensive mechanization.

Our road to Cordoba leads through Ecija, known as 'the frying-pan', since it lies in a shallow dip in the great plain, and, as a result, annually achieves shade temperatures of 120° F.

The powdery, scorched earth cries out for water, and that this is no new thing is revealed by the fact that wherever there is a natural spring in Andalusia it is named after some particular local manifestation of the Virgin Mary.

It is interesting to know that nearly all these fresh-water springs were objects of veneration long before the birth of Christianity, and that since prehistoric times offerings of fruit and flowers for the guardian nymph or dryad had been placed beside them. There is reason to believe that after the official adoption of Christianity the priests found that these pagan offerings were continued and, since the superstition could not be abolished, wisely diverted these beliefs into other channels by arranging for the 'miraculous' discovery somewhere near the spring of an image of the Virgin Mary. To the minds of a primitive peasantry the transition from offerings to a beautiful dryad to reverence for a beautiful Virgin could be achieved during the passage of a couple of generations, whereas by entirely forbidding such pagan offerings the old cult would have been strengthened rather than weakened. The Church of those days was young enough to remember that itself would probably never have survived if it had not been for the tremendous stimulus of persecution and martyrdom.

The road into Cordoba crosses the sixteen-arched Roman bridge that spans the River Guadalquivir, and then skirts the

K

old city walls on the way to the modest but comfortable little Hotel Simón.

This is one of the oldest continuously inhabited cities in the world and, to my mind, has greater individuality than either Seville or Granada, putting me in mind of Damascus more than anywhere else that I have seen. It possesses the same sense of what I can only describe as burned-out splendour, as though illumined by some fierce but fading afterglow from its own tremendous and bloody past, suggested perhaps by the curiously red sky for which it is famous in summer.

So old is Cordoba that we read of its being destroyed—not founded—before the time of Christ, in the course of the struggle for power between Julius Cæsar and Pompey the Great. Though the birthplace of Seneca, the days of its real greatness did not come until the Moorish conquest, when, as the capital of an independent emirate, its University became the main link by which Islamic culture penetrated the Europe of the Dark Ages. From here the world first learned how to manufacture glass and paper, and the art of embossed leather-work was introduced. Not many of London's ancient and respectable Guild or Society of Cordwainers, as the leather merchants call themselves, realize that they are named after a city in Spain, yet such is, in fact, the case. So infinitely superior was the leather-work made in Cordoba in the days of the Moors that Masters of the Trade were known as 'cordovainers', which was soon corrupted into 'cordwainers'. (The remarkable English talent for anglicizing Spanish, however, must have reached its peak when 'Infanta of Castile' became 'Elephant and Castle'.)

It was Abderraman I who began work on the Great Mosque, now somewhat incongruously called the Cathedral, of Cordoba in A.D. 770, and it was finished by his son Hixen twenty-six years later.

Apart from all artistic considerations, the sheer size of the building is breath-taking—roughly 570 feet by 440—but the inside is like a madman's dream of a petrified forest, each one of the 850 red-and-white pillars being different in form, and varying in material from pure alabaster to marble and ordinary

8 Interior of the great ninth-century Mosque of Cordoba, now the Cathedral. Many of the columns were taken from the Roman temple that once occupied this site

stone. Each of the 425 arches is made from one single piece, most of them having been taken from the ruins of the Roman Temple of Janus. For here mankind has prayed to his various gods for well over 2,000 years—the Roman, the early Christian, the Moor, and again the modern Christian—but in this instance it is surely Mahomet, Prophet of Allah, who dominates both the pale Galilean and the Roman! Wandering round this vast, fantastic mosque, I observed an occasional rather gaudy Christian altar as it were tacked on to the Moorish walls, but they all seemed to suffer from an air of pathetic impermanence and almost, if I may say so without offence, of irreverence. This place belongs so wholly to Islam that it cannot be adapted to serve any other creed, and the Church would have been better advised to leave it as a museum, though I suppose that in those crusading days they had either to destroy it or try to make it Christian, and so, wisely, took the only course that could have preserved it undamaged until to-day.

The Great Mosque of Cordoba, more than anywhere else, brought home to me the different physical, and therefore psychological, effects of Christian and Islamic architecture. The fluted columns of a Christian Gothic church almost force you to lift your head and carry your vision upwards towards the sky, and a Christian at prayer is often thus represented, with head uplifted. On the other hand, the universal Islamic arch brings your eyes only a little way from the ground before returning them, with the insistence of endless reiteration, back once more to the earth from whence you came; and, logically, the Islamic attitude of prayer is to abase the forehead to the dust.

The huge courtyard of the mosque, some 422 feet long by 180 wide, was formerly used for the ritual ablutions required by Islamic law, but to-day it is a peaceful garden of tall palms and sweet-smelling orange trees.

If I have devoted too much time to the Great Mosque instead of to the extremely rich art gallery—known as the Museo Principal de Bellas Artes—it is because the former is unique, whereas the latter, however good, is one of many spread throughout the length of Spain. Should you go there, however, you will see one of the finest of all Ribera's works, 'The Flight into Egypt'. Tourists are usually shown the luscious gipsy nudes in the former house of the modern painter Romero de Torres, which certainly do not fail to suggest that he had studied his subject with the most enthusiastic thoroughness.

Only a few miles from Cordoba are the Hermitages of Montes Marianos, where, even in this day and age, a number of Holy Men still seek to live the austere lives of the early saints, with exhausting fasts and all the other masochistic joys that constitute mortification of the flesh. They belong to the Order of Our Lady of Bethlehem, and similar practices are still common in Spain, even among men and women who in other respects live normal working lives.

If you find this difficult to believe without proof, I suggest that you visit a shop beside the Palace Hotel in the fashionable centre of Madrid, where instruments of self-torture are exposed in the window for sale, together with such less remarkable religious objects as candles and Prayer Books. There you will find little whips, with finger-holds and knotted ends of exactly the correct length for beating your own back, and small wire-linked metal bracelets which can be adjusted so as agonizingly to stop the circulation in your arms or legs, and thus, we must suppose, assist you to banish your evil or lustful thoughts. However, if you decide to take some home with you, it might be as well to work out in advance the story you propose to tell the Customs officer! I mention the continued prevalence of mortification of the flesh in Spain as it is such small things which bring home the essential difference between the Anglo-Saxon and the Spanish character and temperament, and the consequent futility of our text-book politicians, who, just because their particular political remedies may have succeeded in their own countries, urge their immediate imposition upon Spain. They take no account of the fact that such remedies cannot be slipped on, like a suit of clothes, by a people still so fundamentally different from us in their whole outlook and way of thought as are the Spaniards.

Cordoba's main charm for me lies in the exquisite private houses that line its narrow and ancient streets, each set round its own vine-hung little patio, which the owners are usually proud to invite you inside to see, even though you are a stranger. The design of these houses is wholly Moorish, but the twentieth-century 'cordobes' is convinced that the ideal kind of residence for his particular climate has not been improved upon during the last 800 years or so. In this he is perfectly right, but again, how profoundly different from our own unquestioning assumption that the passage of time has automatically produced improvement in all things!

While you are in Cordoba you will do well to dine at the Restaurant Hijos de Miguel Gomez—Sons of Michael Gomez—and try the distinctive Cordoba wines of Montilla y Moriles, which are beginning to enjoy an increasing export trade since it has been found that they will travel better than most natural and unreinforced wines.

A pleasant time to visit Cordoba is either for one of the numerous 'romerias', or picnic pilgrimages, that take place in the spring and lead up to the city's Fiesta Mayor on May 25th, or for the Autumn Fair of September 25th–27th.

Cordoba is on the main road to Madrid, some 250 miles distant, and there are Tourist Bureau wayside inns at both Bailen and Manzanares for lunch, depending upon whether you make a late or an early start. You will cross the desolate plateau of La Mancha on your way, the setting for Don Quixote's encounter with the windmill and most other of the tragi-comic adventures created for him by the unmistakably Spanish imagination of Cervantes.

We, however, are on our way to Granada before we can leave Andalusia, and there is a choice of routes. Myself, I prefer to return along the road to Seville for 10 miles, and then turn south over a secondary road, leading through lovely mountain scenery from Aguilar de la Frontera and Lucena to Loja, on the main Malaga–Granada road. The wild stretch between the two main roads is only some 75 miles, which, with the 10 miles from Cordoba and the 35 from Loja to Granada, makes a total of only 120 miles, and Loja, too, is well worth seeing. The recommended, more conventional, and probably quicker route is along the main Madrid road as far as Bailen, 66 miles; then south for 25 miles to Jaen, and a final stretch of 61 miles to Granada, making a total of 152. The Spanish Tourist Bureau have set up one of the loveliest of all their thirty-two State-run hotels in Granada in the old monastery of San Francisco. Tales of its extraordinary beauty and relative cheapness have, however, spread abroad and, since it possesses only a few bedrooms, it is apt to be full unless you make your reservation well in advance—particularly so if you wish to be there between March and June.

However, if you cannot get into the Parador de San Francisco, the matchless view from the terrace of the Alhambra Palace Hotel may do something to console you.

XII

SHERRY

I WAS first introduced to the family of Gonzalez by my friend Toby O'Brien when we were on our way together to Cadiz and the Canary Islands late in November 1950.

After an exhaustive tour of the huge 'bodegas' of the firm of Gonzalez Byass, we had sat down to a very gay lunch, during which—having a memory for dates—I remarked that to-morrow would be Winston Churchill's seventy-sixth birthday. Immediately it was decided to send him a joint telegram, and Carlos Gonzalez offered to follow it up with the gift of a bottle of the famous 1863 Methusalem sherry, by way of a hint that we hoped for an equal demonstration of longevity from him as had been provided by the Old Testament character.

I like to think the Methusalem helped him back to the Premiership before his next birthday. Since that meeting I have kept in touch with Carlos and his kind, unaffected, and hospitable family and, when they heard that I was in Cadiz working on this book, they promised to tell me all there was to be told about sherry, and 'would demonstrate with samples'.

Since sherry is one of the world's great wines, Jerez the heart of the quite small area of country in which it can be grown, and Gonzalez Byass the biggest of all the sherry producers in that area, I felt that most intending visitors to Spain would like to hear about it.

As the crow flies, it was less than 18 miles from my hotel in Cadiz to Jerez, but by road or rail it is double that distance owing to the need to go right round the Bay, through San Fernando, Puerto Real, and Puerto de Santa Maria, before striking inland for the last 8 or 9 miles.

Jerez de la Frontera is one of the most attractive towns in Andalusia, but we are going to do our sight-seeing to-morrow, so, leaving our suit-cases at the Hotel of the Swans (Los Cisnes), we will make our way, like homing pigeons, straight for the 'bodegas'.

The firm was founded in 1835 by the grandfather of Carlos, who, having been told that he had rather weak lungs and must therefore neither work nor marry, promptly set up in business, married, had nine healthy children, and was nearing 80 when he died. The little room where he worked until the day of his death, in the eighteen-eighties, has been left untouched, dust and cobwebs covering the various bottles, which, although corked, have been half emptied by the evaporation of three-quarters of a century. Early in November, just ninety years ago, Queen Isabella II of Spain informed him that she was on her way to Jerez to witness the pressing of the year's vintage. Unfortunately, Her Majesty was apparently not aware that the grapes of Jerez are gathered and pressed during the first fort-night of September. Nothing daunted, Sr. Gonzalez sent off messengers to scour the country and to buy up all the bunches of picked grapes that people in this part of the world habitually leave hanging from the ceiling beams for eating on New Year's Eve.

With these an artificial vintage was duly trodden for the benefit of Queen Isabel, and everyone was happy. The odd part of the story, however, is that the resulting wine was one of the best ever produced, and formed the foundation of the famous wine that now fills the giant casks known as the Twelve Apostles. If there is a moral to the story (which I doubt) I must leave it to my Republican friends to work it out for themselves!

The son of the founder of the firm, who became the first Marquess de Torre Soto, died in 1946, just before his ninety-seventh birthday, which seems to suggest that good wine makes for a long life as well as a happy one. His wife, Carlos' mother, was a Gordon of Scotland, and all the present generation speak English as well as they do Spanish, though the British end of the business is in the hands of the family of Byass. Even in these days of austerity Britain is by far the largest individual purchaser of sherry, taking as much as 70% of the entire world supply.

A heritage of those days still remains in the person of 'Old

Galvez'. When asked how long he has been with the firm, he usually replies, 'I am seventy-five, but I have been with Gonzalez for seventy-five years and nine months because my mother lived on the firm's premises.' He is more or less like a walking puncheon, and has a complexion like a Turner sunset, but there is a light in his old eyes, and I should be a rich man if I could have a penny for every glass of sherry he has 'sampled'. Apart from more or less continual 'sampling', his chief occupation seems to be arranging pieces of fat bacon and cheese on lengths of string attached to the supports of various strategically placed sherry casks. These are for his adored friends, the bodega mice, whom he fiercely protects from any cat unwise enough to show as much as a whisker anywhere on the premises.

Old Galvez still likes to go out for a day's shooting and, rain or fine, always appears for the occasion with an open umbrella, the handle fastened firmly to stand straight up between the shoulder-blades of his back. This unusual adornment is never removed throughout the day, even when eating.

The 'bodegas' are surprisingly cool, with whitewashed walls and sanded earth or wooden-block floors. Each huge room has its triple row of wooden casks lying on their sides one above the other, and each cask is made of oak and designed to hold 108 gallons of wine.

An empty cask costs roughly £20, and there are about 30,000 of them. So, without introducing any question of wine into your calculations, you have over half a million pounds worth of capital tied up in the wooden butts alone!

A full cask holding 108 imperial gallons costs a minimum of £90 when it is sent to England, but before it can be sold to the long-suffering public, the British Government take £270 in duty. Incidentally, American oak is by far the best, mostly from New Orleans or New York, but the Spanish Government will not allow the sherry firms to use all the dollars they earn in purchasing replacements, and they are being obliged to use a certain number of casks made of Persian and Moroccan oak.

At the great Feast of the Vintage (Fiesta de la Vendimia) the first grapes are brought to the cathedral and, in front of the

entrance portico, solemnly trodden to the Glory of God. On
these occasions it is not difficult to discern the faces of still
older gods—a statue of St. Anthony that seems to laugh like
Bacchus, or a beautiful Virgin, the gentle wisdom of whose
smile would be impossible without some knowledge of pagan
joys. As so often happens in Spain, the dark robes of Mother
Church have only to be stirred by the breath of some such
age-old festival as this to disclose the brighter garments of an
earlier world.

But apart from this ceremony, the grapes are picked, left for
twenty-four hours in the fierce sun, trodden, and the 'must',
or unfermented grape-juice, poured into the carefully sterilized
wooden casks, all at the vineyard where they were grown. Owing
to the great heat of the season, fermentation begins within a
few hours, while the casks are still on the way by ox- or mule-
drawn wagons to the bodegas.

The first and most violent fermentation lasts for ten days or
so, and the wine is better if the bodega is cool enough to slow
down the process, which should then continue gradually for two
or three months, during which the yeast has turned all the sugar
into alcohol and carbon dioxide. One of the ways of finding out
whether or not fermentation is still going on is to hold a lighted
match over the bung-hole of a cask. If it is not blown out by
the carbon dioxide, then fermentation is complete. By December the impurities (pips, grape-skins, and lees) have sunk to the
bottom of the cask, and the clear wine is drawn off into fresh
casks and left until the height of the cold weather in February
or early March.

The wine is then 12% to 13% alcohol, and is fortified by
pure vinic alcohol up to 15%. About a month later, starting
as an odd globe and ultimately spreading in a thick grey crust
over the entire surface of the wine, there appears the mysterious
vegetable life known as the 'flor' or flower, which alone gives
the wines of sherry their distinctive flavour and bouquet. Then
begins the great business of classification (which has to be
repeated four times every year), and each member of the
Gonzalez family personally classifies about 100 casks a day.

A whalebone rod attached to a narrow silver cup is used to draw up the wine, which is classified by the sense of smell alone. On the rare occasions when the matter is open to doubt and a few drops are actually tasted, they are always spat out without being swallowed.

The casks containing the best wines are marked in chalk with a single stroke, the next best with two strokes; and there may be a few that get three strokes which are later removed for distilling into brandy.

Now the mysterious part of the affair begins.

For some unexplained reason all wines grown in this district develop into either a 'fino' or an 'oloroso'. Both are dry wines (as all sugar has been turned into producing $12\frac{1}{2}\%$ alcohol), but the fino is paler in colour and less full-bodied to the palate, and lacks the special 'nutty' flavour of the oloroso.

The same vines planted only a few miles away in Sanlucar de Barrameda all turn to the quite distinct super-dry wine known as 'manzanilla'.

There have been various attempts to produce 'sherry' in other parts of the world, notably in South Africa and Australia, but although a quite good sherry-style wine has resulted, there is no denying the fact that they are unmistakably inferior to those grown in Jerez. Apparently science cannot fully explain why this is so, but the undeniable fact still remains, and a similar situation occurred recently when the Americans decided to produce 'Scotch' whisky. The genuine article was scientifically broken down into its chemical components, and the resulting formula exactly followed to produce U.S. Scotch whisky, which, however, did not taste in the least bit like the Scotch whisky that came from Scotland!

The South Africans felt that the indefinable something must reside in the 'flor', and succeeded in getting hold of some from Jerez. It was placed upon the surface of their own sherry-type wine, but after a week it was established that their flor had since become an entirely different form of vegetable life!

A good fino can never be turned into a good oloroso, nor vice versa, but there are always a few dozen casks of two border-line types of wine known as 'Amontillado' and 'Palo Cortado'—the former just on the fino side of the main division, and 'Palo Cortado' just on the oloroso side. If there is a sudden demand for one or the other of the two main types, some young wines can be 'forced' to become one or the other by putting the new wine through the soleras. For example, if they wish to make a young wine into an oloroso, the alcoholic content is raised to 18%, when the flor will not grow, and the fino characteristics gradually disappear.

The wine of both main types is then left to mature for several years in what is known as the 'nursery', after which it occupies the top row of the three tiers of casks I have already described. Those in the second row are eleven years and the bottom row are twelve years old. When an order is received, the wine to supply it is drawn equally from all the bottom-row casks. The bottom row is then replenished from the second row, and the top row from a new supply of the wine of the closest possible resembling characteristics from the nursery.

Incidentally, it has been found that three rows of casks is the effective maximum, both because the weight of a fourth tends to destroy the bottom row, and also because the heat at a greater height than is produced by three rows coarsens the wine. The life of these maturing casks is between 80 and 100 years, though Carlos showed me some museum pieces dating from 1685.

I noticed that the casks had been personally signed by such visiting notabilities as King Alfonso XIII, General Franco, Queen Marie of Rumania, the Duke of Windsor, the late Duke of Kent, and various famous bull-fighters, writers, musicians, and theatrical celebrities; and I was appropriately flattered, therefore, when I was invited to sign a 1907 cask. A certain number of casks of the wine of each year are stored untouched and unblended, and it was interesting to take a sip of the 1850, and to find it almost undrinkable, sour and bitter; but, literally, a drop or two of these ancient soleras in a whole cask of the usual twelve-year-old sherry immediately gives it all the characteristics of a superb extra old wine.

Before finally leaving the subject of sherry it is just worth mentioning how the sweet brown sherry, beloved of so many Englishmen of my father's generation, is produced. A special small sweet round grape is grown locally and, when picked, is left to lie in the sun for no less than three weeks, so that it is almost like a raisin when it is crushed. Because of its dryness, the 'must' only partially ferments, and the result is a very high sugar and very low alcoholic content. This wine is known as PX, and is used only for blending in with the pure olorosos to satisfy the taste for a 'Sweet Old Brown Sherry'. Carlos told me that it contains so much glucose that a glass of it will completely prevent muscle stiffness after a day of excessive exercise.

Spanish brandy is an excellent drink on its own merits, but it is essential not to make the mistake of comparing it with French brandy, which it neither claims, nor seeks, to resemble. Jerez brandy, as made by my host, is distilled from a fully matured sherry wine into a water-white spirit, 65% alcohol, known as 'holanda'. It is then put into oak sherry casks to mature for eight to ten years (for the 'corriente'), from which it acquires its deep golden-yellow colour. Other brandies, such as the excellent 'Lepanto' brand made by them, is matured for thirty years and is, of course, in limited supply. The finished product has an alcoholic content of from 40% to 45%, and it is sold mostly in Spain and South America.

Before I left Jerez, Carlos insisted that I should accompany his nephew Mauricio, who is a crack shot, on a stuffed owl shoot. The use of the phrase 'stuffed owl' carried me back in a single second thirty-five years to my Preparatory School and the voice of old 'Skipper' Lynam jerking me out of a pleasant day-dream by suddenly roaring:

'And you there, Salter: stop gazing out of the window like a stuffed owl!'

But, although I thought it must be some kind of family joke, there really is a stuffed-owl shoot in Andalusia. Actually a live owl is better, as, if loosely shackled to a wire stretched between two trees, its movements serve to attract his natural enemy, the eagle. However, a live owl being unobtainable, we had to make do with 'Egbert'. 'Egbert', before he was stuffed, had been a handsome eagle owl, standing over a foot high, and he was carefully placed to face the wind so that the sun glinted on his glass eyes. If he was placed with his back to the wind his feathers would fluff out in a way which might strike a discerning eagle as 'phoney'. Incidentally, the best times for this peculiar sport are dawn and sunset, and in spring the eagles are particularly belligerent, as they have young in the nest. The guns then conceal themselves in as perfect a 'hide' as can be constructed and observe the behaviour of a small caged shrike (the smallest bird of prey), which will signal the approach of an eagle, kestrel hawk, buzzard, or even a magpie or crow, by becoming excited. All these, being day birds of prey, are enemies of the night birds of prey, and so of the large eagle owl in particular.

As there are only six or seven pairs of the magnificent Golden Eagle left in their game reserve, the Gonzalez family do not shoot them. However, there is the black Imperial Eagle, with white shoulders, which often weighs as much as 15 lb. and can carry off a newly born deer or lamb. He will coast over fairly low the first time, and on the second will dive-bomb straight at his objective. This is the moment to shoot, and if you miss it is just too bad for 'Egbert', as he will look like a storm of sawdust after even one smack. A kestrel hawk will also attack on sight, but a buzzard will sit in a neighbouring tree and make mewing noises for a quarter of an hour before he glides in to the attack at the moment when you least expect it.

Now it is time to begin our regular sight-seeing of Andalusia. My reason for including some pages on sherry, and telling of a form of sport of which, I feel sure, few Anglo-Saxons will have ever heard before, is because these things are not mentioned in the guide-books. Yet, in their unusualness, they are of the very essence of the country and provide yet another example of the unending variety of amusements or interests that await the visitor to Spain if he is prepared to go with me even a little way off the beaten track in search of a holiday that will at least be new and, perhaps, excitingly different from any he has known before.

9 The Vintage

10 Sherry maturing for twelve years in oak casks in one of Jerez's bodegas

XIII

FROM JEREZ TO MALAGA

Jerez—Arcos—Ronda—Antequera—Malaga.

JEREZ DE LA FRONTERA is a prosperous town of just over 100,000 inhabitants, and the whitewashed Los Cisnes hotel, its street-front gaily decorated with pink geraniums, is comfortable without being luxurious or expensive. If you get a room looking out over the little patio garden at the back, you will find that the perfume of magnolias will drift in upon the warm night breeze that rustles the dry fronds of the stately date-palms.

The Los Cisnes (the Swans) is in the middle of the town, and makes an excellent centre for watching the Easter Week processions or the Fiesta de la Vendimia—the Vintage Feast—both of which, in my opinion, are more genuine than the now almost-too-famous Semana Santa and Feria celebrations of Seville. I find the Easter Week processions in Jerez or Granada far more genuinely an expression of the sentiment, faith, emotions, and amusements of the people than those in Seville, where of late I have begun to feel that both are in danger of becoming a show put on, at least partly, for the benefit of tourists. The whole genius of the Spanish fiesta lies in its entire absence of self-consciousness, and in the fact that the people are taking part because they sincerely want to do so, and not, as in most other European countries, in order to be 'quaint' or 'olde worlde', or to raise funds for some worthy but usually dull charitable cause.

In Andalusia the horse is still all-important, and the nightly cavalcades of men and women, all in formal Andalusian riding-costume, is as much a feature of the Fiesta de la Vendimia as are the afternoon bull-fights. The costume is black and severe in cut, but redeemed from being sombre by the white shirt-ruffles at throat and wrist, and the jaunty angle at which the wide, stiff-brimmed hats are worn. Open horse-drawn carriages also parade, with bouquets of really astonishingly lovely girls wearing the many-flounced red-and-white dresses that are more or less the uniform for flamenco dancing. Jerez itself was founded by the Celts somewhere around 2,500 years ago, and was known as Asta Regia under the Romans. It was near here that the Visigoth King Roderick was defeated by the Moorish invaders in 711, and it was not liberated until the time of Alfonso the Wise in 1255. Alfonso immediately ordered the building of the small circular chapel in the Moorish Alcazar or citadel, and here King Philip of Navarre is buried.

The moss-grown, yellowed parish church of San Miguel, built in 1482, is an interesting blend of architectural styles typical of southern Spain. The three main naves are pure Gothic, while the tower, ornamented with 'azulejos'—those shiny, coloured tiles that were introduced by the Moors and which are still manufactured in Spain to-day—is in the 'mudejar' style. Mudejar architecture is a product of the period immediately following the Christian reconquest, when architects and workmen were predominantly Moorish.

In the neighbouring Church of San Salvador the tower of he old mosque has been incorporated unchanged, exactly as with the more famous Giralda tower of Seville Cathedral.

The interiors of most of the churches of Jerez are less striking than their exteriors, and contain few outstanding works of art. One is a fine silver altar in the Church of the Virgin de la Merced.

The bright and animated streets are rich in fine sixteenth-century private houses emblazoned with the coats-of-arms of noble families, of which one of the finest is that belonging to the head of the great brandy (and fighting-bull) producing family of Domecq. Not far away in the Plaza Fortun de Torres there are open-air concerts beginning, on most summer nights, at 11 p.m. There the locals sit and sip their fino and eye the passing parade of girls—these always two and two, since if they walked alone they might find themselves suffering under the extremely severe penalties the present Government has introduced in an attempt to stamp out prostitution. The first time they are caught they are sentenced to a week in prison, the second time to three months, and subsequently to a full year in a reformatory run by nuns just outside Guadalajara. So in the streets of Spain to-day you will not see the spectacle that was once described as 'the procession of lonely Priestesses of Humanity, hurrying slowly to nowhere and back'.

Only some 2 miles outside the remains of the old city walls of Jerez, on the banks of the fast-flowing River Guadalete, the Carthusian monastery, founded in 1477, is being carefully and intelligently restored, and from there you can visit the ruins of the great Moorish fortress of Melgarcijo. An excursion from Jerez that will take you well off the beaten track is by the road through Arcos de la Frontera, Ronda, Cuevas del Bercero, Campillos, and Antequera to Malaga. The total distance is only some 170 miles, but the road is bad after the first 50 miles and I do not recommend it to motorists who are in a hurry, even though it takes them through some magnificent mountain scenery.

I myself did it in easy stages by bus, spending a night in Ronda (Hotel Victoria I.B.) and at the Tourist Bureau's way-side inn (Albergue) in Antequera.

The road from Jerez to Arcos de la Frontera runs through undulating country along a bumpy road lined with tall eucalyptus trees, but the driver obviously knew each pot-hole personally and by name, and the springing mercifully was good. We left half an hour late owing to a farmer having left his hat behind, for which we naturally returned, though the culprit had to stand up to a barrage of jokes at his expense—mostly about how, in the war, he had gone off to the front and forgotten to take his rifle along with him!

The password to the Spaniard's confidence is 'poverty'. If you are travelling by bus or by third-class train, the assumption is that you, too, are poor, which makes you, even though a foreigner, capable of understanding their kind of troubles, and so potentially one of themselves. I remember a train journey in my youth of two days and a night right across Spain when I was quite penniless until I could contact a beneficent sister

L

whose cruise-ship was to touch at Vigo. A patriarch, with the fine hands of an aristocrat and the most beautiful use of the Spanish language, which he could neither read nor write, was diffidently approached by a uniformed guard, after he had first clipped my own third-class ticket. Regarding him coldly, the Patriarch remarked, without heat:

'Retire little man in an absurd uniform, and cease from molesting your elders and betters.'

After the hasty retreat of the ticket-collector, he turned a stern eye upon me.

'May I be permitted to ask, señor, why you encourage these dressed-up obscenities by buying a ticket?'

I explained that I was a foreigner on my way to Vigo, that in my country of England people always bought railway tickets when travelling on trains, and that I had assumed that it was the same in Spain. He thought this over, and remarked:

'It is not for me to comment upon the customs prevailing among the heretics, but if you are a foreigner why do you not travel first-class?'

I explained that until I got to Vigo I had no money. After a pause he beamed amiably, then produced a huge hamper containing bread, tomatoes, sausage, onions, wine, raw fresh eggs, and smoked ham, and offered it to me saying:

'I am hungry, but I will not eat until you have.' When I politely refused, he replaced the hamper untouched, and repeated the process at quarter-hour intervals until, finally, I accepted.

When he got out at a remote, age-old huddle of stone houses, presided over by an immense church that I had seen for the last hour, floating like some vast grey sail above the level of the undulating plateau, he instructed the remaining passengers to look after me, and as they too descended they passed on his instructions to the new arrivals. As a result, for some 800 miles of slow and hot travel I was courteously pressed to share their food and wine which they suspected—rightly, as it happened— that I had not the money to buy for myself. Such courtesy is real, genuine, and without any kind of ulterior motive—but the password was my poverty, and it is almost the only one that is universally recognized throughout Spain.

On the road from Jerez to Arcos there were signs of that same poverty in the primitive, whitewashed, thatch-roofed 'casetas' beside a halting place where the bus and the driver, respectively, took on large reinforcements of water and wine, and I walked over slowly to look more closely at one of them. Poor they were, without a doubt, but the numerous children, though playing bare-bottomed in the dust, were plump and happy, and their mother, singing flamenco fortissimo while scrubbing the family laundry, had none of that beaten look behind the eyes that one finds among the very poor of most other lands. The single low door was curtained with bright blue bells of morning glory, and my hostess, too, looked rather like a morning glory, though possibly during the late afternoon, owing to the too-often-repeated joys of motherhood. She showed me, with pride, the little flower-garden scratched in the sandy soil on the shady side of the house, with its tall hollyhocks backed by a clump of yellow-bloomed cactus plants.

At the crest of a hill the dramatic, fortress-like cliff of Arcos de la Frontera came into view, and soon I was walking up the steep, wide, dead-white street towards the summit. It was early afternoon, the little town was silent, shuttered, and withdrawn, and the door to the fine old Gothic parish church was locked. Nothing loth, I sat on the parapet of the old Moorish castle and gazed down on the huge sweep of the River Guadalete at my feet and away to the tawny mountains of the interior. Countless hawks hovered and swung, level with me, above the rich pasture-land bordering the river. Behind me I could hear the drone of voices from an orphan school—the priest's 'Santa Maria' answered by the children, always exactly five tones higher, with their 'Madre de Dios'. The repetition of these two notes continued with gentle monotony, and looking out across the secret and almost menacing landscape, I realized that nothing I could see or hear had changed materially in the last 400 years or so. Fierce, poor, not only unchanged but deeply resenting change, this strange land often holds the past more dear than the present, and always more glamorous than the future. Its inhabitants are content to live out their lives as though locked within some ancient but still potent spell.

The old sacristan, jingling his bunch of foot-long keys, pointed out to me how one of the golden-brown walls of the church was leaning at a steep angle, as the result of the great earthquake which had destroyed Lisbon in 1755. I enquired whether there was no danger of it collapsing and he replied:

'Yes, it was recently decided to put up those stone buttresses for the wall, and also a metal bar inside to bind together the long Gothic columns.' Curiosity made me look at the date marked on the buttresses, and I gathered, without surprise, that for the sacristan the year 1799 came under the heading of 'recently'.

The vestry contained a number of dark oil-paintings which it might well repay someone to clean and examine, and there was a really fine panel by Alonso Cano, successor to Velazquez and perhaps the last great Spanish artist until the emergence of Goya a century later.

The road climbs into wilder and still wilder sierra country, through El Bosque, with its beautiful Gothic church, to Ubrique, Benaocaz, and, finally, to Ronda, some 60 miles from Jerez.

Ronda, itself 2,500 feet above sea-level, is set in the circle of mountains which provided the hide-out for the last of the Andaluz bandits, and is perched on the edge of a dizzy gorge which at one point is nearly 900 feet deep. Over this 'canyon', at the bottom of which the River Guadalevin flows, there are three bridges—one Roman, one Moorish, and the 'new' eighteenth-century one.

The Church of Santa Maria la Mayor was founded in 1485 by Ferdinand and Isabella upon the foundations of the Moorish mosque when the town was liberated, and is now a strange blend of Moorish, Gothic, and Renaissance architecture.

From the 'House of the Moorish King', belonging to the Duchess de Parcent, you can descend to the bed of the gorge by

11 Arcos de
la Frontera

12 Ronda

367 steps cut in the living rock—but I should not advise it, and I have not myself counted the number of steps!

There are the remains of a Roman amphitheatre 7 miles outside Ronda, where Julius Cæsar is reputed to have fought and subdued the followers of Pompey in 49 B.C.

Ronda has a strange atmosphere of its own, and its setting is unforgettable. If you are a souvenir hunter do not forget that Ronda is justly famous for its wrought iron-work. On the next day, through the same majestic, savage scenery, you will pass Cuevas de Becerro, which is often snow-bound for weeks at a stretch, and of which the local patron is, understandably, the Virgin of the Snows.

Antequera possesses a State-run Albergue, where you will be made very comfortable for twenty-four hours or so, for 125 pts, meals included.

Antequera, at the foot of the Sierra de Torcales, is rich in Roman ruins, and the little Convent of Bethlehem (Belen) contains a Murillo. But, as in Ronda, it is the setting rather than the town itself that makes it memorable.

If you have a taste for such things, take a look at the Cave of Menga—a kind of prehistoric dolmen. Ten miles away there is the Labyrinth of El Torcal, where rocks and red marble give a strange impression of the walls, churches, and streets of some magically petrified city. Most visitors to Antequera come up for the day from Malaga, only 40 miles away, and it makes a pleasant contrast to drop down from the desolate splendours of the sierra country to the comforts of the capital of the Spanish Riviera. Although it has a popular summer season, I myself think that Malaga's greatest charm is as a winter resort.

It is a surprise if you look at the map to see that Malaga is south of such north African resorts as Tunis and, protected from the north by mountains, it has a far better winter climate than either the French or Italian Rivieras.

The Hotel Miramar is rather expensive in the season, but very much the centre of social life and not too far from the excellent modern shopping street of Larios. By the good coast road it is only 80 miles from Gibraltar, and a large British

residential colony is growing up at the little town of Torremolinos, 8 miles outside Malaga, where there is the best of the
various bathing-beaches and also a golf-course. They have
discovered that an attractive furnished villa can be had for £25
a month, and that servants in Andalusia are delighted to do the
marketing, cooking, and all the laundry for a salary of 15s. a
week, so that more and more visitors are contriving to pass the
worst of the British winter months in this inexpensive hide-out.
As a result, of course, prices are tending to go up in the locality,
but if Torremolinos loses its charm, they have only to explore
a little farther afield to find half a dozen attractive little towns
that are still as unspoiled as Torremolinos used to be.

They tell me that you can sea-bathe all the year round in
Malaga. I can vouch for the fact that you can certainly sun-
bathe in bathing-dress on the beach—and get good and brown—
in January and February, but I personally found the sea distinctly cold when I tried it during the last week in November,
though it should be remembered that I have been rendered
sadly unheroic by twenty years in warm countries.

Malaga was a flourishing port in Phœnician times but was
destroyed by the Visigoths. It fell early under Moorish domination as a valuable base for supplies from the near-by African
coast, and was liberated by Ferdinand and Isabella only after a
grim two-year siege in 1487. Some years later it was the scene
of a serious Moorish revolt.

Owing to its relatively late reconquest, the only really ancient
buildings are the eleventh-century Alcazaba, which now contains the Archæological Museum and some very attractive
gardens. Close by is the thirteenth-century fortress built on the
remains of a Greek and still earlier Phœnician one, known as
Gibralfaro, where there is an excellent open-air restaurant. This
is a cool and pleasant place to dine and look across the twinkling
lights of the city and port, and it is so situated that, assisted
by a pair of opera-glasses, I was once able to watch a good deal
of a bull-fight in the ring directly below without having to buy a
ticket! From here it is possible to see the little coastal plain
upon which the city is built stretching from immediately below

to the hill hiding Torremolinos some 10 miles away. Inland, in the uncanny clarity of the light of Andalusia in early autumn, a friend and I once counted no fewer than fourteen ridges of mountains, one beyond the other, until they merged into the blaze of the sunset.

There are so many beautiful cathedrals in Spain that I am reserving a detailed description for the half-dozen or so that are really unique. Unless some such limitations are imposed this will cease to be a book of impressions and become an architectural manual. Malaga's cathedral, though less remarkable than some, is worth visiting, if only for the really extraordinary carving of the choir-stalls by Pedro de Mena. He managed not only to achieve expression and gesture in his figures, but would frequently carve the wood to little more than paper thickness in order to suggest the flow of a robe, so that it is a miracle how his work has survived undamaged for three centuries.

In the early days of the Civil War the worst elements among the local Republicans occupied the cathedral and seized the side-chapels to serve as their homes, using everything made of wood that they could find for their cooking-fires on the altars. Twice they wanted to use Pedro de Mena's carvings in this way, and twice were prevented from doing so in the nick of time.

Malaga Cathedral must be in the running for the title of the oldest unfinished church in the world. Begun in 1528, work was suspended for a century or so from 1631, and in 1783 it was again left, still unfinished as it is to-day, with one 250-foot-high tower instead of two. All three of the main porticos— those of the Sun, the Pardon, and the Chains—are really fine, and one of them is approached up a little avenue of orange trees, upon which the fruit hangs in golden clusters throughout the winter and spring.

There are some fine pictures inside, including a Virgin of the Rosary by Alonso Cano and canvases by Claudio Coello, Morales, Van Dyck, and many other Masters. Historically interesting is the little image of the Virgin Mary which Ferdinand and Isabella always carried with them into battle against the Moors.

Malaga's Art Gallery (the Museo Provincial), although it cannot bear comparison with those of Madrid, has works by Zurbaran, Murillo, Morales, Cano, and—rather surprisingly—Picasso! To my mind two canvases by Ribera, both of old men, stand out from the rest for their forceful portrayal of character.

But Malaga is a pleasure city and sea-side resort, not primarily a place for serious sight-seeing, and the most striking thing about it to most visitors is the incredible profusion of flowers that seem to bloom the whole year round, from the varieties that grow in the cold north of Europe to the frankly tropical and African.

Easter Week produces the biggest fiesta, comparable to that in Seville for its night processions, and from August 9th until the 19th there is a succession of bull-fights followed by all-night dancing in the streets. The celebrations which take place from January 15th until February 15th are more for the visitor, and are primarily of a sporting character, with sailing races and tennis and golf tournaments for cups and various prizes.

Malaga, like most Riviera resorts, is designed for the idle rich. Fortunately for us, however, owing to the favourable rate of exchange, it is not necessary to be rich to enjoy it, and the only remaining obligation therefore is to be idle in the sun.

XIV

GRANADA AND THE ROAD TO ALICANTE

GRANADA has excited the imagination of more generations of travellers than any other city in Spain.

There is so much to see that I can do no more than indicate the atmosphere of the place and briefly mention a few outstanding sights by way of getting you started along the right general lines. For Granada is one of those places, commoner in Spain than in any other country, which everyone must discover for himself—and in discussing it afterwards all who have seen it will reveal that they discovered something different! For in Granada there are three or four quite separate worlds, simultaneously existing side by side, yet themselves scarcely aware of each other, and each is sufficiently absorbing wholly to dominate all subsequent memory of a single short visit.

For some people it is just another ancient Andalusian city, with a dramatic back-cloth of Moorish palace and towering snow mountains, where bull-fighting is a religion, the shops contain too many souvenirs of doubtful medieval authenticity, and the surging life of the dark streets is as vital and intense as everywhere else in southern Spain.

For others it becomes a kind of Thousand-and-One-Nights dream, set against the splendour of the Alhambra, with its mournful gardens and eternally running streams of cool water for its 'leit motif'.

It may also be remembered as the city of the Albaicin, where one first sat outside a gipsy cave and watched the small, fine-boned, flexible hands of a dancing-girl writhing like snakes against her sleek black hair, while the guitars, castanets, and clapping hands seemed to torture her with the wild rhythm of flamenco.

Each of these worlds, and many others less immediately obvious, are capable of being wholly absorbing to anyone, at least for a few days, and yet all are, rather confusingly, blended together within the confines of the single city of Granada.

The origins of the city go back into the remotest antiquity, but the days of its greatness, as with Cordoba, were under the Moors, who, in the Alhambra—the Red Castle—left an example of their domestic architecture as unique in Europe as is the Great Mosque of Cordoba of their religious building.

I say 'unique in Europe' even after having lived for over two years in Istanbul, where the nearest approach to equality is achieved, and though there are Arab buildings in western Asia and northern Africa that can be compared with Granada, the Alhambra still out-rivals them as an artistic conception, if only because of its fabulous setting at the base of the 11,000-foot-high Sierra Nevada.

With hereditary memories of their desert origins, the presence of unlimited fresh and cool water remained the supreme manifestation of both luxury and security to the Moors, even after six centuries in Spain, and when the powerful independent Moorish Kings of Granada realized that, with only a little ingenuity, they could tap an inexhaustible supply from the mountains, it is not surprising that they set out here to build the most beautiful of all their many palaces. But they were, first and foremost, military conquerors, and the original, eleventh-century walls of the Alcazar, which are more than a mile long, were those of a fortress. It was only in the fourteenth century that the more beautiful central part, known as the Alhambra, was built.

Artistically, the Moors of Granada reached their zenith about the middle of the fourteenth century, the Lion Court being built in 1354, and the additions made during the remaining 138 years, before Boabdil the Little surrendered to Ferdinand and Isabella and rode away to a tragic death by treason, reveal the same decadence that, in its more practical manifestations, contributed to their military defeat.

I will not attempt to guide you, step by step, round the Alhambra, for anyway you will see the twelve domestic-looking stone lions spouting water in the court that is named after

them, and the surrounding 124-columned arcade, as well as the
Sala de los Embajadores, richly engraved with texts from the
Koran.

You will be shown in the Court of the Two Sisters the famous
Alhambra Jar—Jarro de la Alhambra—which was found by
Ferdinand and Isabella to be filled with gold; and also the
whispering gallery, known as the Room of the Secrets.

It is more easy to overlook the sad beauty of the Patio of
Myrtles, with its exquisite alabaster and jasper pillars, and
the incredibly lovely glimpses of the white gipsy suburb of
Albaicin, delicately framed through the typical arched windows.

When the American writer Washington Irving lived in the
Alhambra it was well on its way to becoming a total ruin, and it
was largely due to the interest aroused by his *Tales of the
Alhambra* that steps were taken to preserve it. The first culprit
was no less a person than the Emperor Charles V, grandson of
Ferdinand and Isabella, who began the construction of a pom-
pous, bogusly classical palace for himself right in the middle of
the best of the Moorish buildings. He ripped away considerable
quantities of the Alhambra stone for use in his own project, and
its ugly walls seriously mar, in at least one direction, the background to the exquisite Lion Court. The Emperor did not
even justify his vandalism by finishing the work, and his huge
palace still lies open to the sky more than 400 years after its
construction was first undertaken. The next major damage
done was at the orders of Napoleon, whose troops blew up a
considerable section of the old fortress in 1812 before beginning
their long retreat to the Pyrenees.

Most serious sight-seers are so occupied with the Alhambra
that they give only a passing glance at Granada Cathedral, and I
myself was doing little more than taking a look at the pictures,
by Roger Van der Weyden and Botticelli, in the sacristy when
my attention was caught by a small boy of about ten, who was
brandishing an old sword above his head in a purposeful sort
of way, as though trying to get the feel of it. When I asked him
where he had got it, he handed it to me and I saw that, although

the hilt was of gold, it was no ceremonial affair, but was designed for use in battle. He replied, 'It is King Ferdinand's sword—the one he was wearing when he accepted the keys of the city from Boabdil.' I must have looked a bit dubious until he explained that he had been sent to collect it, as it was to be carried in the annual procession that would celebrate the recapture of the last Moorish stronghold in Spain. Seeing that I was interested, my small guide, still occasionally flourishing the sword, postponed his return with it to the Bishop's palace long enough to show me something which I had overlooked when making my cursory examination of the beautiful sixteenth-century building. I had seen the reclining figures of Ferdinand and Isabella by the Florentine sculptor Domenico Fancelli, and the others by Ordoñez of Philip the Fair and Joan the Mad, and I knew that they were buried there. What I did not know, and should not have discovered but for my chance meeting with the sword-waver, was that between the feet of the effigies of Ferdinand and Isabella and the altar there was a narrow stone stairway. Down this I was led to where, in a bare brick vault, lay four black and dusty coffins. Stabbing to the right and to the left, my small guide said, 'Ferdinand' and 'Isabella', and then, indicating the others which were farther back, 'Juana la Loca y Felipe el Hermoso'. Introductions having been completed, he left me.

After the riches and splendour of the cathedral above, with the serenely dignified reclining statues robed in all the majesty of their joint rulership, the contrast with the four plain black coffins in the chilly and unadorned vault was strangely, almost shockingly, dramatic. Each of these four people had led such tremendous or tragic lives that the starkness of their present resting-place, lit only by the unsteady light of two candles, seemed almost intolerably bleak, lonely, and austere.

An entire world away from here, though only ten minutes' journey by car, is the gipsy quarter of the Albaicin, where, for more than 200 years, whole families have abandoned their nomadic habits to live in the famous caves above the Camino del Sacro Monte—the Way of the Holy Mountain. This is the

13 View through one of the windows of the Alhambra, Granada

14 The Lion Court of the Alhambra, Granada

setting for so many strange scenes in Spanish music and romance, and the birthplace of so many of the finest flamenco singers and dancers, that the gipsy colony here has, I am sorry to say, become rather spoiled. When I tell you that some of the caves have their own telephone, and nearly all their own electric light, and that some of the inhabitants are people of wealth and title, who have settled there comfortably with their gipsy lovers after being disowned by their families, you will understand the changes that have taken place there in recent years. Much sought after, not only by tourists but also by film talent-scouts and individual millionaires, who pay them fabulous sums to 'put on a flamenco show' for important society parties, they are getting 'temperamental'. Since a gipsy's interest in money, though momentarily intense, is provoked by his immediate needs rather than by any idea of saving or of buying property, he frequently does not (or perhaps cannot) do his best in an artificial atmosphere, when he does not particularly need to sing for his supper. I had proof of this once at just such a millionaire party. The performers were famous, but their performance had been noisy, mechanical, and rather vulgar. Most of the guests had drifted into another room when I went over to the piano and, playing a few bars from one of Manuel de Falla's works, asked one of the gipsies whether this was not, more or less, the same melody as something he had just been singing. 'So you are an artist too!' he said, and when I explained that I was very far indeed from claiming that, but that I was genuinely interested in flamenco music, he became more animated and interested than I had seen him the whole evening.

It seems that de Falla 'lifted' entire gipsy flamenco melodies for inclusion in his longer works, and that I had stumbled on a case in point. In order to illustrate others, the gipsies gathered around me and got more and more excited about providing fresh examples. As the idea caught hold of them they began to forget their surroundings, the authentic note of passion came back to their voices and movements, and I soon noticed that the other guests had drifted back and were now listening enraptured. I apologized to my host, but he seemed delighted and told me frankly that I had achieved something that his money alone had not been able to secure.

Flamenco is a loose term covering all music of this special and quite inimitable style, but the purest is known as 'canto grande' or 'cante jondo', and it is in this that you will find the highest expression of traditional Andalusian music.

Why flamenco's finest exponents have, latterly, nearly always been gipsies is rather difficult to explain, as it still remains the natural form of musical expression throughout southern Spain. By 'natural' I mean that, if an errand boy or a street urchin in London or New York should decide to whistle or sing, it would be 'natural' for him to produce an air from some popular film. For his opposite number in Spain, it is inevitable for him to produce the strange and involved musical idiom of flamenco.

This may explain why you will find very few really good modern dance-bands in Spain. The living inspiration of American dance-music is negroid; equally, the vital force behind Spanish present-day music is flamenco, and I do not know which would achieve the worst results—a negro band playing flamenco, or a Spanish band playing 'hot' jazz!

It seems that the less civilized races alone are capable of writing great (as opposed to talented, pleasant, or even brilliant) music—namely, the Russians, the Poles, and the Germans. Similarly, it is the least civilized elements in America and Spain —the Negro and the gipsy—that supply all new musical inspiration there.

Bull-fighting and flamenco are as inseparable from one another as Gilbert from Sullivan or Laurel from Hardy, and Granada is one of the great centres for both. You will probably get a far better idea of just what these twin passions are all about if you can obtain a few introductions to Spaniards living in the district. The Andalusian is fantastically hospitable, and if it is known that a 'foreigner' is in the district and anxious to see something of their way of life, you will not lack invitations for long. Usually these parties are given in one of the surrounding country houses, starting in the late afternoon at the improvised

bull-ring, where small, two-year-old bulls are 'played' by any
enthusiastic amateur who feels the urge. At these shows there
are no picadores, and the bull is not hurt in any way, so that the
show would not upset even an R.S.P.C.A. inspector, though I
can assure you, from experience, that a two-year-old bull can
knock you most comprehensively flat if you give him the
chance! It was at this party that I first realized that the bull-
fighting world has an aristocracy of its own. One of the guests
was the Duke of Pinohermoso, who, in addition to being one of
the greatest 'rejoneadores'—bull-fighters on horseback—is also
a rich and influential grandee. Marvellous though he is on
a horse, he is not so good on foot, or at least was not on that
particular afternoon, and he was not making the most out of the
opportunities being offered him by a spirited young bull.
Suddenly a professional bull-fighter—a penniless foundling
from a local orphanage—could stand it no longer, jumped into
the ring, and, seizing the 'cape' from the surprised Duke,
jerked his thumb over his shoulder and said a single word:
'Fuera'—'Get out'! The young professional did some superb
passes, then threw the cape back to the Duke, who shame-
facedly apologized to him for having been so bad! Later, the
party gathered on an open terrace to hear the woman who, in
her day, was probably the greatest of all the flamenco singers
and dancers—Pastoria Imperio. By the time I saw her she was
fat and in the middle fifties, and her voice was smoky-sounding
and tired, but she still made the young ones who came on for a
turn now and again (while she took a long, strong drink) look
like amateurs. Her voice and feet could still convey the essence
of the dance, even though she hardly moved her body; but it was
her hands above all that fascinated and held quiet even this
sophisticated crowd.

While I was in Bali in the East Indies in January, 1942, I
took pains to see as much as I could of the dancing, in which the
incredibly expressive hands alone tell a detailed story, which
can be read by the people of the island as easily as we can read
a newspaper. In flamenco, too, the quality of the dancer is
usually revealed by the supple movements of the hands, which

are held just above the head during certain phases of the dance.

When you have had your fill of the ancient city of Granada there is a complete contrast to be had very close at hand.

Granada itself is over 1,800 feet above sea-level and, incredible though it sounds, you can take a bus to the mountain village of Maitena, at 5,000 feet, and continue on a good road to a height of over 8,000 feet. And within 30 miles of the city, at 4,000 feet, is an excellent hotel at Güejar-Sierra, where skiing and other winter sports are organized.

For those who are interested I should perhaps mention that winter-sports facilities are also available quite near Madrid, but that the best-developed resort, complete with ski-lifts, &c., is at La Molina in the Pyrenees. With the Swiss franc making their old haunts too expensive, more and more winter-sports enthusiasts are now finding what they want in the Guadarrama, the Sierra Nevada, and the Catalan Pyrenees.

The day we leave Granada, and also Andalusia as well, is long and rather tiring, but, with so much that is worth seeing in Spain, I personally advise you to make an early start and do the 233-mile hop direct to the Mediterranean at Alicante. This does not sound a great deal, but it is in fact a very full day's run. There is a Tourist Department Albergue at Puerto Lumbreras, 131 miles from Granada, which is a good place for lunch. Many people decide to stay in Murcia, 52 miles short of Alicante —but they usually regret it!

The first place along the way is Guadix, which has a large colony of gipsy caves. The road then climbs to the Sierra de Baza, with peaks to the south rising to over 6,000 feet. This is wild and desolate country, though I remember the roadside, even in January, being bright with wild orchids.

After lunch at Puerto Lumbreras we come to Lorca, presided over by a fine fifteenth-century castle. The town suffered great destruction when 6,000 people were drowned in 1802, following the collapse of the neighbouring water reservoir of Puentes.

The first time that I drove along this road was in late November, and I was badly puzzled to observe that the slopes of most of the surrounding low hills were covered with what looked to me like red snow. When I finally stopped the car and went to investigate, I discovered that my red snow consisted of millions of 'pimientos'—red peppers—that had been placed thus in the autumn sun to complete their ripening, since the production of this important ingredient in Spanish cooking is a speciality of the province.

Murcia itself, the capital, possesses a fine fourteenth-century cathedral, and its Easter Week processions are among the finest to be seen anywhere in Spain; but to me it is a town without what the Spaniards call 'simpatía'. Perhaps the secret of my dislike lies in the character of the 'murcianos'. They enjoy—and rightly so, I fear—the reputation of being the most illiterate and bloodthirsty people to be found in all Spain, and I can answer for the fact that most of the church-burning and other atrocities of the early days of the Civil War were carried out by men and women from this province. If you should want to hire a thug to push some rich but excessively long-lived relative over a cliff, you hire a murciano, and in every case of murder, robbery with violence, or rape that comes before the Spanish Law Courts, you will inevitably find that the gang responsible contains a high proportion of them.

From this you must not get the impression that Murcia is unsafe, for that would be entirely false. Knowing the propensities of the locals, the district is well stocked with Civil Guards—and even the murcianos prefer not to tangle with them.

Visitors to Spain frequently carry away an entirely mistaken impression of the function performed by these tough and well-armed men. They either assume that their presence is an indication of 'terrible Fascist oppression', or else an admission that the country is seething with revolt and bandits. Both assumptions are completely false. Even the most casual glance at the Civil Guard's tricorn hats must reveal a Napoleonic, rather than a Franco, inspiration, and the traditions for courage and incorruptibility of the force are second only to those of the Royal Canadian Mounted Police. Far from having fascist leanings, the Guardia Civil is traditionally monarchist and legitimist,

M

and at the outbreak of the Civil War the majority of them fought for the Republicans—not because they approved of them, but because, for better or worse, they then constituted the 'de facto' government of Spain.

The reason for their existence is much the same as that which accounts for the existence of the Royal Canadian Mounted Police : immense areas of thinly populated country where, if someone is wanted for a serious crime, his first reaction (and that of his entire village) is to take to the hills with his gun rather than give himself up to the authorities.

The basic instinct of the Spanish is anarchistic, i.e. against all forces of authority or control, quite regardless of whether they are good, bad, or indifferent. Although anarchy and communism are frequently confused in people's minds, they are fundamentally opposite ideas, the former appealing to the incurable individualist and the latter, as its name implies, to those who wish totally to submerge their individuality in the largest political mass movement in history.

Only 14 miles short of Alicante the road takes us through the little town of Elche, which is unique for several reasons. First, and most obvious, because it possesses the only palm-forest in Europe, some of the trees being over 100 feet tall. It supplies the entire country with the long palm-branches that are carried to Mass to be blessed on the Sunday before Easter, and are then tied to the balcony of most Spanish homes until the following year.

Second, this is the site of the discovery of the famous statue known as 'The Lady of Elche', which is on exhibition in the Prado Museum in Madrid and is believed by archæologists to be of Celtic origin, and not less than 3,000 years old.

Lastly, and most important, it is the Church de la Merced in Elche that, on August 14th and 15th every year, gives representations of an unchanged thirteenth-century musical miracle play, which attracts many people from the surrounding countryside.

The Hotel Victoria in Alicante is not luxurious, but it is by far the best available, and from its windows you will be able to look over the fine palm avenue and across the port to the open Mediterranean. If there is a moon and you have a corner window facing north, you may perhaps also glimpse the huge dark bulk of the ruined castle of Santa Barbara looming against the bright sky.

XV

A CHEAP MEDITERRANEAN HOLIDAY

From Alicante via Valencia, Tarragona, and Sitges to Barcelona.

THE long day's journey from Granada to Alicante bridges the gap between Andalusia and the coast, where you can enjoy a Mediterranean holiday for half the cost of a fortnight at Black-pool—if you know how!

The coast road north from Alicante leads to the great spur of land that juts out towards the island of Ibiza. South of that the climate is wholly tropical, and it is a land of palms and cactus where, even in the heart of winter, the sun can burn you attractively brown—or unattractively red. Once that corner is rounded the land looks towards Europe instead of towards Africa; the palms give way to oranges, and the cactus to flat squares of shrill green rice. North of Alicante, it is only 5 miles to the city's bathing resort of San Juan, where the second-class Hotel Playa will feed you well, with a room looking directly on to the sandy beach, for 75 pts, or less than 15s. a day.

Next comes Villajoyosa, a fishing village since Roman times, sleeping among its crumbling medieval walls and turrets. On rounding a corner, the road runs past an oasis of tall palms towards the picturesque little port of Benidorm. Here sun and perfect bathing, and the simple comforts of the Hotels Bilbaino, Planesia, and Villa Marconi, offer everything needed for a memorable family sea-side holiday. There are none of the sophisticated pleasures such as cinemas, piers, or smart bars, but the fishing round the little island a half-mile or so away is full of strange rewards, for recently some Scandinavian visitors uncovered a chest of golden 'pieces of eight' hidden among the rocks by Barbary pirates a couple of centuries ago. Almost on the tip of the great land-spur the road leaves the sea, and it is necessary to turn off to the right to discover one of the strangest and loveliest places on the entire coast. The few who do turn off are effectively stopped by the ugly little town of Calpe, which

15 The ancient island fortress town of Peñiscola

16 In the foot-hills of the Pyrenees on the road to Huesca and Jaca from Lerida

seems to me never to have recovered from the dark day in the seventeenth century when Moorish pirates left it empty of all life—the men and older women lying dead where they lay, while the young women and children of both sexes were carried off for sale into the harems and brothels of North Africa. Should you continue another mile or so you would reach the Parador de Ifach, not a State-run hotel, in spite of its name, but comfortable, clean, and placed between two sand-bathing beaches, backed by the mysterious, towering 1,000-foot rock known as the Peñon de Ifach.

There used to be an old sailor living in a tavern there who told me stories, in the peculiar English that he had learned in Cardiff, about the villagers who had climbed the Peñon on the night of the full moon, and returned with crazy babblings of having witnessed strange and unholy rites there, performed before the throne of an immense black goat, of which they could remember nothing but their fear of his shining, blank white eyes!

However, when I was last in Ifach at Easter-time I found he had gone, and enquiries revealed that he was in prison for smuggling, so do not blame me if you fail to find him there.

The sea is so warm and still round this fantastic headland that on my last visit I swam out for about half a mile and, lying on my back, went as nearly to sleep as is humanly possible without sinking. My stillness led to an odd experience, for when I raised my head to turn over I found that I was one of a party of eight turtles, all apparently equally enjoying the occasion. For some reason or other it made me think of the *New Yorker* drawing, showing ten ostriches with their heads buried in the sand, while the eleventh gazes anxiously around and exclaims:

'Where in hell have all the other chaps got to?'

The memory caused me to swallow a certain amount of Mediterranean, but I recovered sufficiently to secure one of my companions to form the basis for a memorable soup.

This is the land of carnations. They grow like weeds, twining from gaily coloured pots on every windowsill, and, although I did not believe it until I tried it myself, their fragrance is discernible in the local pale red wine.

Back on the main road you must climb steeply to Ondara, from which a track leads for 2½ miles to the forgotten village that was once the city of Denia. There are three simple inns, the Morera, the Fornos, and the Comercio, where for 55 pts a day, including all meals, you can stay among the relics of the ancient Greek founders, the Phœnician fortifications, and the remains of the mighty Temple of Diana. From there you can venture out with the little fishing fleet on moonless nights, when the black waves glow with phosphorescent stars, brighter even than those that wheel slowly above your head towards the dawn. The fishermen will welcome your company if you bring a goat-skin of wine and do not disturb the watery silence with too much talk.

Gandia contains the exquisite Palace of Osuna, once the residence of the Dukes of Gandia, and a fourteenth-century church possesses paintings by Paolo de San Leocadio sent as a gift from the Borgia Pope Alexander VI, for we are now near the town of Játiva from which this strange but enormously gifted family came, and of which I will tell you a little when we visit the orange-farm of El Realengo. After Gandia we drive across the richest rice-growing province in Europe—flat and muddy, and with tall yellow irises clustering thickly in every ditch. Away to the right is the Lake of Albufera and one of Spain's two best areas for shooting duck, mallard, and other migratory water-fowl, while ahead of us is the important but unlovely city of Valencia, 114 miles from Alicante and roughly 220 from both Barcelona and Madrid. You will not be long in Valencia before you become aware of the fact that the character and appearance of the people have changed for the worse. It seems that the 'valenciano' is a blend of Semitic Phœnician and Barbary pirate, which, while certainly not his fault, may justify most of the rude stories that are told of his sly, acquisitive character.

No Spaniard is ever upset by noise, but the valencianos actively worship it, and they have now established a kind of commercial monopoly over all the more deafening devices produced by man. These are displayed to the full in March during the famous 'Fallas de San José', which, if you can stand the din, are amusing. For weeks before, even the usual, slight pretence of doing any work is abandoned, and the entire population devotes itself to the construction of giant papier-maché figures, often of popular bull-fighters and footballers. These usually have an ironical twist, and reveal a real talent for caricature. On the big night, to the sound of fireworks (which make the barrage that opened the Battle of El Alamein seem like birdsong at eventide by comparison), all but the prize-winning figures are set on fire, and battles of flowers and parades of local belles in their attractive regional costumes set the stage for all-night dancing in the streets and plazas. Apart from shipping oranges from the port from November until April, the only staple industry appears to be organizing fiestas, which attract not only foreigners but Spaniards from all over the country— and all leave a good deal of their money behind them!

Like every other town in Spain, Valencia has its full share of old buildings, and the Museum of Fine Arts is one of the very few, outside Madrid, that should stand high on the list of anyone interested in Spanish art, as the Valencian School of Joanes Macip, Ribalta, Espinosa, Vicente Lopez, and Cubells is better represented here than in the capital. The same building also contains some fine canvases by Van Dyck, Murillo, Velazquez, El Greco, and Goya.

The cathedral, begun in the thirteenth and finished in the fourteenth century, replaced an earlier building with an unusually chequered history. First a Temple of Diana, then a Visigothic Christian Church, it became a Mosque on the arrival of the Moors. El Cid liberated the city in 1095 and made it a Church again, but a few years after his death the Moors recaptured it and turned it back into a Mosque. It is not surprising that, on Valencia's final liberation in 1238, it was decided to pull it down and build a new one without its predecessor's complex background. The chapter house contains the chalice believed to be the authentic Holy Grail, for which

Parsifal and our own legendary Arthurian knights were always in search. The bell tower, 213 feet high, contains the famous 500-year-old bell affectionately known as Little Michael (Miguelete).

From a long list of places and sights to see in Valencia, the two most interesting are the little-visited Church of San Juan del Hospital, founded by the Knights of Malta in 1300 and containing the tombs of the Byzantine Empress Constance of Nicea and her daughter Irene; and the 1,000-year-old Water Tribunal, still held every Thursday under the Cathedral entrance of the Apostles in the Plaza Mayor.

Having satisfied your æsthetic tastes, do not ignore your gastronomic opportunities, but visit the popular bathing-beach of Levante, some miles away, and there order a 'paella' at the fountain-head of this excellent and savoury dish, in the Restaurants La Marcelina or La Pepica.

Valencia's first luxury hotel, the Excelsior, was opened in 1952, but the Alhambra and the Victoria are both adequate. The general run of hotels in Valencia is surprisingly poor and stuffy, so this is one of those few occasions when I advise visitors to aim for one of the three more or less expensive establishments that I have mentioned.

In these days of currency restrictions it surprises me that no one has tried a holiday on one of the countless orange-farms in the surrounding countryside, in most of which anyone prepared to live the simple life in an ideal winter climate can find clean, if unluxurious, accommodation (and unlimited paella) for something like £3 10s. a week per person.

I made my first acquaintance with an orange-farm late in 1945, when I was sick in body from six years of the strange foods, drinks, and climates of Persia, Iraq, Syria, Turkey, Egypt, India, Burma, and the East Indies; sick in mind from a close-up of a Russian 'liberation' and from the certainty of our then Allies' long-term plans for World War III; and sick in pocket because I could not write, as fashion and my employers demanded, of the long and loving honeymoon with Russia upon which we were officially just entering. It was at this bad moment that I ran into my very best of friends, Lucas de Oriol, who in half an hour diagnosed my condition and prescribed as follows:

'What you need is a dose of El Realengo.'

Two days later I took the night 'sleeper' to Valencia and there boarded a Walt Disney train, with open benches on the roof and slightly square wheels, which fumed its way south and inland for some 30 miles to the little town of Carcagente. From there I was bounced over an atrocious road for another 8 miles, and found myself at the orange-farm of El Realengo, and in another world from that which had ruined my duodenum and morale.

El Realengo was my home for two months. Old Antonia brewed delicious 'paellas' for me, Carmen sang fortissimo while making up the sitting-room and bedroom that were all of the long, low, whitewashed former monastery that my wife and dog and self disturbed; and promptly at sunset we would hear the heavy clank of massive wooden doors being securely bolted against the perils of the night.

During the days of mild winter sun we would walk through the orange groves, where most of the red-gold fruit was already ripe, to the corner where fat yellow grapefruit were growing. Occasionally we would climb up through the pine forests to the crest of the bare brown mountains, from which we could make out the distant sea.

I learned quite a lot about oranges and consumed, in solid or liquid form, about two dozen a day. First there were the flatter, smaller 'mandarinas', 'tangerines', and 'clementinas'. The first two I had met at Christmas in my early youth, though I then imagined that they grew already wrapped up in silver paper; but the 'clementina' was a new and particularly delicious variation. Most of these were ripe by late November, but orange-growers, experimenting with the Golden Apples that caused Hercules so much trouble, have now evolved methods for 'staggering' the harvest so as to spread it over half the year from early November until late April. The great period of anxiety is in mid-January, when a single night of frost may halve the value of the season's crop, and this occurs fairly frequently in the northernmost orange-growing province of Castellón de la Plana. It happened, too, at El Realengo on the night of St. Anthony, January 16th, when the jubilations attending huge bonfires in the courtyard (through the flames of which the small boys of the neighbouring village must leap until their eyebrows are singed, or else risk the dreadful charge of cowardice) were tinged with anxiety. Next day, sure enough, the red-gold skins of some of the fruit were bruised as though by a blow from a stick, and later dropped to rot in the rich soil. The almost overwhelmingly sweet-smelling orange-blossom appears before the last of the fruit is gathered in April and, driving after dark through the endless groves of fruit, silver instead of gold in the moonlight, it is easy to recapture the pagan intoxication of ancient and forgotten lands.

From Realengo I called on the Borgias, though historical memories suggested that it might be dangerous to stay for dinner! The Spanish name was Borja, which Alexander Italianized to Borgia when he became a Cardinal, and Játiva was the family's native town. Although chiefly renowned for two bad Popes, Calixtus III and Alexander VI, the family later produced a very great Saint, and the towering castle above the town is one of the most romantic looking in Spain.

Játiva was the Roman Setabis, and also the birthplace in 1588 of one of Spain's greatest painters, José Ribera. It is one of the many historic old towns in Spain that seems outside the usual tourist's range, but if you decide to try it you will find the little Fuente Roja Hotel both charming and cheap.

My dose of El Realengo certainly cured me of feeling sorry for myself. A similar stay would not be difficult to arrange for any youngish couple, with a child or two, who wished to escape the worst of the English winter, and their combined currency allowance would suffice for two or three months.

North from Valencia the huge fortress of Sagunto soon towers above the coast road. It was the scene of the ghastly siege by the Carthaginians under Hannibal, when the inhabitants, loyal to Rome, committed mass suicide when surrender was inevitable. When this took place in 219 B.C. the fortress

was already old, yet well over 2,000 years later it was still able
to hold up Napoleon's march for several weeks.

From here a road climbs inland to Teruel and the 5,000-foot
peaks of the Sierra de Albarracin, of exceptional wild beauty.
Although it adds a couple of hours' driving to the journey from
Barcelona to Madrid, I usually choose this route in preference
to the more direct road through Saragossa.

Castellón de la Plana is of no great interest except for the
export of oranges. There the road forks, and you will be well
advised to stick to the coast one, which leads through Alcalá de
Chisvert to the small but attractive State-run Albergue just
outside Benicarló.

From there you can see the unbelievably ancient fortress
island town of Peñiscola, 5 miles away, yet few tourists ever
seem to bother to visit it, though it is one of the most strangely
beautiful places in the Mediterranean anywhere from Smyrna
to Gibraltar.

The town is built on a sharp 200-foot-high rock and is linked
with the mainland only by a ridge of sand, submerged at the
whim of wind or tide. A settlement even before the Phœnicians,
it was already an important fortress by the time Rome and
Carthage were struggling for the mastery of the known world.
Liberated from the Moorish occupation in 1233, King James
the Conqueror presented it to the Knights Templar, and later
it was the refuge for ten years of the anti-Pope Pedro de Luna
before he moved to Avignon in 1424 to become Benedict XIII.
As late as 1814 it was held by the French against a Spanish
bombardment of 6,000 cannon-shots, which severely damaged
some of the still lovely rooms of the fourteenth-century castle
built by the Templars. This ancient knightly order owned
enormously rich property at the beginning of the fourteenth
century and, perhaps because of this, fell under suspicion of
practising black magic, and were dispossessed.

The small image in the Santuario de la Virgen Ermitaña is
supposed to have been brought there by St. James the Apostle,
and is certainly very ancient indeed.

Peñiscola, with its steep, narrow streets of time-weathered

stone suddenly framing both sea and landscape, is an artist's paradise, and the modest little Fonda Cabomar is clean and feeds you well for 55 pts a day.

Vinaroz, famous for its immense and savoury grilled 'langostinos' and excellent table wines, is only 5 miles beyond the Albergue de Benicarló and, like Peñiscola, was the property of the Knights Templar in the thirteenth century. Beyond it the character of the country changes as the sharp hills, clothed with vine and olive, give place to the delta of the Ebro, Spain's greatest river.

Most people turn inland to Tortosa, but if, like myself, you prefer to stick close to the sea, then take the shorter road through Amposta; although marked on your road-map as being very bad, it was fully repaired in 1952.

Once across the Ebro it is a straight run through pleasant country for some 50 miles to the famous Roman city of Tarragona.

Tarragona always seems to me to be a happy town, bustling and busy as a port, despite its great antiquity, and many a memorable meal have I eaten on the terrace that overlooks the bluest of seas. Should you decide to stay the night, the Hotel Europa is excellent, and the sandy bathing-beach of El Milagro only a quarter of a mile away.

The biggest of Tarragona's many fiestas starts on September 23rd, when you will see plenty of attractive folk-dancing and costumes.

As so often happens in Spain, the twelfth-century cathedral replaced an earlier Mosque and a still earlier Temple of Jupiter, and the huge marble baptismal font started life as a bath for a stout and un-Christian Roman governor!

I promised to try to limit my comments upon cathedrals, but that of Tarragona is particularly fine, and I think the carving round the main entrance, finished in 1475, is beautiful of its kind. The gentle, lovely face of the Virgin Mary was obviously taken from life, and by someone who surely loved his model as a man loves a woman rather than as man loves the Mother of God.

17 The prehistoric cyclopean walls of Tarragona, upon the top of which can be seen the smoother Roman masonry

In 1952 Tarragona surrendered many of its royal dead, including Don Jaime el Conquistador, and they were carried in great state to the Monasterio de Poblet, which has been made the official burial-place for the Kings of Aragon and Catalonia of the period before the unification of these provinces with Castile by the marriage of Ferdinand and Isabella.

For me the old walls of the city are its greatest attraction, greater even than the Roman circus or the aqueduct known as the Devil's Bridge. The base is of 'cyclopean' origin, containing single stones as heavy as a locomotive, which even massed slave labour could not possibly have laid so neatly in their place. Above these are the Roman fortifications, to which Moors and Christians periodically added. Looking inland from these walls, towards the blue peaks of the Sierra de Almusara, is a view not easily forgotten.

North of Tarragona you may overlook an attractive roadside Roman tomb, but you cannot miss the triumphal arch of Bare, perfectly preserved despite some 1,700 years of sun and rain. When first I saw it the road still led under it, but now it loops round the arch itself—a precaution induced by the apparent determination of all lorry-drivers to knock it down.

At Vendrell the main road to Barcelona turns inland to Villafranca del Panades, and again I urge you to turn right along the sea. You will be rewarded by pleasant hilly country, rich in vines and occasional crumbling fortresses. Villanueva y Geltru is rather a blot on the landscape, but, once that is passed, it is only 5 miles to Sitges.

Since Sitges was my home from 1948 until 1950, I feel justified in writing of this little Catalan fishing village and sea-side resort in some detail.

It lies 25 miles south of Barcelona, and spreads along the 2-mile-long half-moon of sandy beach which ends at the church, perched on a high rock. This is the fashionable beach, beside which Barcelona's millionaires have built strange-looking houses primarily designed to impress their business rivals. At the opposite end to the church is the luxury Terramar Hotel. Beyond the church there is another far smaller sand-beach, with the more modest but newer Hotel Miramar. The little bay is ringed by converted fishermen's cottages, in one of which I lived, with the pleasant postal address of the Street of the Happy Port No. 11 (Calle del Puerto de Alegre), and paid a rent of £15 a month, fully furnished, to my kindly landlord and friend Manolo Vidal Quadras.

Despite this seeming cheapness, Catalonia in general, and Sitges in summer in particular, is a good 25% more expensive than anywhere else in Spain. But with direct B.E.A. communications to neighbouring Barcelona, a month's holiday there is well within the range of the present British travel allowance of £50. My pleasantest memory of Sitges is of the fiesta of Corpus Christi, which usually takes place in early June and coincides with the great annual carnation show.

For days there is a house-to-house collection of flower-petals of all colours, the pale pink of the commonest kind of carnation (which grows like weeds in this part of Spain), the purple of bougainvillæa, scarlet or white of roses, brilliant yellow of sunflowers, and all the other hues that Nature permits to a Mediterranean spring. Then, on the night before the big day, the population gets busy forming these into a pictured carpet a quarter of a mile long. Geometrical patterns, religious pictures, ships a-sailing, flags a-flying, and even bars of music, all made with flower-petals, succeed one another as each householder seeks to outrival his neighbours and win one of the coveted money prizes.

No one must tread upon this flowery carpet until the procession from the church has passed along it. People kneel on the narrow pavement as the Host is carried by, but it is followed by the 'gigantes' that are an integral part of most Spanish fiestas. Fifteen-foot-high Ferdinand is docilely followed by 15-foot-high Isabella, both arrayed in fine velvet, and behind them bob the South American Indians brought back by Columbus. When they reach the open sea-front the King and Queen dance a stately measure together and then take a seat, while the populace forms into the ever-growing circles that announce the 'sardana'—the fascinating local Catalan dance. Beneath their feet the last of the flower-petals are crushed into perfume, and the exciting nasal whine of the flutes throbs through the night air until the stars turn pale above the still branches of the palm-tree avenue.

Perhaps because Spaniards are less self-conscious, a fiesta anywhere in Spain is alive and exciting, free of the ghastly blight imposed upon such efforts in England by the climate, the arty and crafty Vicar's wife, and the crashingly dull Good Cause which has occasioned the whole affair.

My first winter in Sitges was enlivened by the activities of the 'fantasma negro'. Now, as everyone knows, a black ghost is far worse than the common-or-garden white or grey variety, and requires a whole collection of bells, books, candles, and bishops before it can be successfully exorcised.

To begin with, it was only a few old women who staggered in babbling complaints to the Civil Guard (and some unkind souls even suspected that it was an act put on just to obtain a large free brandy). But when one of the town's two doctors—a man of scientific training—was brought in, pale and trembling, the authorities decided that they must act. The doctor had been returning late from Villanueva when one of the front tyres of his car went flat near a railway bridge. Getting out to inspect, he was aware of a voice behind him that said:

'To-night you have saved a life. Meet me here at the same hour to-morrow, or you will pay me back with your own.'

Wheeling round, the good doctor perceived a tall black figure motionless beside him. The next thing he knew was that he was driving as fast as he could on his flat tyre, regardless of the ruin of the outer cover. Of course he did not believe in ghosts, black or otherwise, but really it was difficult to accept the idea that anyone would play such a profitless practical joke!

The Captain of the Civil Guard did some hard thinking and announced, 'Well, whatever it was that you saw, it gave itself away when it told you to meet it to-morrow night. You will keep the appointment—and so will I and my entire company of ten men, and we will put an end to all this "fantasma negro" business once and for all.'

Well before the appointed hour the Captain had posted his men in strategic olive-groves with Napoleonic precision, while he and his sergeant took cover under the railway arch. Above their heads the doctor—a shivering morsel of live bait—waited, apparently alone, for his unpleasant visitor.

The hour came, and passed. For an hour longer the waiting men stood in the cold wind and swore under their breath. The party was then called off and returned to the village feeling somewhat unkindly towards the doctor and his old woman's tales. But the Captain was not satisfied, and the following night he and the sergeant came back alone, and stationed themselves as before. It was a moonless night, and it was some time before the sergeant's eye caught sight of something darker than the darkness among the olive trees. He rushed forward, with rifle at the ready, calling upon the figure to surrender. Nothing happened, the black shape seeming only to flap derisively in answer. Scenting promotion or martyrdom, the sergeant hurled himself forward and bore the figure to the ground.

By this time the Captain had caught up, and together they examined their victim. It consisted of a black silk, skin-tight costume, in the pocket of which they found a packet of Chesterfield cigarettes and a hand-printed note. By the light of his torch the Captain read as follows:

'Thanks, Captain, for your co-operation. We landed 5,000 cartons of these last night in the bay just below your quarters while you were out here catching cold—but not the
                                        Fantasma Negro.'

While it is only 25 miles from Sitges to Barcelona, it takes an hour by road or rail, and the 10-mile stretch, known as the Costas de Garraf, is narrow, twisting, and dangerous. If you need a break, look out for a mad fairy-tale kind of house on your right, built by the unbearably Hans Andersen Gothic Catalan architect Gaudi (also responsible for Barcelona's monster unfinished Cathedral of the Holy Family, which looks like a drunk organist's nightmare about a Christmas tree). A hundred yards before reaching it a steep earthen road turns right and, if you follow it under a railway arch and then up a hill, with some bathing bungalows on your left, you will come to one of the most attractive restaurants in Catalonia. It is called the Club de Garraf, but do not let the idea that it is a club mislead you, as anyone with the price of a drink or a meal is a member. When Barcelona is unpleasantly hot this is an ideal escape place for dinner and dancing in the open air beneath the illuminated double palm, for there is always a breath of cool air from the sea directly below.

Soon after Garraf the hills move away from the coast and the road enters the fertile valley of the River Llobregat. It then joins the main one from Saragossa and Madrid, and the top of the next hill reveals the great port and city of Barcelona, spread out between the heights of Mount Tibidabo and the sea.

N

XVI

BARCELONA AND MONTSERRAT

THIS is not Spain but Catalonia, with a different race speaking a different language and with a wholly different character from that possessed by the Castilians. Catalans are often called the Scots of Spain, and up to a certain point the description is just. They possess the Scots reserve in their personal relationships, and they are hard-working, hard-headed, thrifty, independent, and extremely culture-conscious. Rather surprisingly perhaps, they are also artists and musicians of the highest order, as the names of Picasso, Sert, Dalí, and Pablo Casals in the present generation alone are sufficient to prove.

Separatism has always been strong in the provinces geographically farthest from Madrid—namely, among the Catalans, the Basques, and in Andalusia. The weakening Monarchy allowed them some form of local autonomy which, under the Republic, came near to a promise of complete independence if only they would fight against Franco, and Barcelona was the head, if Madrid was the heart, of the Republican resistance throughout the entire Civil War.

But the Catalan Separatists are not primarily anti-Franco, as many hopeful newspaper correspondents of the Anglo-American Leftist Press have delighted their editors by suggesting; they are simply anti-Madrid, quite regardless of whether a King, a Republic, or General Franco rules from that new and upstart capital. Barcelona, the Catalans point out, was a great port and city when Madrid was a huddle of grubby huts clustering around a Moorish fortress; Catalonia, they state, pays three-quarters of the entire nation's taxes because of its people's industry; and, culturally speaking, they feel themselves superior because of the greater interchange of ideas with France, due to their common frontier.

All this can be made up into the kind of case which arouses the ready sympathies of the professionally freedom-loving

Anglo-Saxons, but for the same reason as led Lincoln to fight the Civil War, and Queen Elizabeth, the advisers of Queen Anne, and finally George II to scheme or fight against the claims to independence of Scotland, no honest Madrid Government could ever consent to Catalan independence. The reason is that the smaller nation could not be an economic unit without the help of the larger and, even more important, would soon fall under the economic influence or political domination of some foreign Power anxious to weaken the nation as a whole. It was French meddling in Scotland that led to its loss of independence, French meddling in Mexico (while the American Civil War was in progress) that stressed the absolute need for union, and it is the threat of French Communist meddling in Catalonia that to-day makes Madrid so hard on Catalan Separatists.

But these are political considerations which need not concern the visitor, and I give them only because they supply part of the explanation of why Barcelona is so different from the other great cities of Spain.

Superficially, at least, it is a pleasanter place for foreigners than Madrid. It is on the Mediterranean instead of in the middle of a bleak plateau, French is understood everywhere, and English increasingly so; it can equally be reached direct from London or Paris by B.E.A. and Air France, and it is the jumping-off place for such ideal holiday resorts as Sitges, the Costa Brava, and Majorca. The shops, though notably expensive, have a wider and more attractive display of most kinds of luxury goods, and the night-life, though severely purged under the present régime, is still more varied than is to be found in the capital.

Although Barcelona is an ancient city, as the thirteenth- and fourteenth-century cathedral (replacing an eighth-century Church of Santa Eulalia) and the eleventh-century San Pablo del Campo and Santa Maria del Mar amply demonstrate, it has suffered some severe ups and downs during the last century. Between 1880 and the Great Exhibition of 1928 it reached a position of world importance as the largest Mediterranean textile manufacturing centre. Vast fortunes were made, and the inhabitants became conscious of the need to enlarge and beautify their city. Almost the whole of the modern town which lies above the huge Plaza de Cataluña, and includes the really magnificent shopping street of the Paseo de Gracia and those running parallel with or at right angles to it, was built in the last quarter of the nineteenth century. Increased labour troubles and frequent bomb outrages were Catalonia's methods of drawing attention to her separatist claims, and these coincided with the world slump of 1931. Just for good measure, in October 1934 the Catalan lawyer Companys selected this moment to declare Catalonia's independence.

It was the Republican Army, not that of General Franco, which swiftly smashed the revolt, and business, bad since 1930, had almost ceased to exist by the time of the outbreak of the Civil War in July 1936. For the next two and a half years it was the primary objective for German and Italian planes stationed in Majorca, and after Franco's victory it suffered both from the effects of World War II and from a certain amount of special hostility on the part of Madrid as having been the focal point of the resistance which, right or wrong, had certainly been responsible for a million Spanish deaths.

But Catalan doggedness and industry allied to Barcelona's unchangeable geographic advantages began to tell after the collapse of Germany, and in the last eight years she has regained most of the prosperity of a quarter of a century ago.

Until recently Barcelona's main trouble was shortage of first-class hotel accommodation to cope with the tourist flood that began in 1950, as the result of Luis Bolín's successful fight to introduce a special tourist rate of exchange, and which increased during subsequent years. However, when the Pope decided that the 35th Eucharistic Congress should be held there in May 1952, an immense building programme was begun in order to cope with the million pilgrims from all over the world who wished to attend. Eight new hotels resulted, including two luxury ones that far outshine the old Ritz in splendour, so I advise you to make sure that your list of Barcelona hotels dates from after June 1952 before making your final choice.

Culturally, Barcelona is going through a powerful fit of

nostalgia for the palmy days of fifty years ago, and the arch-priest of this movement is the septuagenarian millionaire Vizconde de Güell.

When he was in his thirties and forties the Vizconde used to have a lot of fun being mistaken for King George V, to whom he bore a really extraordinary resemblance, and the Duke of Windsor, then Prince of Wales, used habitually to greet him with a wink and a 'Hallo, Dad' when they met at parties. To-day, white-haired and rather fuller in the face, he looks exactly like Edward VII in about 1908.

If you go into the lounge of the Ritz any morning between noon and 1.30 p.m. you will find His Late Majesty ensconced in the left-hand corner as you enter, a bottle of French champagne eternally beside him in a silver bucket of ice. He is the presiding genius of the delightfully 'fin de siècle' club next door to the Liceo Opera House, where plush sofas and water-colours of beautiful ladies with hour-glass figures and hair arranged to look like a disorderly bird's nest successfully re-create the atmosphere of an almost forgotten age. He is also president of the Artist's Club in the Plaza de Cataluña, where beards and naked models recall the Quartier Latin of du Maurier's *Trilby*, and of a very select lecture club, with premises in the Ritz Hotel, where visiting literary lights glimmer for the benefit of culturally minded ladies wearing pearls and enormous hats and energetically talking indifferent French.

The Heir Apparent to Barcelona's cultural throne is Alberto Puig, good-looking, delicate, and 45, who became fabulously wealthy from his silk factory during the last decade, has a special passion for flamenco music and private bull-fights, and was recently responsible for the visit to London of a party of gipsies to play a part in a film. He tells a delightful story of how he pacified the manager of the Savoy when it was discovered that his gipsies had built a camp fire in the centre of their sitting-room floor!

Barcelona has charm, apart from the old-world charm of its prominent residents, though I advise you to avoid the sticky heat of July and August. To appreciate its real beauty you will

do well to take the funicular railway to the top of Mount Tibidabo and then, from a height of 1,600 feet, look down upon the
city spreading away from your feet to the very blue sea. If you
walk to the other side you can look across pine forests to the
incredibly romantic peak of Montserrat, rising sheer and
mysterious for over 3,700 feet to the spot where Parsifal, at
long last, found the Holy Grail.

Although the Catalans are notoriously anti-clerical and always
seem to begin their efforts to achieve independence by burning
down the churches, the cathedral has escaped and is well worth
visiting, though many other beautiful old buildings were
destroyed or badly damaged during the first days of the Civil
War. There was a day in July 1936 when, from a friend's flat
in the suburb of Bonanova, I counted no less than sixteen
simultaneously on fire, and I witnessed some of the atrocities
committed in the name of Liberty upon harmless nuns and
monks. Many superficial observers ascribed this church-burning complex to disillusionment with and disbelief in Catholicism. Nothing could be farther from the truth, since it is obvious
that no one bothers to destroy a thing of which he is not afraid,
and no one is afraid of a thing in which he does not believe.

Perhaps a short incident from those far-off days is not out of
place in explaining the position of the Church in Spain and its
power over the minds of every Spaniard, regardless of his politics.

It occured in August 1936, when a wild crowd, of which I
was one, pressed into the Plaza de Cataluña to hear the great
Anarchist leader Buenaventura Durruti make a speech. He
concluded something like this—'. . . and I swear to you, I,
Buenaventura Durruti, that I will never rest until every church
in Spain has been burned to the ground and the power of the
Church lies finally and completely broken. This I solemnly
swear to you in the Name of the Father, Son and Holy Ghost.'

No one, except myself, thought that he had said anything in
the least bit peculiar!

The best explanation of the Catalan propensity for church
burning is their primitive feeling that, before they can really let
themselves go, they must remove, or at least temporarily blind,

18 The mountain monastery of Montserrat
perched 3,700 feet above the plain near Barcelona

the one great controlling force whose anger they fear infinitely more than death. In short, they do not destroy because they do not believe, but precisely because they believe so completely, even against their own desire.

But these are sombre thoughts for a holiday, and Barcelona to-day is certainly far from being a sombre place, even though it is not quite the rip-roaring strip-teasing, wide-open city of pre-Civil War Republican days.

The jugular vein of Barcelona's day- and night-life is the Ramblas—the wide, shop- and tavern-lined avenue that leads down from the Plaza de Cataluña to the docks, from where the boats follow the pointing finger of Columbus on his tall statue and obediently leave every evening for Majorca. The whole street is called Las Ramblas, although different sections of it have different names, such as Ramblas de los Estudios, Rambla Canaletas, Rambla de las Flores, &c. The top section is filled with sellers of cage-birds—canaries, red-polls, love-birds, and parrots—plus a few depressed-looking kittens and puppies. Next come the stalls of the flower-sellers, on a morning in May or June one of the loveliest sights in the whole city. Where this ends you may notice the surprisingly attractive Gaudi-designed Palace de Güell, now used as a museum. By its side are half a dozen wooden boxes looking rather like confessionals, where sit the professional letter-writers. In literate Catalonia it is a dying industry, but the learned scribes have now brought themselves up to date and abandoned their quills for typewriters. I eaves-dropped on one occasion, when an angry peasant mother said:

'You tell that shameless rascal my son that if he does not come home at once I'll have the police on him.' After a flurry of typing the scribe read back:

Distinguished Sir,
    I am writing to you at the wish of my egregious client, your lady mother, who wishes me to inform you that if your absence from home is further prolonged you may become involved in tedious and costly legal proceedings. . . .

I think he earned his 10 pts!

A little farther down, a narrow lane to the left leads to the Barrio Chino, where, even to-day, the police prefer to patrol at night in pairs. This rabbit warren is full of shady hotels, dark little café bars, and one outstandingly good and inexpensive restaurant. You will soon spot Caracoles (which is run by Spain's Wallace Beery, Señor Bofarull, whose family have owned the establishment for a century and a half) because, if it is anywhere near meal-time, you will suddenly come across a number of chickens turning on a spit before a charcoal fire let into a corner wall of the street. Inside there is a long bar, rich in the tasty but preferably anonymous thirst-provokers known as 'tapas'. You then go down a couple of steps and through the huge kitchen, up a couple more steps and into one of the many small rooms which together comprise the restaurant. It is hung with strings of garlic and signed photographs of film celebrities. Señor Bofarull, who is 6 foot 2 and immensely fat, habitually drives himself from his restaurant to the film studio in a smart pony-trap.

The bouillabaisse, or fish soup, served at Caracoles makes the best that Marseilles can produce look like prison-fare. The lobster is always excellent, and occasionally you can obtain that greatest of all Spanish fish dishes, 'angulas a la bilbaina', which you must eat only with a wooden spoon and fork. The menu is printed in English—rather quaint English, but understandable.

Returning to the Ramblas and continuing towards the port, you will pass or, far better, fail to pass the Bar Sanlucar on your left. This is a favourite haunt of bull-fighters and their current girl-friends, and the walls are plastered with scenes at countless corridas, many of them signed by the most eminent members of the profession.

This summer I was sitting there quietly, eating snails and drinking a half-bottle of manzanilla (price 1s. 6d.), when I observed a very nervous young bull-fighter, obviously awaiting the return of his manager from the allotment of the respective bulls among the three matadores in to-morrow's fight.

A gloomy-looking individual with a pronounced limp and wearing a hard, wide-brimmed Cordoban hat came in and

slumped down beside him. Their conversation during the next
half-hour consisted of four words.

MATADOR: 'Son grandes?' (Are they big ones?)

MANAGER (sadly): 'Muy grandes!' (Damned big!)

If the noise and bustle of the Ramblas are too much for you
it is only 100 yards to the lovely eighteenth-century Plaza Real,
where immensely tall palms reach towards the moon and all is
quiet, though there are two good restaurants in this surprising
backwater.

It was in this square that, many years ago, I attended the only
public poets' competition I have ever seen.

In the centre were three judges on a dais, upon which Barcelona's budding Byrons had to climb and read their effusions
to a crowd of several hundred. When the poems were bad—
and they were frequently very bad—the crowd would moan
very slightly and the judges would take another swig out of the
wine-skin they were sharing. When they were good—and two
or three were excellent—you could have heard the proverbial
pin drop. But, Catalan poetry aside, the thing that charmed me
was the system of prize-giving. The third best was given a rose
made of silver, the second best a rose made of gold, and the
winner a perfect, natural bloom!

Being of a cynical turn of mind, I enquired whether this did
not occasionally lead to the winner stoutly insisting that the
poem by his runner-up was really even better than his own, but
I was assured that to the first prize of the natural bloom was
added the proceeds of a silver collection!

Almost opposite the exit from the Plaza Real into the
Ramblas is the Liceo Opera House, the largest in Europe with
the sole exception of the Scala in Milan.

If you have any ideas about Grand Opera being out of fashion
you should attend one of the performances at the Liceo. You
will see enough diamond tiaras to make even M. Cartier's mouth
water, and evening dress is compulsory everywhere except in
the gallery. This is not quite exact, for actually on the stage,
though invisible to the audience, is a luxurious box, with a room
for drinks leading from it, which is the property of a very

exclusive male club, known as the Twelve Apostles. Here I was once invited to sit through the whole of *La Traviata*, wearing a lounge suit and drinking champagne—a most indigestible, æsthetic-sartorial-alcoholic combination! The Twelve Apostles were all elderly, and I suspect that their enthusiasm for opera dated from the bad old days when it was customary for the 'jeunesse dorée' to send round their cards to any promising-looking soprano inscribed with the simple words:

'Où, quand, et combien?'

and to receive the satisfactorily inexpensive and epigramatic reply:

'Chez-toi, ce soir et pour rien!'

It is rather fun in the gallery—if very Grand Opera can ever be described as fun—as you will see many individuals who look as though they had cut a meal or two in order to buy their tickets. Quite half the audience there follows the singing from a tattered musical score, and if the prima donna funks a high C there is an audible rustle of shocked disapproval which would never occur in the bejewelled stalls, where a high C obviously only suggests rough weather aboard the yacht.

The Plaza de la Universidad leads into a not quite first-class shopping street called the Ronda de San Antonio, which, in turn, becomes the Ronda de San Pedro and runs parallel to the lower part of the Ramblas. Here you will find most of the girl-shows and night-clubs—but most of the girls weigh upwards of 200 lb., and most of the night-clubs are pretty shabby.

Barcelona is full of good restaurants and you can eat well without penetrating into the 1890 Quartier Latin atmosphere of the Barrio Chino (by the way, there have been no Chinese anywhere in Barcelona for the last century, but the name has stuck). Superb though expensive meals can be obtained at Parellada, Cau Ferrat, Hostal del Sol, and, if you have a taste for oysters, lobster, or langostinos, cheaply and safely at Cantabrico in the Calle Santa Ana, just off the Plaza Cataluña—but these are just four names out of forty. Most people seem to enjoy a visit to the gardens of the fortress prison of Montjuich—once held by the British, and latterly the lodging-place of Laval after his escape from Germany in 1945. Parts of the Great Exhibition of 1928–9 are still on view, and the 'Spanish village' is attractively done for the benefit of those who prefer a copy to taking the trouble to go and see the original.

Barcelona is a large and highly civilized city equipped to satisfy the holiday tastes of anyone with a little money to spend and, as is the case with all such places, you can make what you choose of it, so that, without a knowledge of your individual tastes, detailed suggestions from me would be pointless. No. 1 sight-seeing excursion from Barcelona is undoubtedly that to the mountain monastery of Montserrat, some 30 miles inland from the city, with a chance to do the last 2½ miles by aerial railway, which is exciting but safe.

This strange serrated peak, towering dramatically out of the Llobregat plain, is so rich in legend that even though it can be visited by charabanc it has somehow still managed to preserve a certain kind of Shangri-la atmosphere of mystery.

It is the setting, far more than the buildings, that is remarkable, with huge petrified fingers of rock pointing accusingly towards the sky.

If it is anything like a clear day you will see the whole snow-capped mass of the eastern Pyrenees piled up over 100 miles away on the northern horizon, even before you reach the monastery itself, which is built in a small clearing at the base of the towering stone fingers.

The main 'plaza', with its restaurant and souvenir shops, may strike you as distinctly trippery (and on high days and holidays it is); but here you have touched only the outer, commercial fringe of the place, which is scenically very beautiful but about as spiritually interesting as Margate or Coney Island.

It is only when you penetrate into the not particularly beautiful, recently restored church, and find yourself in the presence of the little Black Virgin, that you will begin to understand why this mountain has always been a place of pilgrimage. I have been to many such, including those in the Holy Land, but nowhere have I felt the same sense of power as radiates from that small, and to me slightly sinister-seeming figure. A small stairway behind the High Altar allows you to see it close, level, and face to face, and even to touch the orb that it holds in one of its hands.

Since the whole story of Montserrat is linked up with this strange image, I must tell you something of its history.

Tradition ascribes it to St. Luke, but critical examination discloses unmistakable Byzantine characteristics, probably from the fifth or sixth century. Nothing positive is known about it until the late tenth century, when it was already much venerated by the Benedictine monks who established themselves on the Holy Mountain in A.D. 986.

At a time of Moorish persecution the Black Virgin was hidden in the mile-long tunnel which ends in the Santa Cueva, where it was re-discovered and taken to the oldest of the existing buildings on Montserrat, the eleventh-century Chapel of St. Michael. The still older ninth-century Monastery of St. Cecilia was at that time in ruins, though it has since been intelligently restored to its original form.

Pilgrims came from all over the world, and the importance of the abbey increased accordingly, providing at least one Pope to the throne of St. Peter in the person of Cardinal de Rovere. So great was its prestige that it was granted a kind of extra-territorial independence, with its own flag, rather like the present-day Vatican City State. The boys with the best singing voices in Spain are still sent to Montserrat to join the choir, in the same way as the best from all over Italy go to the Sistine Chapel, or in England to Magdalen College School in Oxford.

But adversity overtook the devotees of the Black Virgin in the nineteenth century. First Napoleon sacked and burned all the monastery buildings in 1811, and then, during the Carlist Wars, the whole of the immense monastery treasure was stolen to provide the contestants with the sinews of war. There were anxious days, too, during the Civil War, and near the church are the graves of Montserrat's modern martyrs, killed by the Anarcho-syndicalists from Barcelona in 1936.

Only male visitors are allowed to visit the buildings and

gardens behind the church, but it is not very difficult for them
to obtain permission to visit the monastery proper. If you have
qualms about leaving your womenfolk for half an hour, a kindly
Brother will gladly show them the countless drawers full of
gorgeously embroidered and jewelled robes worn for High Mass
on the Black Virgin's festivals of April 27th and September 8th,
or for the fabulously rich Mass of New Year's Night.

If you are alone and would care to do so, you can stay actually
in the monastery, though near the times of these festivals you
are unlikely to obtain a cell unless you have written well in
advance to the Padre Aposentador to make the reservation.

If you do penetrate behind the scenes do not miss the
beautiful 100,000-volume library, which includes the first books
ever printed in Spain—the work of the Montserrat Press during
the last years of the fifteenth century.

The Holy Mountain is dotted with ruined hermitages dating
from the thirteenth to the sixteenth century, and honeycombed
with vast caves which are the supposed places of worship used
by the Knights of the Holy Grail during the days after the
collapse of Rome and before the Christianization of Spain's
Visigothic invaders. Others, filled with stalactites and stalag-
mites, can be reached by hiring donkeys from the little village of
Collbato.

You should not miss Montserrat. The buildings you will see
are neither very old nor particularly beautiful, but the matchless
setting and the glimpses of another world far below you in the
plain, whence the sounds of everyday life ascend with dis-
embodied clarity, or of the snowy mass of the Pyrenees, alone
make it unforgettable. To this must be added the aura of legend
and hidden power that unquestionably surrounds the small,
black, and malevolently ancient figure of 'La Virgen Morena'.

XVII

THE BALEARIC ISLANDS AND THE
COSTA BRAVA

Majorca—Palma—Ibiza—S'Agaro—Tossa.

I WAS rather shaken when in London recently to discover that people looked blank when I mentioned the Balearic Islands, and it took a minute or two before a friend patiently explained on my behalf: 'He means Majorca'.

Everyone has heard of Majorca (even though the inhabitants call it Mallorca and pronounce it 'my-yorker'), it being the best known of all Mediterranean holiday islands with the possible exception of Capri. However, the group includes Menorca and Ibiza, and the latter at least has great charm, not to mention several smaller islands of less touristic interest.

Still, Majorca is the largest, best-known, most important, and, in my opinion, most beautiful of the islands. Unfortunately, 30 million Frenchmen can't be wrong, and they all seem to think so too. As a result it suffers from Gallic overcrowding during July and August and, if I have occasion to be in that part of Spain at the height of summer, I have lately preferred Ibiza. But for most of the other ten months of the year Majorca is still my choice.

Air France now runs a through service from Paris to the island's capital of Palma, and B.E.A. will accept payment for the whole return trip in London. However, most people come by overnight ship from Barcelona or Valencia and, if they are early risers, they are wise to do so, in that the first glimpse of the Bay of Palma from the sea is every bit as beautiful as that of Naples.

Majorca was an Iberian settlement even before the arrival of the Celts, and was an important Phœnician trading base between 1200 and 1000 B.C. Whether or not it was the site of the Garden of the Hesperides and Hercules' capture of the Golden

Apples, or oranges, is problematic, but it seems fairly certain
that it was a matriarchy at the time of the Argonauts, and that
the High-Priestess-Queen lived in the Caves of Drach—one
of the five officially accepted entries into the pre-Christian
Underworld.

The Carthaginians followed, only to be ousted by the Roman
general, Cecelio Matelo, in A.D. 125. Under Rome the regiment
of Balearic stone-slingers became world-famous; but the Vandal
hordes seized the island in A.D. 455, though it was liberated for a
brief space by the great Byzantine General Belisarius. The
Moors, however, did not reach there for over eighty years after
they had overrun most of the Spanish mainland, and it was
from them that the islanders learned the secrets of the high
seas. By the eleventh century Palma was the favourite lair for
all the most skilful and bloodthirsty of the Barbary pirates, who
made such a nuisance of themselves that the Catalan king was
forced to seize the island and make it an independent kingdom.
Its fourth and last monarch fought desperately to retain its
independence, but it again fell to the Moors, who were not
finally ejected until New Year's Eve 1229. There was more
trouble with King Pedro IV of Aragon in 1343, and it only
passed to the united Spanish Crown with the marriage of
Ferdinand and Isabella.

During the wars of the Spanish Succession Majorca took the
side of the Austrian Archduke against the grandson of Louis
XIV, and so, while incurring the subsequent displeasure of the
first of the Spanish Bourbons, escaped the wrath of the all-
powerful British fleet which seized Menorca in 1708.

The campaigns of the great Duke of Marlborough are still remembered. All over Spain small children to-day sing a little
song about 'Mambrú'—which is the nearest approach to Marlborough that can reasonably be expected. It goes as follows:

Mambrú se fué a la guerra,	Marlborough is off to the war,
(Que dolor, que dolor, que pena!)	(What a pity, what a shame, how sad!)
Mambrú se fué a la guerra	Marlborough is off to the war
Y no sé cuando vendrá.	And I don't know when he'll be back.

Si vendrá por la Pascua?	Will he be back for Easter,
(Que dolor, que dolor, que pena!)	(What a pity, what a shame, how sad!)
Si vendrá por la Pascua	Will he be back for Easter
O por la Trinidad?	Or for the Trinity?
La Trinidad se pasa	Trinity Sunday is passing
(Que dolor, que dolor, que pena!)	(What a pity, what a shame, how sad!)
La Trinidad se pasa,	Trinity Sunday is over,
Mambrú no viene ya.	And still Marlborough's not back.
Por allí viene un paje	And now a page approaches
(Que dolor, que dolor, que pena!)	(What a pity, what a shame, how sad!)
Por allí viene un paje,	And now a page approaches,
Que noticias traerá?	And what is the news he brings?
Que Mambrú ya se ha muerto	That Marlborough's already dead,
(Que dolor, que dolor, que pena!)	(What a pity, what a shame, how sad!)
Que Mambrú ya se ha muerto,	That Marlborough's already dead,
Lo llevan a enterrar.	And now they are burying him!

As a result of 'Mambrú's' activities, Menorca remained in British hands continuous exceptly, for one short spell, from 1708 until the Treaty of Amiens in 1802, and the British left their unmistakable imprint upon the port and capital of Mahon.

Palma de Mallorca, to-day a thriving city of 150,000, with hotels to meet every pocket, is very noticeably cheaper than Barcelona in all respects. The smart hotel and residential quarter of Terreno, at the west end of the Bay, is a good 3 miles from the port and is dominated by the superbly placed Hotel Mediterraneo, from the terrace of which there is one of the loveliest views in the world, and below which it is possible to bathe from the rocks. Unfortunately the Mediterraneo has suffered too long from being Palma's No. 1 hotel, and as a result many people now prefer the Victoria or the Principe Alfonso—both also classed as 1a—while the new super-luxury Maricel, a few miles farther on, has effectively skimmed the financial cream off the American tourist milk.

Most people upon their first visit are surprised by the size of Majorca, which covers some 2,200 square miles and contains

mountain peaks rising to 5,000 feet. Being so mountainous has
meant that the railway communications are limited, and most
exploring of the island must be done by road. The hire of a
private car is ruinously expensive unless you arrange to share
the cost with one or two other passengers, but there is a fairly
comprehensive network of buses. The great majority of
summer visitors never stir beyond Palma and its immediate
surroundings, and unless you have a taste for exploring there is
really no need to do so. The shady Paseo contains every kind
of shop you may require, together with gay pavement cafés,
cinemas, and a diverting kaleidoscope of people to watch, while
the excellent Restaurant Lenes is also close at hand.

In Palma, too, there are pleasant open-air dances in the Yacht
Club on most of the purple velvet Majorca summer nights, and,
last but by no means least, the factory where they can watch the
justly famous green Majorcan glass being made, and where those
with a little money to spare can pick up bargains that, once they
get them home, will make their neighbours turn the same colour
as the glass, with envy! There are bull-fights on most Sundays
and on national or religious holidays, and folk-music and dancing,
particularly during the Fiesta Mayor around August 3rd. Most
important of all, there are no fewer than three sand bathing-
beaches that can be reached by tram.

For the serious sight-seer, too, there is much of interest in the
Lonja Museum, formerly the Exchange, which itself is a flawless
example of fifteenth-century Gothic. However, the two land-
marks that first strike you, as your ship draws in towards the
exquisite Bay of Palma, are the round fourteenth-century turrets
of Bellver Castle at the western end and the huge golden sand-
stone Gothic cathedral at the opposite end. Later and closer
acquaintance confirms that first unforgettable impression.

The cathedral was begun towards the end of the fourteenth
century, and although there is some matchless old brocade in
the Royal Chapel (where two of Majorca's four kings are buried),
its austere interior is in disappointing contrast to the rich,
warm glow of its golden outer walls. However, its sheer size is
impressive—the central nave being 245 feet long by 150 wide.

o

The Kings' residential palace was the Castillo de la Almudaina, almost next door to the Yacht Club, but their fortress home was the Castle of Bellver, built early in the fourteenth century and set among pine-forests high above the sea. Being of an almost white stone, it stands out against the blue sky with the appeal of all the stories you have ever heard that begin with the magic words, 'Once upon a time . . .'

However, even though there are all the necessary ingredients ready to hand in Palma itself for the perfect Mediterranean holiday, it tends to become a little too much like Juan-les-Pins during the summer, at least for those who do not share the enthusiasm for their fellow-men that was responsible for the admission to heaven of Abu ben Adam (may his tribe increase).

To the west of Palma a pleasant road leads through almond and olive-groves for 12 miles to the little town of Andraitx, and then on another two to its port. The name 'Andraitx' may shake you a bit, but the Majorquin patois resembles Catalan and specializes in producing hideous names for beautiful places.

I spent a sailing and fishing holiday in Puerto de Andraitx in August 1946, and although the little hotel at which I stayed is now closed, I can enthusiastically recommend the Hotel Camp de Mar 5 miles away where, for 100 pts a day, you can live like a pre-Income Tax Lord, and bathe from a sandy beach bordered by pine-woods. Almost next door is the tiny Cala Fornels, which charges 75 pts a day.

Puerto de Andraitx is at the head of a 'cala', and if you are interested in either the Balearic Islands or the Costa Brava you had better get used to the word as soon as possible, as you will meet it very often. Calas are long, fjord-like rifts in the coastal rock, into which the sea has thrust its inky-blue fingers. A cala makes an ideal bathing place because it is waveless and windless. As the surrounding rock is usually either red or white you can see to a great depth in the water, and experts say that the under-water fish-shooting (with a harpoon-gun, frog's feet, and a breathing tube) is better in Majorca and the Costa Brava than anywhere except in the West Indies.

Do not be alarmed if you see an occasional squid which,

magnified by several feet of water, may assume the proportions of a small octopus. Although repulsive, they are too small to do anything worse than squirt a little ink in your eye, and if you capture one and hand it over to your cook she will make a popular dish of him, known as 'calamares en su tinta' or, if you don't like the colour of ink on your plate, then 'calamares salteados', with tomato and garlic sauce.

Andraitx is on the western tip of the island and is backed by the 3,300-foot Mount Galatzo, so that you must return to Palma before exploring the steep, cliff-like, north-western side of the island to Soller. There are two roads, and the secondary one is my choice as providing the most beautiful sea and mountain scenery I have seen anywhere, outside Greece and the Dalmatian coast.

I do not like Puerto de Soller, as it makes me feel uncomtably shut in to have a 1,000-foot cliff at my back, but there are many people who swear by the little Hotel Marisol at 75 pts a day.

Eleven miles from Palma, on the main road to Soller, is the village of Valldemosa with its much-restored fifteenth-century Carthusian monastery, which attracts visitors who still find romance in the relations between the be-trousered George Sand and the effeminate, dying Chopin. The cells they occupied during their unhappy stay there in 1838 are unchanged, together with the great composer's piano, clothes, and other personal belongings. One wonders why the good monks made no attempt to return these valuable possessions!

Eight miles away there is further evidence that nineteenth-century Austrian Archdukes must have made Lewis Carroll's March Hare seem, by comparison, the very essence of sober sanity. The evidence is supplied by the Gothic Cocktail built as a residence by the Archduke Luis Salvador and named, with true Hapsburg originality, Miramar! The setting is lovely, but the building is almost a justification for Austria having elected to become a Republic.

Most visitors to Majorca find time to cross the island at its narrowest point, the 40 miles from Palma to Alcudia. This leads through Inca and passes many of the typical Balearic windmills, some of the sails of which are made of cloth, like those of a ship, not of wooden blades. Inca has a fine thirteenth-century church but is still more famous for its beautifully painted and glazed pottery and for its specially expert performances of the local folk-dances 'L'Estandart' and 'Els Cavallets'. People come from all over the island for Inca's fiestas on January 20th, Corpus Christi, and August 2nd. Do not fail to visit the picturesque wine cellars of Inca and try the local vintage.

An excursion that I once made on the back of a motor-cycle was the 21 miles from Inca to the Sanctuary of the Virgin of Lluch upon the slopes of the island's highest mountain of Puig Mayor. The image was discovered in 1208, but belongs to the sixth century and has been the object of pilgrimages for the last 700 years.

Puerto de Pollensa had quite a vogue with foreigners before the Civil War and is still well supplied with hotels, the Maricel being well worth the 100 pts a day that it charges for full pension. If you happen to be rich, then continue your journey for another few miles to the northernmost point of the island at Cape Formentor. There, in the almost closed circular Bay of Alcudia, facing south from among pine trees, is the almost legendary Hotel Formentor.

It is a place I visit only when I am invited by a rich friend, and as I seem to be running a bit low in rich friends lately I have not been there since 1950. On that occasion only two yachts were there, but, as it was late in the season, I did not feel that this deplorable absence of privately owned shipping quite justified me in asking for my rich friend's money back.

It was built some twenty years ago regardless of expense, but the Civil War and World War II accounted for nine of them, and it fell into bad disrepair from which it is only now emerging. The cooking and the wine-cellar are as good as anywhere in Europe, and the bathing and climate everything that even a poster designer could invent, but its distance from Palma and its reputation for being expensive seem to make it a dubious financial propostion in these dreary days of currency controls.

Naturally, it is subject to the Spanish Tourist Bureau's rule of a top price of 180 pts a day—but the 'extras' are still enough to shake even the richest of my rich friends!

The other main excursion from Palma is the longest, since it is nearly 60 miles by road to Cala Ratjada, on the easternmost point of the island, but despite its menacing name (Stinging Ray Creek), it provides perhaps the best bathing in Majorca. The road to Cala Ratjada passes through the town of Manacor, famous for its cultured pearls, 32 miles east of Palma, and if you turn off there it is only a quarter of an hour's run to the really extraordinary Cuevas del Drach. I have never been a great enthusiast for the caves and grottos that so delighted the late Victorians, but I gladly stifled my claustrophobia for a full hour to explore these, which far excel anything of the kind that I have seen anywhere else.

As already mentioned, the Ancient World believed this to be one of the only five certain entrances to the Underworld, and without the excellent concealed electric lighting with which the caves are now lit I should be quite ready to believe it myself. Model cities, huge organs, petrified forests, Gothic cathedrals succeed one another as one walks, literally miles, through this incredible mad architect's nightmare. Here and there the roots of a living tree hang down from the ceiling like fossilized snakes, but the crowning oddity is the huge underground lake, in which the fish are born dead white and without eyes, owing to countless generations having lived in darkness. Upon this lake a first-class orchestra gives concerts of classical music every Saturday and Wednesday, the acoustic properties of the place apparently being perfect. I did not discover whether the blind fish preferred Verdi or Wagner!

The least-known part of Majorca is the south and if you want to try the relatively simple life I suggest that you pay a visit to Santañy, with its sixteenth-century walls, and then go on to the sleepy little town of Felanitx, dominated by Santueri Castle and set amid hills dotted with ruined hermitages.

I have only been to Menorca once in my life, and it struck me as by far the least attractive of the three main islands of the group. Port Mahon is the capital, and it possesses only third-class hotels, the Bustamente and the Sevilla. If you like prehistoric dolmens, cromlechs, and rather scrappy Roman remains this is the place for you—but not for me !

Ibiza, on the other hand, is very much to my taste. Perhaps it is just that I really prefer my islands rather smaller than Majorca: certainly I love the human race more when there is no danger of its trampling on my feet. You will find plenty of other visitors there if you go to Ibiza in summer, but you will not find yourself being hemmed in by ping-pong-playing hearties, as now, alas, occasionally happens in Majorca and the Costa Brava.

Ibiza is a gentler island, despite tree-clad hills 1,000 to 1,500 feet high, and is less dramatically, self-consciously beautiful than her big sister, and a great deal more restful. There are really only three towns: the capital Ibiza in the south-east, San Antonio Abad 10 miles away on the west coast, and San Juan Bautista 14 miles to the north, though there is also the village of Santa Eulalia del Rio a few miles up the coast from Port Ibiza.

There are ships going direct to Ibiza from Barcelona and Valencia as well as from Palma de Mallorca, but there is no air service yet, though I am told that one may be opened before long.

Ibiza itself has the pleasant little Hotel Restaurant Ibiza, charging 75 pts a day, and there are two sand bathing-beaches to choose from. Although slightly farther, the one called D'En Bosa is the better of the two, and pines come down to its fringes, as at Formentor in Majorca.

Most people who travel a great deal form a mental picture in advance of the places they are going to see. Usually the reality is less satisfying than the picture, but occasionally it turns out to be just right. My own mental picture of a Mediterranean island was perfectly fulfilled in only two places: one was in the Greek Peloponnese, and the other was when I first saw Ibiza.

On that occasion I bought a small sail-boat for £15 and pottered right round the island, fishing, bathing, and stopping

19 The Costa Brava (Aigua Blava)

20 The Costa Brava (between Tossa and S'Agaro)

the night at any village that presented itself towards the end of the day. I caught a great many fish during four weeks, achieved a mahogany tan, and spent—with some difficulty—£12 during the period. The boat I sold again for exactly what I had paid for it.

Each day would dawn in absolute calm, and I would have to row out to my fishing-place. From around 8 a.m. until noon the fish would bite continuously, mostly small red mullet, with an occasional 3-lb. hake to liven up the proceedings. By noon I would have twenty or thirty fish flapping round my bare feet and, as though by the stop-watch, precisely at 12 the fish would stop biting and the first puffs of the breeze would take the edge off the heat. The wind would freshen steadily until between 5 and 6 p.m. I would usually be making a good 8 knots and then it would gradually die away, with a few last violent puffs, and I would run into harbour slowly, trying to see whether I could just make it before the fall of the dead calm of every summer evening.

I know that I have never been so physically fit as I was at the end of my four weeks' pottering round Ibiza, and I am almost sure that never before, or since, have I been so nearly perfectly happy. Certainly, I have never met so many friendly, honest, and helpful people in so short a period of time.

The 'fiesta mayor' of Ibiza is from August 5th until the 9th, and the costumes and local dances are as beautiful as any. I particularly recommend 'La Curta' and 'La Llarga', in which the girls are grouped in threes and fours, and the youths circle round them, leaping as high as they can into the air to attract the girls away from the group, one by one, for the final dance together. Although its origins are probably Phœnician and are certainly lost in antiquity, it always reminds me irresistibly of the mating dance of a cock and a hen pigeon.

The thirteenth-century cathedral was restored in the six-teenth century, but its great beauty lies in its position on the edge of the steep cliff, towering above the more modern port, upon which the old walled city of 10,000 inhabitants is built.

San Antonio Abad, 10 miles away, is the most popular

summer resort on the island, and is at the head of a good natural port dotted with the enchanting small islands known as the Cunilleras. It has the first-class Pension Parador Playa, which charges 55 pts a day for any one of its seven rooms, and the larger second-class Hotels Portmany and Ses Savines, charging 75 pts a day.

Santa Eulalia del Rio, just north of Ibiza, also has the small first-class Pension Marimonte, and in all the sea-side villages you will find small, simple, but spotlessly clean little fondas, or inns.

In all that I have said of the Balearic Islands I have tried only to tell you what, and what not, to expect, and so have said little or nothing of the very special quality possessed by both Majorca and Ibiza, which is a compound of ancient civilizations, matchless climate, red rock, blue sea, vines, pines, and age-old songs and dances. The Mediterranean belonged to the pagan gods, but the pale Nazarene drove them into hiding. Still, being a merciful God, He has let them live on unmolested in a few out-of-the-way islands, and there you may still hear the Pipes of Pan being played by a shepherd, and perhaps even catch a glimpse of fleet-footed Diana the Huntress among the writhing shapes of the 1,000-year-old olive trees. If you do not care for these things—well, Palma is still fun from any point of view!

THE COSTA BRAVA

The British 'discovered' the Costa Brava in 1951 and, since it is the nearest stretch of Mediterranean coast apart from the now fabulously expensive French Riviera, they have adopted it for their very own.

The Costa Brava begins 40 miles north of Barcelona at Blanes, and stretches from there to the French frontier. Wild and rocky from the sea, inland it is a jumble of small hills thickly covered with umbrella pine trees. It has remained unspoiled so long largely because of the fact that the railway leaves the coast at Blanes to run through Gerona and Figueras to the frontier at Port-Bou. Additionally, the roads are so bad that motorists rarely turned off to explore these dusty avenues of cork or eucalyptus trees, and kept straight on to Barcelona or Perpignan.

By car or railway it is not necessary to touch the expensive city of Barcelona in order to reach the Costa Brava but, since B.E.A. and Air France run home-paid return flights to the Catalan capital, quite a few Britons arrive that way. The train entering Spain at Port-Bou (where the howling chaos of former days is now considerably reduced), stops at Figueras, which is only a few miles to the Costa Brava resorts of Cadaques (Salvador Dali's village), Rosas and Puerto de la Selva. The next big station is Gerona, and from there it is easy to reach Palamos, Llafranc, Aigua Blava, Tamariu, and Calella. The next stop is Caldas de Malavella for those bound for S'Agaro, Tossa, and San Feliu de Guixols, while Blanes is the station for Santa Cristina.

All these places are little more than fishing villages—the smallest, such as Santa Cristina and Aigua Blava, being of not more than 100 inhabitants, and the largest, such as Palamos and San Feliu de Guixols, of not more than 6,000.

It is difficult to define the tremendous charm of the Costa Brava, which is a thing of the senses rather than of words. There are no bays or views to equal those of Mallorca; few ancient castles, monasteries, or other historic attractions; just a string of whitewashed fishing villages facing the brilliant blue of the sea, with small, sandy bathing-beaches, modest, clean inns, and little hotels. There is the security of brilliant sun, bathing in water so clear that you can see the fish 30 feet down during the day, and soft nights with the croaking of bull-frogs as a background to the intricate-stepping dance of the 'sardana' and its pensively-gay, reedy music. It is a place of bountiful semi-dry white wines and superb lobsters, prawns, and the rare and subtle-flavoured 'dorada'; and of modern dancing under the palms and the sky in the luxurious Hostal de la Gavina in S'Agaro.

The setting is perfect—and only man is vile. In other words, it is up to you!

The show place of the Costa Brava is unquestionably S'Agaro, and S'Agaro is what it is because of the vision and courage of Don José Ensesa. Few millionaires have visions, except perhaps of further millions, and still fewer employ their millions in turning their visions into reality. Don José had a vision of the kind of village he wanted, the kind of people he wished to live there, and the kind of houses in which they should live. He was able to build most of it himself and, being the ground landlord, he could refuse people whom he considered undesirable, and sell to the desirables only if they were prepared first to submit their architect's plans to him. In order to prevent the gradual infiltration of undesirables, he also insisted that if, through death or financial difficulties, one of his tenants wished to sell his house, then he himself always had the first offer at a previously agreed price.

I am sure that such methods would be considered feudal by our town-planners, and so, of course, they are! However, I do not accept the word 'feudal' as being the name of something necessarily bad. It was no doubt a bad system, because it permitted a bad feudal lord to do great harm and, history being what it is, we have naturally heard all about the bad ones and nothing about the good (of whom there were many) who presided over their vassals with patriarchal care, intelligence, and sympathy.

Don José does just that, and though the reformers would no doubt prefer to see long lines of slate-roofed, semi-detached suburban dwellings, I, for one, am glad that S'Agaro is a model village of attractive whitewashed buildings, bright with purple bougainvillæa and scarlet geraniums.

S'Agaro is the heart of the Costa Brava, which is at its loveliest 14 unbelievably twisting road miles south to Tossa, or 19 bumpy miles north to the cluster of villages reached through Palafrugell—Llafranc, Aigua Blava, Calella, and Tamariu.

Tossa, with its twelfth-century castle walls, has two good hotels, the Casa Blanca and the Ancora, charging 100 pts a day. The Hostal de la Gavina at S'Agaro is the Costa's only luxury establishment, though its annexe, the Playa, is pleasant enough. For the rest, the entire 50-mile stretch from Blanes to the

21 A typical Spanish side street in Palma de Mallorca

frontier is thickly sown with pleasant little 'bistros', new examples of which are being opened almost every week, where you can live well if simply, and eat really excellent food.

Being near to the Pyrenees, the Costa Brava is rarely too hot; it is in fact the most temperate stretch of the Mediterranean that I know, and its season is therefore short. The Spaniards stick strictly to their calendar, and are to be found there only in July and August, but June and September are, in my opinion, even lovelier, and certainly less crowded. For the other eight months of the year all but the Hostal de la Gavina, or the principal hotels in each of the larger towns—such as the Mediterraneo in Blanes, the Trias in Palamos, the Muria in San Feliu de Guixols, or the Ancora in Tossa—are closed.

I glimpsed the Costa Brava as far back as 1931 and promptly made a firm resolve to return, but it was not until 1945 that I really got to know it. Now it is so well known that its special, brilliant beauty needs no further description.

XVIII

THE HEARTY BASQUES

Andorra—Lerida—Panticosa—Pamplona—San Sebastian—Bilbao.

To these they add a name so long and strong
That even Hearty Basques pronounce it wrong.
(with apologies to Hilaire Belloc)

PERHAPS they pronounce it wrong, but they can reel off names like Ormaiztequi, Zumalacarregui, Iruretogoyena, and Uriaguereca without turning a hair, which is more than Mr. Belloc's 'pious people of Pretoria' could have done. And with them there is no period of silence,

'. . . when no more is heard
But sounds of strong men, struggling with a word.'

To reach the Basque country from the Costa Brava or Barcelona it is best first to get to the most attractive Catalan Pyrenees frontier town of Puigcerda (this Puig that keeps on cropping up is merely the Catalan for peak, and is pronounced Pooch, for reasons unknown to lesser breeds). The main road from Barcelona intersects with the rather bad, but picturesque, one from Figueras at Ripoll, where there is an eleventh- to sixteenth-century Benedictine monastery, of which the loveliest part is the cloisters containing 440 columns of jasper and granite of Byzantine workmanship. Ripoll is already 1,200 feet above sea-level, though by the road from Barcelona you are barely aware of climbing until you reach the attractive old town of Vich. The vast cathedral there dates from 1040, but the present structure is eighteenth-century baroque, and is chiefly notable for the gold-and-black mural paintings by José Maria Sert, who completed them just before his death in 1946.

Sert, whose nephew Paco was one of my first friends when I arrived in Spain, is a very much discussed painter who studied in Paris at the same time as his fellow Catalan Picasso, and who is known to Americans primarily for his murals in the dining-room of the Waldorf Astoria Hotel in New York. Personally, I find the room he decorated in Barcelona's Ayuntamiento, or Town Hall, in which he tells the story of the Catalan invasion of Constantinople and their King's death by treason, to be his best work. Sert, latterly, seemed to lay too great a stress upon anatomy and the play of muscles, and in Vich Cathedral the eye loses sight of the theme in the endless contortions of heroically striving masculinity! He always chose to use the largest possible surfaces, employing generally nothing but black, gold, and ochre for his colours, and it was only when I saw a quite small painting in his nephew's flat (of Don Quixote engaged in deliciously didactic argument with some obviously Catalan types) that I realized how competent he was with more ordinary media and colours.

On the way from the Costa Brava to Ripoll, via Figueras and Olot, you will pass the really beautiful castle of Besalu, which should console you for the very bad surface of the last 20 miles or so.

From Ripoll both the road and the electric railway which links Barcelona with Toulouse climb steeply through Ribas (where a branch line leads to Nuria, a winter-sports resort at 6,500 feet above sea-level) and over the 6,000-foot Tosas Pass to La Molina, which is undoubtedly Spain's best winter-sports resort, with good hotels, ski-lifts, &c. From the head of Tosas Pass the road winds down into the wide and beautiful valley of Cerdaña to the quaint little frontier city of Puigcerda, perched on a low hill. Just across the valley lie the French frontier towns of Bourg-Madame and Le Tour de Carol, and I am continually surprised that summer tourists to and from Barcelona or the Costa Brava, travelling by either train or road, so rarely use this alternative route, which is not only infinitely more attractive but also very much cooler than the dull, hot road from Perpignan via Le Perthus and La Junquera.

Puigcerda, 105 miles from Barcelona and standing at roughly 3,750 feet, has been a place of escape from the city heat for generations of 'barceloneses'. It has two luxury hotels: the

Lago in the town itself, where the noise of the bullfrogs in the lake will lull you to sleep, and the new Golf Hotel, a couple of miles along the valley. The golf-course is one of the most attractive in the country and possesses real grass 'greens'— a rarity in Spain, where sand greens are almost universal owing to lack of rain.

The route to the Basques lies along a secondary but most attractive road for the 33 miles to Seo de Urgel on the River Segre, one of the most ancient cities in Spain. Its craggy eleventh-century fortress cathedral somehow looks its age, battered equally by Pyrenean storms and medieval raiders, but it has the exceptional dignity of its Bishop being co-ruler, with the President of the French Republic, of the small semi-independent Basque state of Andorra. It is 13 miles to the Andorran capital, and after that the road rises to nearly 8,000 feet, to become the highest in Europe, before entering France. High though this is, there are peaks on every side soaring up to over 10,000 feet.

Andorra's independence dates from the ninth century, and it is administered by a patriarchal Council of Elders who meet in the Casa de lo Valt and discuss weighty matters to do with thirteenth-century grazing rights in a language which is a baffling mixture of Catalan and Basque. All this seems very idyllic, but it is generally admitted that Andorra's only staple industry is smuggling. In the good old days it was silk, spirits, and tobacco, then, under the Republic and during the Civil War, arms and ammunition. During World War II there was a brisk trade in escaping Allied airmen seeking internment and repatriation through neutral Spain, and now it is motor-car spare parts and tobacco again.

This applies not only to Andorra but to all the country from here to the Atlantic coast, for the obvious reason that the Franco-Spanish frontier cuts across the ethnic unity of the two million or so Basques who had made the Pyrenees their home long before the gentlemen in Paris and Madrid had decided to draw certain arbitrary lines upon the map. Knowing every goat-track and patch of cover in their immediate neighbourhood, the Basques can always find a way to fool the guards if they wish to visit their cousins in the next valley (which often happens to be in France), and when paying the call it is only practical to take something along with them that can be sold profitably, and to bring back something else that is in short supply on their side!

Climbing to the head of any of the Pyrenees passes brings home the fact that four-fifths of the mountain range is in Spain and only one-fifth in France. From most of the Pyrenees frontier posts, if you look towards France the land drops away quickly to a distant glimpse of fields under cultivation, while, turning towards Spain, you look into range after range of mountains, to a depth of 30 or 40 miles.

There were complaints during the summers of 1949 and 1950 that the Spanish authorities at Seo de Urgel were frequently closing the Andorran frontier without previous notice. This was true, and was due to a considerable infiltration of Civil War voluntary exiles from Toulouse entering Spain in the guise of French hikers—with French passports. These men were next heard of when a bomb would explode in a Barcelona church or Underground station, wounding or killing a number of people who certainly had nothing to do with Franco having won the Civil War. The improvement in Franco-Spanish relations since U.N.O. withdrew its ban upon the exchange of Ambassadors has stopped this flow of explosive hikers, and the frontier is now open at the advertised times.

Many people like Andorra, and the fact that I myself do not is due to my claustrophobic dislike of having my mountains right on top of me. In most places in Andorra, even in June, the sun always appears to emerge from behind one set of peaks at about 11 a.m. and to set behind another at about 3.30 p.m. This I find depressing.

From Seo de Urgel the road runs directly away from the frontier along the River Segre for 85 miles, through Pons, Artesa de Segre, and Balaguer to Lerida, on the main road between Barcelona and Madrid.

Lerida is a large and prosperous city with the 1b Hotel

Palacio, a fine thirteenth-century cathedral, and a dominating castle which played an important rôle in the lives of two conquerors as far removed from one another in time, if not in reputation, as Julius Cæsar and Napoleon Bonaparte.

If you are just on your way through Lerida you will find that the Restaurant Zazurca or the Taberna Vasca will feed you both well and inexpensively.

But to return to our Basques, we must take the secondary road through Binefar, Monzon, and Barbastro (73 miles) to Huesca.

This little town of 20,000 inhabitants was the capital of the short-lived Iberian Republic established by the renegade Roman general Sertorius, and was the scene of the beheading of no fewer than four Moorish kings before its liberation in 1090. It contains a startlingly large number of twelfth- and thirteenth-century churches, and one, San Pedro el Viejo, dating from Visigothic times and maintained as a place of Christian worship even under the Moors.

Our road climbs 33 miles to a point where there is a choice between two passes into France. By carrying straight on to Biescas there are two more interesting alternatives. The first is the side road east to the National Park and game preserve of Ordesa, where the Spanish Tourist Department recently completed another of their inns. In this huge area, bounded by the 11,000-foot Mount Aneto—the highest peak of the entire Pyrenees—there are eagle, brown bear, wild boar, red and fallow deer, and a score of other types of lesser game. Ten miles beyond Biescas there is another turning to the right leading to Panticosa 6 miles away.

Panticosa is pure Shangri-la, with no less than four first-class hotels. The reason for this sudden outburst of comfort at a height of 6,000 feet is the outpouring of some of the best medicinal waters for anæmia to be found anywhere in Europe. From Panticosa you look eastwards into the very heart of the Pyrenees range, with its peaks piling up against the clear summer sky, many of them still wearing their crowns of snow.

22 The semi-independent Republic of Andorra's Parliament House

Back on the main road, it is only a short run to the 6,000-foot Portalet Pass into France.

However, our road turns left 33 miles from Huesca and leads to Jaca, 9 miles away. North, both road and railway lead over the 5,300-foot Somport Pass to France. There is a good hotel— the Cadanchu—20 miles up this road at a height of 5,600 feet. Jaca, with its great fortress built by Philip II and its weather-worn eleventh-century cathedral, is of real interest, and its Romeria de la Victoria in May, when its liberation from the Moors is celebrated, includes a religious play, 'El Conde de Aznar', performed by the inhabitants on this date for many centuries.

But the Basques, whom we left far to the east in Andorra, lie to the north-west, and our next stage is 63 miles to Pamplona, capital of the ancient Kingdom of Navarre.

The Moors succeeded in capturing and holding the city from A.D. 738 until 750, but the tough Navarese, who had taken refuge in the Pyrenees, then struck back and liberated it. However, Moorish pressure soon became intolerable, and the Christians called upon the mighty Emperor Charlemagne for help. This he sent, but only in order to serve his own aims, and he caused such devastation during his attempts to capture Saragossa that the Navarese turned upon him in the famous Battle of Roncesvalles in 778, where the great knight Roland died in covering the French retreat against the attacks of Oliver ('a Roland for his Oliver'). In 905 Navarre became an independent kingdom and remained so until the ageing King Ferdinand finally conquered King Jean d'Albret in 1512 and annexed it. It was only in 1841 that it ceased to be at least nominally a kingdom and became officially a province of Spain.

Pamplona's eleventh-century cathedral was rebuilt during the fifteenth and sixteenth centuries in the purest Gothic style, and its outstanding treasures are the hundred choir-stalls, beautifully carved in English oak during the reign of the Emperor Charles V by Anchietta. There is also a much-venerated fragment of Christ's robe at the time of the Crucifixion (reputedly brought to Pamplona from the Holy Land

P

by St. Luis), and the eighth-century image known as the Virgen del Sagrario.

Next door to the cathedral is the so-called Beautiful Room (Sala Preciosa) where Navarre's Parliament held its sessions in medieval times. There are also many attractive mansions dotted around the city, built by nobles in the days when this was the Court of the Kings of Navarre.

Many visitors like to drive the 50 miles up to the 3,450-foot Pass of Roncesvalles, where there is a fine old monastery containing relics of the great eighth-century battle. It is one of the eight main passes through the Pyrenees, and winds its way to the most attractive little French frontier town of St. Jean Pied-de-Port.

But Pamplona's greatest claim to modern fame is its world-famous fiesta of St. Fermin, which lasts from July 6th until the 12th. In fact, this differs from other fiestas in only one particular, though admittedly an important one. This is that the bulls to be killed in the daily bull-fights are not taken in the usual closed stall to the bull-ring, but are turned loose through the main streets of the city and coursed towards the Plaza de Toros by fifty or a hundred youths, who run ahead of them and, when overtaken, have an opportunity to display their skill and courage before their dutifully impressed girl-friends watching from the balconies.

This mad flight before the horns of the angry black bulls carries a real and contagious excitement which the professional performers of the afternoon can rarely induce, and it attracts the hearty Basques in their thousands from their neighbouring provinces of Alava, Vizcaya, and Guipuzcoa, just north and north-west of Pamplona. It is rare that anyone gets killed, though there are usually a dozen or so more or less seriously hurt.

The main road from Pamplona to San Sebastian, 67 miles away, lies through Tolosa, but during the last days of October 1952 I had offered to accompany an American journalist and writer who wanted to witness various forms of Basque sports, beginning with the pigeon-netting in Echalar. Accordingly, we drove 30 miles north to Mugaire and, instead of continuing through Elizondo to the frontier, turned left to Irun—that not very interesting town that is so many visitors' first glimpse of Spain as they cross the River Bidasoa, by the International Bridge, from Hendaye on the opposite bank in France.

There are few things that I dislike more than getting up at 6 a.m. on a chilly autumn morning, but such is transatlantic enthusiasm that before it was fully light I found myself not only driving inland for the 16 miles or so to the little village of Echalar, but also doing my best to answer a number of questions about the Basques. The first was, 'What are the principal Basque sports, and why are they special to this part of Spain?'

I explained that they were an entirely separate race from the Spaniards, with a totally separate language and appearance, being on the short side, barrel-chested, bullet-headed, and with the short, thick, slightly bow legs of the mountaineer. Probably because of the climate, they were much bigger eaters and drinkers than the Spanish and, also probably because of the climate, they, like the British, worshipped all forms of violent exercise. As a result we might witness log-chopping, stone-piercing, beer-drinking, and steak-eating competitions, upon which heavy betting takes place, not to mention the national Basque game of 'jai-alai' (the happy festival), more generally known as 'pelota', which is the fastest and most exhausting ball game in the world. This has, with good reason, become so popular that 'frontones', or public courts, have sprung up all over the country, and it is even catching on in Cuba and Mexico, though the best players are still nearly always Basques. This same extreme heartiness was the motive for the pigeon-netting that we were now on our way to see, as there are obviously numerous other, and easier, methods of killing pigeons if the obtaining of pigeons was really their principal object. Being Basques, however, they had thought out a uniquely complicated method which involved dozens of people swarming up and down mountains at an hour when they ought to be in bed.

This slightly undergraduate attitude towards life, combined

with their really remarkable capacity for 'carrying' hard liquor, and the fact that they are superb rough-sea sailors, so endears them to the average Anglo-Saxon that he can almost forgive them for being devout Catholics. We like to feel that our foreigners are simpler than we are, and we are always a little uneasy about supposed Latin subtlety; but the Basque, well, he was a sportsman and knew how to hold his liquor—definitely a 'pukka sahib', as Continentals go!

Since the scene of operations was right on the frontier, we had come provided with special permits. We soon climbed by a tricky winding road to the head of the 1,500-foot pass, where there is a simple restaurant and a few mountain huts connected with the sport, and there we left the car.

Climbing on foot a further couple of hundred yards, we gazed down at the French village of Sare and, as the light strengthened, away to the sea at Biarritz.

Between mid-October and mid-November every year tens of thousands of wild pigeons leave their summer breeding-grounds, mostly around the Baltic, and begin their great migration to northern Africa. Their direct line takes them across France to the north-east corner of Spain. They avoid traversing long distances over the sea—the narrow Baltic and the Straits of Gibraltar do not take them out of sight of land—and they now find themselves confronted by the huge mountain wall of the Pyrenees, through which Echalar is the lowest pass. Although thousands cross by other routes, the majority make for the narrow break where we were standing, which had been rendered even narrower by the planting of tall trees on either side of a grassy gap, across which were stretched nets 80 feet high. These drop to the ground as soon as a flock or covey strikes it, imprisoning the pigeons in its ample, falling folds.

Ingenious though this is, the birds would rarely fly into the nets if they were not intentionally panicked into doing so. Far down the narrowing opening to the pass men were stationed in masked coverts and, as a flight of two or three dozen birds drew level, they blew bugles, beat drums, and made as much din as possible in order to scare them in the desired direction.

If the birds were flying too high to be caught by the nets, these men flung flat white wooden disks, looking like badly made ping-pong bats, curving through the air above them. Mistaking these for diving hawks, the pigeons swerved away and downwards while continuing upon their same line of flight.

There is a kind of breathless excitement in waiting for the next flock to appear against the northern sky, and it is unquestionably sporting, in that quite half the birds escape. Anyway, I am extremely fond of a lunch of pigeon stewed in a savoury sauce, particularly when I have been made to get up at 6 a.m. and have missed my breakfast, and I was glad personally to reduce the morning's bag of 368 birds by three.

From the frontier at Irun to San Sebastian is only 12 miles, and San Sebastian in July, August, and September is Madrid-on-Sea, even the Government moving there for at least two months, while Franco goes giant tunny-fishing off the coasts of his native Galicia, farther west.

Spain has few really first-class sea-side resorts. There are Palma de Mallorca and Malaga on the Mediterranean, and San Sebastian, Santander, and, perhaps, La Coruña on the Atlantic, but it is only in San Sebastian and Palma that you will find the authentic, fully organized holiday town. Until twenty years ago San Sebastian was competing not wholly unsuccessfully with Biarritz 30 miles away on the opposite side of the frontier, but one of the many reforms introduced by the Republic was the abolition of roulette, which immediately put the Spanish resort at a fatal disadvantage. Then the Civil and World Wars, followed by political disagreements and currency restrictions, put Spain more or less out of tourist bounds, and it only came back into its old stride in the summer of 1951. However, it is now the simplest and most obvious place for a cool summer holiday, being geographically the nearest point to London and Paris where the favourable Spanish rate of exchange can be enjoyed, and catering for all tastes except perhaps those of the real sun-bathing addict.

There are two very famous bathing-beaches, and on one of them (since they are urban beaches) the regulations against skimpy costumes are rigidly enforced. On the other, known as the Diplomatic Beach, you can wear, or not wear, more or less what you like. Apparently the fact that members of the Embassies are apt to disport themselves here is the reason for this distinction. Morals are morals in Spain, but the complications likely to arise from the arrest of a foreign Ambassador for indecent exposure will not bear contemplation even there!

There are forty-two listed hotels in San Sebastian, ranging from the three luxury ones—the Continental Palace, the Londres, and the Maria Cristina charging the full permitted 180 pts plus 12% per day (and with a special increase during the Semana Grande beginning on August 15th), to the modest 55 pts of a first-class pension. However, for the forty-two recognized by the Spanish Tourist Bureau, there must be at least 142 that are not, so any attempt at selection by me would be invidious.

The delights of San Sebastian are the obvious ones expected from a first-class sea-side resort. Apart from bathing, there are sailing regattas, golf, tennis, dances, pigeon-shooting (disapproved of by the English as unsporting, as indeed it is), three good theatres and five cinemas, horse-racing, countless 'frontones' for watching pelota, boxing matches, concerts, art exhibitions, and, of course, bull-fighting upon every possible excuse presented by the religious or secular calendar.

San Sebastian, though its origins are ancient, is a relatively modern town, having been almost completely destroyed by the British General Graham while expelling the Napoleonic garrison. Rebuilt in 1816, it was again badly knocked about during the Carlist Wars, and it was really only the liking for the place displayed by the Queen Regent, mother of Alfonso XIII, at the turn of the present century, that produced the San Sebastian of to-day. There are a few good pictures in the Museo de Pintura, but San Sebastian is not the place for sight-seeing and, rightly, does not attempt to compete with the historic cities of Castile or Andalusia from that point of view.

Really, apart from bathing, my principal occupation in San Sebastian always seems to be eating, in which the Basques are also profoundly interested and, being interested, possess real talent.

There are not only an infinite variety of restaurants but even a number of eating-clubs (women are barred, since their presence would inhibit the free and light-hearted expulsion of gases engendered by extensive eating), where members have the run of the kitchen to prepare their pet dishes for themselves and their male friends.

The list of Basque gastronomic specialities is too long to recount here but, as mentioned elsewhere, 'angulas a la bilbaina' is one of the world's really great dishes. For a cheap but tasty and filling meal you can hardly improve on 'bacalao a la vizcaina', and if you like hot curries or highly spiced or flavoured foods you will certainly like 'callos'. These are small squares of tripe cooked in an earthenware dish with tomato, garlic, and red pepper. At their strongest, they will reduce fire-eating Anglo-Indian ex-colonels literally to tears! I love callos, but sadly abandoned them when it became apparent that they caused me to fire, simultaneously, upon all four duodenal ulcers. However, if you are young, healthy, and heavily insured, you can do no better!

The Basques, too, seem to be the only people in Spain who understand cheese. One of my earliest memories is of the Stilton cheese (occasionally varied with a Blue Cheshire or a Wensleydale) which used to arrive for my father at Christmas and which he used happily to corrupt with a glass of his best port before putting it to bed every night under a napkin soaked in fresh milk. I also remember the hunted look that came into his eye when, around March, he perceived my mother sniffing in a marked manner, and the final great tragedy when, early in May, she announced that either she or the cheese must leave the house, never to return, within the next twenty-four hours.

Since those remote days, just before the outbreak of World War I, I have rarely encountered a cheese that I felt capable of coming between man and wife and, in the nineteen-fifties, nowhere except in the Basque country.

From a list as long as my arm, I can personally recommend the Restaurants Casa Eusebio, La Nicolasa, and Anabitarte; and, in the matter of setting as well as food, the Monte Igueldo, which is perched on the top of a hill that gives you an appetizing vision of the town, harbour, and sea.

Despite the many alternative distractions that are on offer, do not fail to go to a fronton to watch a pelota match. Not only is the game itself, on its huge cement flood-lit court, as exciting as any, but you will be amused by the system of betting. The 'bookies', wearing white jackets, stand with their back to the wire-netting that separates the court from the public in their tiered seats, and yell the odds that they are currently offering. If you raise a hand one of them will lob a soft rubber ball with a hole in it to you, with a nonchalant accuracy that is uncanny, and you will insert inside it the sum you wish to bet.

The players, usually two on each side—a 'forward' and a 'back'—always wear either red or blue sashes, so that you enclose a scribbled slip bearing the word 'rojo' or 'azul' to indicate which team is your choice, and then return the ball (probably less accurately) to the 'bookie', who at once makes a note of the amount and the odds, and throws you back a carbon copy. With this you collect—if you are lucky—when the game is over.

Only the Basques, one feels, could have invented a game complicated by the need to catch a hard ball travelling at the speed of a bullet in a narrow, foot-long, curved wicker basket, worn as an extension to a glove on the right hand—but they do it amazingly well, and the game is so strenuous that a player is already a veteran at the age of 30.

San Sebastian is the capital of the Basque province of Guipuzcoa (pronounced Gipscoya, with a soft 'g'). But the largest and most important Basque city of all is Bilbao, capital of Vizcaya, which the British call Biscay with the same Empire-building logic that turned the inhabitants from Vascos to Basques.

The main road runs within sight of the coast, passing the

thriving sea-side resorts of Zaraúz and Zumaya, in both of
which there are large 1a hotels and a plentiful selection of
cheaper ones. Both these fishing villages, respectively 16 and 23
miles from San Sebastian, struck me as ideal for those who wish
to be within easy distance of a big city, but without the social
obligations, verbal and sartorial, which a first-class resort
demands. Only 10 miles farther on is Deva, which, although
less picturesque, has an even better bathing-beach than Zaraúz
or Zumaya.

At Deva the main road turns inland to Elgoibar, Eibar, and
Durango, near which there are some enormous prehistoric rock
paintings, and it is here that I always turn off to the south,
along a good secondary road that leads to Vitoria. Before it
joins the main road from Bilbao at Villareal, our secondary one
climbs the 3,500-foot Urquiola Pass, through typical Basque
country—green, highly cultivated, and interspersed with ancient
grey stone churches, perched upon the belfries of which there is
always at least one stork's nest.

My frequent references to storks may seem a little strange,
and it would be as well to admit frankly that I find these grave,
sagacious birds particularly fascinating. Everyone has his pet
lunacy. Those who read Tschiffely's delightful book *Round and
About Spain* will recall that his consisted of a consuming passion
to be photographed on one of the wooden horses used as a
'prop' by Spanish street photographers. In my case it is
storks, and my interest in them occasionally leads to peculiar
discoveries.

When my wife is with me in a car, she knows my fatal
weakness when confronted with the temptation of a side-road
and she does her best to keep the radiator pointing towards
our supposed objective. But, running down from Madrid to
Lisbon last June, I was alone. That main road west across
Extremadura to Badajoz is hot, and rather dull once the lovely
old palace of the Dukes of Frias, now the State-run Parador of
Oropesa 93 miles from Madrid, is passed. Some miles short of
Merida, therefore, I yielded to the blandishments of a peculiar-
looking road to the left, and within twenty minutes of crossing

the River Guadiana was magnificently and comprehensively lost!

However, this was obviously good stork country, and I was quite content to discover, after a couple of hours' driving, that a ruinous-looking village with a fourteenth-century monastery fortress was called Hornachos. As I neared it I observed a number of large dead birds in the surrounding fields, and I got out to investigate. They were mostly storks, but I counted four large eagles, two of them transfixed right through their bodies by the long beak of a stork. I spent the next hour questioning villagers, including a priest, and I am convinced that the story they told me was substantially true.

This is what I learned.

A large number of storks have always nested in the crumbling ruins of the monastery, and this year the usual little colony had hatched their eggs, and were engaged in raising two or three slightly bald but already endearing youngsters. Suddenly one morning, without warning, a flock of eagles flew out of their eyries in the Sierra del Pedroso to the east and attacked the stork colony, killing many of the young and also two parent birds which had tried to protect them. Two days later the same thing happened again, and that evening the entire adult stork community gathered on the roof of the old parish church. There was much voiceless clapping of beaks and, just as the light was failing, eight birds flew off to each of the cardinal points of the compass, and disappeared into the barren immensity of Extremadura. Nothing happened for two days, and then storks by the score came flapping in from all directions until, according to local estimates, there must have been well over eighty birds reinforcing the resident colony of about twenty. Further beak-clapping conferences followed, and then all was quiet for another three days.

Then, on the morning of my arrival, twelve eagles had repeated their previous tactics—but with remarkably different results. Groups of from three to five storks took off and each, as a team, tackled one eagle. The eagles, of course, were faster, more manoeuvrable, and heavier gunned—forgive me, better

armed—and the stork making the direct attack did not stand
a chance of survival, but while he was being torn to shreds by
his adversary the eagle was momentarily vulnerable to the
attacks of the rest of the team and, after a full five minutes of
aerial combat (which spattered the gaping inhabitants below
with blood), eight eagles and twenty storks had crashed to their
death. The remaining four eagles, with storks still swarming
round them from every angle, had had more than enough and,
for the first time, sought only to escape. It was then that two
storks drove their closed beaks right through an eagle's body
and, still living, voluntarily fell to the ground with their victims.

The two surviving aggressors disappeared eastwards, one of
them with a badly damaged wing and both still being attacked.
Their ultimate fate will never be known. An hour or so later
the fifty-odd surviving storks flew away heavily, and disappeared in the direction from which they came. I took the
trouble to write to Hornachos in August to ask whether there
had been a sequel. From that day in June, I was told, no
eagle had been seen within 20 miles of the village.

However, you may not share my enthusiasm for storks, so let
us return to Vitoria, the capital of the Basque province of
Alava, 1,800 feet above sea-level and only some 70 miles from
San Sebastian. It is the smallest of the three Basque provincial
capitals, and to my mind possesses more character than either
of the others.

For a while it formed part of the Kingdom of Navarre, but
voluntarily united with Castile in 1332. During the War of
Independence, as the struggle against Napoleon is called in
Spain, it was the base of operations for Pedro Mina, one of the
most famous of all the guerrilla leaders. On June 21st, 1813, it
witnessed the decisive battle in which Wellington defeated
Marshal Jourdan and Joseph Bonaparte, causing them to suffer
10,000 casualties and to fall back upon Pamplona and, from
there, to cross the frontier in the retreat which led the British
Peninsular forces all the way to Toulouse.

Not only is Vitoria full of Wellingtonian associations, but it is
oddly British in appearance, the large bow windows of many of

its grey stone houses closely resembling those that we associate with Regency London or Bath. The climate too, rainy and with frequent cold winter fogs, strengthens the illusion!

It is an older town than either San Sebastian or Bilbao, and the White Virgin, who is carried in procession from the twelfth-century Church of San Miguel on the eve of the Fiesta Mayor on August 5th, has been the city's patron for a thousand years or more.

While rich in excellent restaurants, like everywhere in the Basque country, Vitoria's hotels are unambitious, though the 1b Fronton, charging 100 pts a day, has the charm of an old posting-house.

Of the restaurants, the Hermanos Ande, Fernandez, and La Parra are all outstanding. Though without pretensions to luxury, they understand and take a pride in serving good food, excellently cooked, at reasonable prices. Vitoria is only 50 miles or so from Logroño, which is the heart of the area that grows the best table-wines to be found anywhere throughout the length and breadth of Spain, and Rioja and Haro wines are correspondingly cheap and plentiful, even though they do come from just across the border of the Basque country.

The road from Vitoria, 41 miles to Bilbao, crosses the ring of mountains, that everywhere bar the way to the sea, by the easy 2,200-foot Barazar Pass, and it takes only an hour or so to reach the outskirts of what was, for a short time, the capital of the semi-independent Basque Republic.

The Basques, like the Catalans and the Andalusians, have always dreamed of independence from Madrid, and fought for the Republic against Franco in exchange for promised autonomy. But the iron-ore deposits and the great blast-furnaces that ring the first-class port play too vital a part in the economy of the whole country for any strong central government ever willingly to agree to these separatist ambitions, and the intensely pious and orderly Basques had little but their separatism to bind them to the Church-burning anarchists of Catalonia.

Bilbao is a relatively modern, thriving, industrial city of a quarter of a million inhabitants, though it has been a port since its foundation in the year 1300. The sea is 8 miles away, but the River Nervion enables ships up to 4,000 tons burthen to come right to the city docks.

Being a large and prosperous city, Bilbao has two luxury hotels, the large Carlton and the small Torrontegui, and, in the 1b class, the Excelsior and a list of sixteen others recommended by the Tourist Bureau. Again, it is the food in Bilbao that remains longest in the memories of most visitors. The restaurants may have jaw-breaking names like Chacoli Uriaquersea, but the food they serve will repair the damage. Angulas, lobster, crab, and prawns are superb all along the north coast of Spain, but a local speciality is the grilled fresh sardines, washed down with the super-dry, only slightly alcoholic wine known as 'chacoli', and followed by 'pil-pil' and 'bacalao a la bilbaina'.

Bacalao is the staple diet here, as in Portugal, and you must not be discouraged by its appearance as sold in the markets. It arrives looking like an overgrown finnan haddock, has the consistency of a wooden board, and, if it is just boiled in the normal way, is either uneatably salty or, alternatively, quite tasteless. However, the Basques understand a number of ways of treating it—with tomato, garlic, chips of peppery sausage ('chorizo'), and, occasionally, deliciously tender broad beans. It is not only cheap and filling, but extremely appetizing.

Though all the comforts are available, Bilbao is neither physically beautiful nor climatically attractive. Visitors and well-to-do residents live during the summer in Santurce or Portugalete, the sea-side resorts at the mouth of the River Nervion, and come into the city by train, tram, bus, or car for their work, shopping, or indoor amusements. The bathing-beach of Las Arenas can be reached by a funicular railway, and the social life of the place centres round the excellent yacht, tennis, and golf clubs, which during the summer months are crowded with fashionable people from Madrid, as well as visitors from abroad.

The most attractive local fiesta is on July 10th, when the Virgin of Begoña is brought down the river and along the coast at the head of a procession of gaily decked ships, though Bilbao's

'Semana Grande' is centred around August 15th, when there
are the usual bull-fights and typically Basque exhibitions of all
the more exhausting forms of exercise. One of these latter
—the stone-piercing competition—has now been suspended
since it recently produced no fewer than three deaths from heart
failure in a single day's 'sport'!

Despite their apparent preoccupation with physical prowess,
the Basques, like the Welsh, are natural-born singers, and I
have heard better massed choral performances there than
anywhere else in Europe, though, being Basques, the songs
they sing all tend to be fortissimo.

Perhaps I have said too much about the Basque cities and
people and not enough about the countryside, which, inland
and in summer, is green, fertile, and gracious, with avenues of
tall trees. Many people tire of the tawny, austere, empty-
seeming uplands of Castile, or the arid, sub-tropical Mediterranean coast, and the contrast with the small, highly cultivated
green fields and rushing streams of the north comes like a balm
to sun-tired eyes. For the Anglo-Saxon, too, the punctual,
hard-working, reliable Basque is far less difficult to understand
than the more reserved, formal, and complicated Spaniard,
and that greater understanding, consciously or not, usually
makes for a happier holiday.

While I must admit that I never visit their green and pleasant
land unless I have to, I equally must admit that the Basque
and his mountains undoubtedly possess a powerful charm of
their own.

XIX

THE COOL NORTH-WEST

Santander—Picos de Europa—Riaño—Oviedo—La Coruña—Santiago
de Compostela—La Toja—Vigo and Leon.

SANTANDER, 248 miles by road due north of Madrid and 70 west
of Bilbao, is Castile's only outlet to the sea.

I am frankly a sun-worshipper, so from choice I go south for
my summer holidays; but during August 1952 I felt I should
refresh my sixteen-year-old memories of Spain's cool Atlantic
coast, if only because it is now enjoying a new vogue of a
rather specialized kind, of which I wished to know more.

This vogue is for families from northern Europe with young
children. They want to come to Spain for their holidays in
order to benefit from the favourable rate of exchange and to
enjoy sea-bathing in a climate warmer than their own. The
Mediterranean holiday appeals to the adult, but, with the exception of the Costa Brava, it is rather too hot for small children
from Britain, the Low Countries, and Scandinavia. Santander
and Asturias in the north, and Galicia in the north-west,
exactly meet their needs, and every class and type of hotel,
pension, and inn has now been opened along this 400 miles of
coast in order to cope with the growing annual influx.

The train service from the French frontier is good, though
there is an obligatory change at Bilbao. From Madrid it is an
overnight journey and, if you find the direct road through
Burgos monotonous, there is an only slightly longer alternative through the castle-country of Valladolid and Palencia to
Reinosa, where there are the ruins of the Roman–Cantabrian
capital of Juliobriga.

The popularity of Santander was established by Alfonso
XIII in the first ten years of this century, rather as that of San
Sebastian was the result of his mother's patronage during the
nineties, and there is a small royal palace there, presented to
him in 1910. In these days, however, with the government

going to San Sebastian farther east, and Franco to his native Galicia farther west, Santander has surrendered first place to its Basque rival with, in my opinion, the happiest of results for itself.

I do not wish to belittle the obvious charms of San Sebastian, but at the height of the season it gets rather too overpoweringly excursionistic for my taste. Santander, on the other hand, being 150 miles from the French frontier instead of 11, attracts what, in my father's day, used to be called 'a better class of visitor'. It is what Frinton or Cowes is to Southsea or Ryde.

The comparison to Cowes is apt, in that Santander possesses Spain's No. 1 Yacht Club, founded because of the Spanish Royal Family's enthusiasm for sailing, just as Cowes' Royal Yacht Club developed from George V's similar passion, and there always seems to be a regatta going on. Santander, I found, is one of the few cities in Spain that is unashamedly and yet attractively new. Nearly all that was not destroyed in the ammunition-dump explosion in 1893 was burned in the great fire of 1940, so that it has a wholly modern aspect lacking in new, but late Victorian, San Sebastian.

It is a great place for clubs—yacht clubs, tennis clubs, golf clubs, even fishing clubs and swimming clubs—and I found that it was worth joining a couple, the Yacht and the eighteen-hole Padrina Golf, as most of the social life of the 120,000 inhabitants seemed to originate from one or other of them. As a foreigner you can become a temporary member for a month, or even a week, for a nominal fee.

There are as many as six luxury or first-class hotels, all within easy reach of the really superb sand bathing-beach of El Sardinero, but I was lucky enough to get into the first-class pension known as the Parador del Cantabrico. I say lucky not only because it served me with some of the most exquisite sea-foods I have ever eaten for 55 pts a day, but because it possesses only ten bedrooms! Although called a Parador, it is not one of the State-run inns.

One of the few relatively old streets in Santander is the Paseo

23 The Cathedral of Santiago de Compostela said to be the burial
place of St. James the Apostle, Patron Saint of Spain

Pereda, where you will find the authentic atmosphere of a port
if you take your 'sundowner' sitting outside any of the numerous
pavement cafés. Here I habitually consumed with my drink
so many 'tapas', composed of delicious fat prawns, shreds of
dressed crab, and 'percebes' (a marine growth of repulsive
aspect but admirable flavour), that I was quite unable to compete with my ten-o'clock dinner. The days of Santander's prosperity were when it was the principal port for Spain's South
American colonies, in the eighteenth century, but it has a long
tradition of trade with Britain across the stormy Bay of Biscay
and displays a prosperous air, due partly to the large zinc
deposits found quite recently in the neighbouring mountains,
and partly to its new-found tourist trade.

I arrived after the Semana Grande—which, incidentally,
lasts for twelve days from July 25th—but in time to see the end
of the yacht race from Southampton, in which the first two
places were taken by Spaniards, and the third by a British
crew.

I rather blotted my copy-book in the Yacht Club when I
suggested, in reply to a concrete statement to the contrary,
that Britain's Drake was *not* the first person to circumnavigate
the globe, and that this had been achieved by Spain's Juan
Sebastian Elcano in 1522, before Drake was born. It was a
social 'gaffe' on my part because the Spaniards already knew it,
the British had never even heard of J. S. E., and the fact that
impartial history (even including the *Encyclopædia Britannica*)
confirmed my statement was of satisfaction to absolutely no
one, including myself!

Quite a few people are now just discovering that several of the
unadvertised Spanish spas, such as Solares, not far from
Santander, were good for whatever ails you long before
Edward VII popularized those of Germany, Austria, and
France, and in fact have been so ever since Roman times.
Many of the best of these lie just inland among the mountains
that encircle Spain's northern coast.

Number one excursion from Santander (if the absence of an
R in the month prevents you from taking a motor-boat trip to
Q

eat oysters on the Isle of Mouro) is to Santillana, 18 miles away, where the Tourist Department have the particularly attractive old Parador de Gil Blas, built in a sixteenth-century nobleman's palace. It is a sleepy little village full of crested mansions dating from the lordly days of Charles V and Philip II, but it was only a long lifetime ago that the discovery of the Altamira Caves brought it back into the limelight.

Although I had heard a great deal about them, I had never myself seen them until my last visit, chiefly because of my unreasoning dislike for being some distance below the surface of the earth. The huge 30-foot-long panel of brown and black wild boar, bison, deer, and horses, painted some 20,000 years ago, during the last Ice Age, is really impressive. If you like this sort of thing I would recommend the rock shelter of Navazo near Teruel, which, although almost unknown, impressed me more than that at Altamira. My preference is not entirely accounted for by the fact that it was not necessary to penetrate underground in order to see it, but because, in addition to brown and black, both white and red had also been employed by the prehistoric artist, and he had painted human figures, with snake's heads, as well as animals. These cave paintings are fairly common all over Spain, but usually in remote places difficult of access.

Probably the finest bathing-beach on the whole northern coast is that of the little village of Suances, 20 miles from Santander, and there are half a dozen 50-mile excursions into the surrounding 8,000-foot mountains inland. For myself, I was particularly anxious to visit the Tourist Department's Parador at Riaño, opened in 1952 on the southern flanks of the Picos de Europa mountains, and accordingly took the coast road west from Santillana through San Vicente de la Barquera to Unquerra-Bustio. There the Peña Santa and Peña Bermeja tower up to 8,500 feet, guardians to the eastern limits of the small and desperate Christian kingdom that, nearly 1,200 years ago, barricaded itself into its remote fastnesses to defy the all-conquering hordes of Islam.

There I found one of my favourite side-roads to Panes,

Puentenonsa, and Potes, climbed the 4,500-foot San Gloria Pass, and then followed the rushing river Esla to Riaño, 107 miles from Santander. The scenery from the extremely comfortable Parador defies all attempts at description, with the northern and eastern sky ringed with a whole series of 8,000-foot peaks, but peaks as I prefer them, not close enough to block out the sun, as happens, for example, in Andorra.

Another of my almost unmarked mountain side-roads led me through the easy 4,000-foot Tarna Pass to Sama de Langreo and Mieres, and then on for 66 miles to Oviedo, capital of Asturias. The whole journey was unmatched in my experience, resembling, though exceeding in grandeur, parts of the Austrian Tyrol.

Less unreasonable people stick to the first-class coast road, which I left at Unquera-Bustio, and continue through Llanes and Ribadesella before turning inland to Arriondas and the Asturian capital, covering 132 miles to my 173—but they miss a great many things, besides punctures, by doing so.

An easy compromise between my long detour from Unquera-Bustio through Riaño and their rather dull main road, is to follow my route only for the 8 miles to Panes, and then turn west, through Carrena de Cabrales and Cangas de Onis, to rejoin the main Oviedo road at Arriondas. The advantage of this is that they can take a look at the Sanctuary of Covadonga, built on the site of the famous eighth-century battle which constituted the first real check that the Moors had ever received in their triumphant penetration into western Europe.

Most people seem to have heard of the great French victory over the Moors at Poitiers, but no one seems to know that what Charles Martel did for France and Europe in 732, Pelayo did for Spain and Europe at Covadonga thirteen years earlier—but Spain has no talent for Public Relations!

From Covadonga you may climb to the lovely little Lake Enol, or visit the shrine which is the burial-place of both the victor and his son Alfonso I. Beyond it is the small sixteenth-century monastery, of which the entrance is the only remaining part of its thirteenth-century predecessor. Backed by the highest of the Picos de Europa, over 8,500 feet, you will probably feel, as I did, that King Pelayo did not repose all his trust in the Virgin of Covadonga and the plain wooden cross on his saddle-bow (now covered with gold and silver and guarded in Oviedo Cathedral), but also possessed the born soldier's eye for the lie of the land. This was as well, as he was to fight a battle in which (miracles apart) defeat and extermination must have seemed almost certain; in short, it seems to have been another case of God helping those who help themselves.

Oviedo itself is an ancient and historic city, but with the discovery of important coal deposits it has become somewhat industrialized. I stayed only two nights at the very comfortable Hotel Principado, but had time to catch at least something of the atmosphere of these most independent and unconquerable of people.

Because it never came under Moorish dominion, the heir to the throne of Spain was always given the title of Prince of the Asturias, and it was to Oviedo that all the most precious Christian relics were brought in order to save them from falling into the hands of the Infidel. As a result, the cathedral, begun in 1388 but not finished until nearly a century and a half later, contains the most amazing collection. This includes a bone of Moses, a sandal of St. Peter, the heart of St. Bartholomew, one of the thirty pieces of silver paid to Judas for his betrayal, a piece of the True Cross, a fragment of the bread with which the multitude was fed as the result of the Miracle of the Loaves and Fishes, a fragment of the winding-sheet in which the dead Jesus was wrapped, and some strands of the hair of Mary Magdalene! Requiring a less unquestioning faith in its authenticity is the famous eighth-century Cross of Victory, already mentioned. I had time, too, to go round the fine private collection of pictures in the palace of the Duque de Parque, now the property of the Marquess de San Felix, which includes three particularly fine Grecos, and to visit the interesting ninth-century Church of Santa Maria de Naranco, just outside the city. This contains some unusual statuary, in which the Byzantine influence is clearly evident. However,

I did not go out to Oviedo's port and popular sea-side resort of Gijon, 17 miles away, scene of fierce fighting when the Asturians rebelled against the Republic in 1934.

The cause of the revolt was the unsatisfactory working conditions of the coal-miners who, to-day, are among the most satisfied of all Franco's subjects. The reason for this is the personal crusade which was fought by the present Minister of Labour, Giron, who, an 'asturiano' himself, has made them among the best-housed, paid, fed, and insured of all Europe's miners.

For those who are interested, it is worth noting that it is from Oviedo that they will set out upon both their salmon-fishing and their shooting- or hunting-trips organized from the Tourist Department's mountain refuge of Aliva, after chamois. The fishing preserves are on the rivers Eo, Narcea, and Deva-Cares, but both fishing and big game can only be organized through my good friend Max Borrell, who, as Technical Adviser on Sport to the Tourist Department, is the king-pin of all such activities and, incidentally, himself a crack shot and dry-fly wizard of international fame.

It is an easy day's run west from Oviedo to La Coruña, and 80 of the 205 miles journey are close above the deeply indented coastal cliffs. As a northern resort, I place La Coruña second only to Santander.

The capital of Galicia had changed enormously for the better since I had last seen it. Unscarred by the Civil War, having given its immediate support to 'gallego' General Franco (born just across the huge bay in El Ferrol), it seemed prosperous and gay. Perhaps it was just the contrast with Asturias, for if the 'asturianos' are the Scots of Spain, the 'gallegos' are assuredly the Irish. Both climate and blood strengthen the comparison, for Galicia is a lush, green land of misty sun, Atlantic gales, deep scored creeks and sea reaches, fat cattle, broad-beamed women, and charming liars! As to the blood, it was from just outside La Coruña that the Celtic leader Breogan set out in the armada that was to conquer and populate Ireland and part of Scotland. On my first visit to Galicia before the Civil War, I was with a Scot and his wife, who, while enjoying themselves, were a little inclined to consider everything Spanish as distinctly odd. I shall never forget their faces when they heard the skirl of the bagpipes being played by a shepherd in very 'gallegan' and un-Scottish attire. My friend suspected the musician—if that is the correct word—of being an eccentric compatriot, and I had to do a lot of rapid translating. The unkindest cut of all came at the end, when the peasant said:

'I had not heard that you had the bagpipes in your country too, but, of course, we must have taken it with us when we moved on with Breogan'!

La Coruña, or Corunna, has many other associations with Britain—most of them unpleasant. It was from here that Philip II's 'Invincible Armada' set out to conquer Protestant Elizabethan England in 1588, and later the city paid the penalty of almost total destruction. Again, in 1809, it was in La Coruña that the British General Sir John Moore ended his desperate retreat before the armies of Napoleon. He lies buried in the pleasant little garden of San Carlos, where there is a statue to his memory.

It is a strong-minded British visitor who can resist the temptation to declaim:

> Not a drum was heard, not a funeral note,
> As the corpse to the ramparts we hurried.

I was not strong-minded, and continued until I noticed a certain nervousness on the part of a group of inhabitants whose presence I had not previously observed.

Just for good measure, the city was once again much damaged in 1836, during the First Carlist War.

La Coruña, I found, has many really excellent hotels, including two large luxury ones, the Embajador and the Finisterre, and two smaller ones of the 1b Class, the Atlantico and Palas. The Finisterre is only open from the beginning of July until the end of September.

I arrived at the tag end of the 'Semana Grande', which

officially ends on August 10th, but actually continues, at a slightly calmer tempo, until the 17th, so that I saw some of the very special Galician folk-dances and costumes.

Despite all its disasters in the past, there is still an old quarter in this city of 150,000 inhabitants, lying to the north of the harbour. Here I found quiet and empty streets, and the famous sun-galleries that have earned for it the name of 'The City of Glass'. The Church of Santiago dates from the eleventh century, and both it and the twelfth-century Santa Maria del Campo are well worth visiting.

The Tower of Hercules is a remarkable monument, though it is difficult to see just how the Greek hero-god got mixed up in it. Apparently the Celtic leader Breogan, to whom I have already referred, built a tower there some 2,500 years ago to mark the site of his embarkation for Ireland, and the Spanish-born Roman Emperor Trajan, some 700 years later, used the ruins to build a lighthouse. Although it has been patched up here and there, it still retains its original form, with the exterior ramp up which the wood was carried to feed the warning fire at the top of the tower.

Since La Coruña, like Cadiz, is built on a long, narrow peninsula, it is surrounded by excellent bathing-beaches—the Riazor, Santa Cristina, and the more distant Bastiagueiro—and it seemed to me to have all the usual amusements and facilities of a first-class summer resort. As everywhere along the coast, the sea-food is superlative, and the Restaurant Salto do Can served me with a notable meal of 'centollos'—dressed crab, but dressed, most emphatically, in the regional costume—washed down by Galicia's pleasant 'ribeiro' (white wine), followed by one of the rich local cheeses.

The local cider, though less well known than that of Asturias, is a remarkably cool and refreshing drink, for Spain's north and north-west coast is the one area where rainfall is both regular and plentiful, and so the one and only place in the country where the apples do not taste of cotton-wool. This sometimes, touristically, unwelcome rain also produces ample pasturage, and so fat cattle and unlimited fresh milk and

butter. It is not uneconomical, as elsewhere, to allow calves
to grow into cows and bulls, and replace the eternal veal with
beef, as good in quality as anything from the Highlands of
Scotland. Even so, the besetting Spanish gastronomic sin of
ensuring that even the best meat is tough by killing one day and
eating the next still holds good, and there is the similar tendency
to eat their tomatoes green and their fruit unripe! However,
both the quantity and the quality are available here, and you
can soon arrange for your special tastes to be met—though only
after much shaking of heads over your odd preference for
eating things when they have reached the point when they
ought to be thrown away!

The country surrounding La Coruña is very typical not only
of Galicia but of all European countries that border the great
ocean. For this is Finisterre—the end of the world—beyond
which, until less than 500 years ago, there was officially only a
watery nothingness.

Here, as in Ireland and the western isles of Scotland, there is
a haunting sense of being upon the fringe of the fabulous. This
is not just Celtic Twilight, but some compound of immense
space and timelessness, of shadows on the sea that might be
legendary islands, of the dreamy, misty sun, and the vague
haze that, between breaths, can turn the familiar scene into
something wholly strange. If this seems unduly fanciful,
make your way alone one day, as I did, to fourteenth-century
Betanzos, 15 miles from La Coruña, and then walk along the
flowery banks of the Rivers Mandeo and Menda.

Running south for 40 miles to Santiago de Compostela, I
was only the same distance from Cape Finisterre itself, but,
though I have seen it so often from the sea, I have never been
there. It can be reached by a secondary road that makes a
wide half-circle covering 110 miles from La Coruña to Santiago,
through real end-of-the-world scenery, and I shall most
certainly take that road one day before I die.

On this occasion I was in a hurry, as some friends who had
followed the ancient Pilgrim's Way all the 500 miles from Jaca
in the Pyrenees wanted me to meet them at their pilgrimage's

end before the Tomb of St. James the Apostle, Patron Saint
of Spain.

Compostela, with its arcaded streets, is set on a low hill, with
mountains filling the horizon. For 600 years it was one of the
principal objects of Christian pilgrimage, literally millions
finding their way here on foot along the route which is still
unmistakably marked by the chain of hostels, chapels, and
bridges erected by pious monarchs and prelates to assist their
journey. To-day it is a town of 55,000 inhabitants possessing
no fewer than forty-six churches.

The legend is that St. James the Apostle, son of Zebedee,
landed at the port of Padron, 51 miles away, and for seven
long years walked the length and breadth of Spain converting
the heathen inhabitants. He then returned to Palestine, where
he died a martyr's death. His disciples Anastheseus and
Theodore, however, brought his body back to Spain and buried
it in the Holy Mountain, not far from where Compostela now
stands.

In the year 811 peasants claimed to hear angelic voices and
also to see mysterious lights in the neighbourhood, and in due
course the Saint's body was discovered, and housed in a small
crypt. Unfortunately, the Normans, and later the reconquering
Moors of Almanzor, completely destroyed the town in 997, but
during the following two centuries every effort was made to
build a worthy resting-place for the Saint, whose more ancient
name of Iago has never been changed in Spain to Jaime, or
James. The final result was the magnificent twelfth-century
Gothic cathedral of to-day, though its present baroque overlay
almost completely masks its original purity of line.

There are those who decry the baroque, but, although its
ornateness may be bewildering, at its best—and this is its very
best—it can be more emotionally impressive than any other
architectural style.

But the already much-travelled Saint was not destined to
rest in peace (after his victorious appearance at a critical
moment in the Battle of Clavijo in 844), and in 1589, with the
arrival of Sir Francis Drake to destroy La Coruña, he was

hastily removed to Orense, where the body was lost for 200 years. The pious Spaniard is fond of pointing out that it was during precisely those 200 years that Spain fell from a first to a third-class Power.

However, his rediscovery in 1789 was soon followed by the Napoleonic invasion, and Compostela was sacked in 1809, though the Saint was, rather surprisingly, left undisturbed in his solid silver casket.

Our visit was nearly a month too late for the great fiesta of July 24th and 25th, which I had witnessed in 1935.

My chief memory is of a brilliantly glittering procession of the Knights of Santiago following the Archbishop, dressed in silver, and passing into a great, candle-lit nave from the roof of which a giant incense-burner swung through a 260-foot arc with a motion that made me certain that it would surely bring down the whole building upon our heads. This was the famous 'Botafumeiro', which normally reposes in the Chapter House.

The High Altar, covered with gold, silver, and precious stones, is surmounted by the image of Santiago surrounded by the kneeling figures of Spanish kings, while before it always burns the silver lamp presented by Spain's greatest soldier, 'El Gran Capitan', Gonzalo de Cordoba, in 1503.

July 24th–25th is the big day every year, but when the 25th falls on a Sunday the year is declared a Jubilee, as in 1954, and the Puerta Santa, or Holy Door, is opened at midnight.

While the choir-stalls carved by Juan Davila in 1606 are exquisite, I found my own and my friends' interest soon riveted on the three-arched Portico de la Gloria—the central one representing the Catholic faith, and the other two the Jewish and the Pagan. Here you can pick out prophets, apostles, the twenty-four ancients of the Apocalypse, the seven deadly sins, and scenes from the life of Christ, but, dominating them all is the Tree of David, its stone trunk worn with the finger-touch of millions of long-dead pilgrims.

Splendid though its interior is, Santiago de Compostela's 'pièce de résistance' is the twelfth-century Platerias, or silver-

smith's portico, which is reached up a particularly graceful
double stairway. The west front, known as the Obradoiro,
completed in 1738, is a mass of carving right up to the cupolas,
246 feet above the pavement, and is generally regarded as the
supreme masterpiece of the baroque style, not only in Spain but
in all Europe.

After a brief look at the Tapestry Museum, with beautiful
designs by Goya and Teniers, we were all temporarily overcome
with the complete exhaustion of those whose capacity for receiving new impressions had long since passed its limit.

On such occasions the restaurant opposite the University,
known by the amiable name of El Asesino (the Assassin), is a
great comfort. Two hours there restored us sufficiently to
pay a visit to the Monastery of San Martin Pinario, where the
Old Pretender, James II of England's son, once lived for
several years. A quick look at the Archbishop's Palace ended, as
all things do in Santiago, with a short but heavy rainstorm,
and we were almost glad of the excuse to retire to the un-
demanding quiet of the 1b Hotel Compostela, swearing, as we
have all so often falsely sworn, that we would never again try
to do so much sight-seeing in a single day!

The next day I continued alone to the once-important but
now forgotten town of Padron, in the primitive little church of
which St. James the Apostle is traditionally supposed to have
officiated in the first Christian service ever held in Spain. This
was destroyed by the dreaded Almanzor at the end of the
tenth century, and replaced by the present seventeenth-century
Church of Santa Maria, where there are the tombs of seventeen bishops.

Next came Caldas de Reyes, with its feudal castle and Roman
bridge, and one of the best radioactive anti-gout thermal springs
in Europe. There I turned off towards the sea for a run of
20 miles through Villagarcia de Arosa to Cambados, where I
took the little ferry-boat to the island resort of La Toja.

Reverting to Caldas de Reyes, you may be surprised at the
dozens of obscure villages all over Spain with the honorific 'of
the Kings' tacked on to their original names. The explanation

is that the title was always conferred upon the place where a King of Spain first met his bride by proxy, in order to conduct her to his capital. The custom was that the place of meeting should be freed from taxation for the period of his reign, so the monarchs, with an admirable sense of economy, always arranged that these meetings should occur in some extremely modest hamlet or village!

Villagarcia de Arosa is situated upon one of the most beautiful of Galicia's famous 'rias'. Exposed to the ceaseless pounding of the Atlantic, the sea has driven fjord-like reaches deep into the rocky coast, where the water is often so still and the sea so distant that they look like calm mountain lakes rather than offshoots of the stormy ocean. Although the comparison with the fjords of Norway is inevitable, the rias of Galicia are fundamentally different, in that they often run between quite low hills instead of towering cliffs. This makes them less dramatic but, to my mind, sunnier and less oppressively Wagnerian.

My reason for going to the Island of La Toja was not the guide-books' assurances that it produced a mineral water of un-rivalled efficacy for the cure of venereal diseases and scrofulism, but because I had heard that, within the last two summers, it had become a very popular summer sea-side resort. I found that although the one luxury and four 2a hotels were all named 'Balnearios', not one of their occupants was there for any purpose other than to spend his time bathing on the various lovely sea-beaches. The place is only open during July, August, and September, but was well patronized by Scan-dinavians with large families, who certainly did not appear to stand in any need of the medicinal waters.

Returning after lunch to the car at Cambados, I continued by the pleasant coast road for the 20 miles to Pontevedra. This is a sleepy provincial capital, occupied by the British in 1386 and largely destroyed by 'the pirate Drake' (as the local history books describe him) in 1589. It possesses a fine old church, which apparently escaped the attentions of the Elizabethans, in which there are a few good pictures, notably a 'Triumph of

the Church' by Rubens, a really lovely diptych by Quentin
Metsys, and, my favourite, 'St. Bruno' by Zurbaran, who was
unequalled in his representation of King Lear types.

Another 28 miles brought me to Vigo, the 1a Hotel Alameda,
and the atmosphere of a thriving transatlantic port. For my
personal holiday taste it thrives, perhaps, a shade too much,
but the view from the old castle on the hill across the mouth
of the great 'ria' to the picturesque little fishing-ports on the
other side, and with the attractive little islands of Cies and the
bathing-beach of Samil in the foreground, was still Galicia at its
best.

Since I was leaving the sea the next morning, I chose the
Restaurant Cantabrico for an all-crustacea dinner: mussels in a
strong sauce with my manzanilla, a thick prawn soup, and a
large cold lobster plus a bottle of 'ribeiro', coffee, and 'anis'—
not brandy after fish, since at the age of 21 the combination
robbed me of victory in the finals of a tennis tournament!
The bill for this disgraceful orgy was 8s., but, then, of course,
lobster is always expensive!

Make a note that wherever you see a 'Cantabrico' restaurant,
even if it is in Barcelona hundreds of miles away from the
Cantabrican Sea, it will specialize in sea-foods and, if only there
is an R in the month, in oysters at 3s. or so the dozen.

The thought of oysters being only a week away and the fact
that on the last Sunday of August Vigo has its picturesque
Romeria de Santa Tecla appealed to both my æsthetic and
gustatory tastes, but I had to return to Madrid, 410 road-miles
distant, and so contrived to resist the twin temptations.

The next morning I was running due east, only 10 miles or
so north of the Portuguese frontier, for the 65 miles to Orense,
through pleasantly mountainous country simply bubbling with
mineral springs, many of which, by the way, are bottled and
sold all over the country. Orense itself has been famous for its
cures for rheumatism since Roman times, its medicinal springs
at a temperature of 150° F. being identical in composition to
those at Carlsbad.

Orense's thirteenth-century cathedral is second in Galicia

only to that of Santiago de Compostela and is famous for the mysterious carved 'Christ on the Cross', traditionally the work of Nicodemus and once the property of a remote mountain hermitage near Cape Finisterre, where it was rescued from the sea. The old city's other claim to fame is its seven-spanned Roman bridge over the River Miño, of which the central span is 124 feet long. The whole structure was restored 'recently' in 1449.

Having made an unusually early start from Vigo, I felt that I could allow myself the dissipation of a side road, and pushed on south through Albariz and Ginzo for 47 miles to Verin. Each one of these places—none of them even mentioned in any guide-book that I have ever seen—is a discovery in itself.

The walled town of Albariz contains the lovely Convent of Santa Maria Clara, founded by Doña Violante, wife of Alfonso the Wise, in the thirteenth century. Ginzo de Limia, although itself modern, is dominated by the medieval Torre de Pena, and just outside Verin is the tenth-century Church of Santa Maria de Mixos, containing a fine twelfth-century fresco and unusual Byzantine carvings.

At Verin I found that I was again only 9 miles from the frontier, and for the next 62 miles the mountains of the Royal Portuguese province of Braganza thrust up into the southern sky on my right. At the provincial frontier of Galicia and Leon I climbed sharply to the 4,200-foot Canda Pass, to reach the Spanish Tourist Bureau's Albergue de Sanabria for a rather late lunch, having covered an eventful 174 miles through wild mountain country since leaving Vigo.

Sanabria, a medieval frontier garrison town, is the centre of some of the best game-shooting country in Spain and not far away in Lake Villachica there is excellent trout-fishing.

Forty-five miles of indifferent road brought me to the main Madrid–La Coruña thoroughfare at La Bañeza, where there is another State-run Albergue, from whence I turned 15 miles north to Astorga before a final 30 east to Leon for the night.

Pliny described Astorga as 'a magnificent city', and its fifth-century walls still hint at its former greatness.

Once installed in the comfortable, old-fashioned 1a-class Hotel Oliden at Leon, I still had an hour of daylight to explore the ancient, dreaming city, and it is precisely at the sunset hour that it is at its enchanted best. Perhaps the softer light hides the scars of poverty, even as candle-light conceals the wrinkles in the face of an ageing beauty, but, whatever the reason, it is the right hour in which to see Leon. The pure Gothic lines of its immense thirteenth-century cathedral soar above the stained houses and the bare plateau that surrounds it, and recall that this forgotten city of barely 45,000 people once played a mighty part in the history of a nation.

Founded by the 7th Roman Legion in A.D. 70, it was already a Bishopric 100 years later and, although utterly destroyed by the Moors in 845, was then the capital of Christian Spain for nearly 300 years until, in the wave of reconquest led by El Cid, liberated Toledo usurped Leon's place.

When I had last been there many years ago I had witnessed the city's Romeria to the Virgin del Camino, a few miles outside the third-century walls, which is held every September 29th. Then I had seen some of the best folk-dancing I ever remember, followed by the centuries-old form of competition, peculiar to Leon, known as 'aluches'.

Inevitably, I was now drawn towards the cathedral, which many people consider the loveliest in Spain and the equal of Chartres or Amiens, and I was pleased to find it still open. I remembered Van der Weyden's moving 'Descent from the Cross', and the image of the Virgin that is supposed to bleed whenever an unrepentant gambler enters her chapel.

I had forgotten the thirteenth-century rose windows, or perhaps it was just that this time the last of the sun shone straight upon them so that they blazed with a light that seemed unearthly.

This was the eternal Spain—a strangely coloured enchantment of ancient and half-forgotten glory. Here a man easily slips away from this Brave New Atom Age, and dreams his way back to the white-hot crusade that once followed the giant, fabulous figure of El Cid. The blues, reds, and golds that now dazzled my sight were the banners of rich brocade that fluttered before his small, devoted band as they stormed across the bleak and tawny uplands of Castile. For here the centuries have no meaning, and all time is eternal, so that the past becomes more real than the present, and the future lies eternally hidden in the womb.

Here I shall stay, until the last light has faded, and the grey walls are lost in the gathering darkness.

APPENDIX I

NOTES ON SPANISH FOOD

'*Paella valenciana*' and '*Arroz marinera*'. This dish comes from the rice-growing province of Valencia, but has spread, with minor variations, all over Spain, though in the north it is only known in the better-class restaurants. The foundation is rice, yellowed with saffron, which is boiled in oil in an iron dish (and served and eaten from the same dish). At the moment when the rice begins to become crisp (but not dry) the dish is ready, and the period should be twenty minutes. Cooked in the rice are fragments of rabbit, chicken, pork, artichokes, red-peppers, green peas, nuts and unbroken garlic cloves.

The fishy variety substitutes prawns, Dublin Bay and ordinary, lobster, baby octopus or squid, small clams (almejas) and whiting for the meat ingredients, but is otherwise identically the same.

'*Angulas a la bilbaina*.' This has (as far as I know) no English equivalent, though I am told that where the River Severn becomes tidal 'angulas' are caught and eaten under the name of elvas. It is a really great dish. The dictionary translation of 'angulas' is the unattractive one of 'eel-spawn', but they are so small—smaller even than whitebait—that there is nothing unpleasant about their appearance. These are cooked and served in an earthenware dish, with an unbroken clove of garlic and a sliver of red-pepper (neither of them to be eaten) among them. They must be eaten with a wooden fork, as under no circumstances must 'angulas' be touched by metal.

'*Callos a la madrileña*.' These are small cut squares of tripe, cooked in fine oil with fresh tomato sauce, red-peppers, and a trace of garlic. Anglo-Indian Colonels who are still lamenting the really hot curries they used to get will find 'callos' bringing (literally) tears to their eyes!

'*Pulpitos salteados*.' I know that the idea of baby octopus or squid is unattractive to the conservative minded, but if they are young and tender enough they are delicious 'salteados'. Try anything once! The larger 'chipirones en su tinta' are apt to be rubbery, and, anyway, I am not myself particularly keen on ink for purposes other than writing—but many visitors love them.

'*Cochinillo asado*', roast suckling pig, is a Castilian speciality, being particularly excellent in Burgos, Segovia (Restaurant Casa Candido) and Madrid (Restaurant Botin). They are so small that there is virtually no fat on them, so that they are not over-rich—and the 'crackling' is pure joy!

'*Corderito asado*', roast baby lamb. Rather heavier than 'cochinillo'; and make sure that it is not baby goat, which is tougher.

'*Perdiz estofada.*' Partridge, stewed in white wine, with half a dozen different sorts of fresh vegetables.

'*Langostinos a la parrilla.*' The langostino is a 5-inch-long prawn, found plentifully on the Mediterranean coast north of Valencia (and particularly at the Albergue de Benicarló). These are fresh grilled in fine oil and served as an 'aperitif' with your very dry 'manzanilla' wine—a kind of sherry from Sanlúcar de Barrameda.

'*Bacalao a la bilbaina.*' This is dried cod, sold in most grocer's shops, and possessing the consistency of a board. However, soaked for at least 24 hours to remove the salt, and then cooked in oil, with fresh tomatoes, and onions in an earthenware dish, it tastes rather like a spicy finnan haddock. Cheap, nourishing, and never dull.

'*Cangrejos.*' A particularly delicious fresh-water crayfish, usually only about 3 inches long, found in the rivers in the Burgos area.

'*Zarzuela de pescado*'—literally 'a musical comedy of fish'—a fish fry particularly plentiful around Cadiz and Catalonia. It should contain at least six varieties of fresh sea-fish, cooked in oil until it is almost dry.

'*Centollo*'—a large sea-crab which, properly dressed, is delicious. At its best (like oysters at 3s. a dozen) along the 400 miles of north and north-west coast from San Sebastian to Vigo.

Two outstanding *soups* are the 'bouillabaisse' of Barcelona, and the cold Andaluz 'gazpacho'.

Turtle, venison, hare, fresh salmon, and trout are excellent and plentiful in their seasons.

'Almejas' (clams) and 'percebes' (a kind of barnacle) are highly prized by those with strong digestions and a taste for sand. Better are the 'cigalas' (Dublin Bay prawns), 'gambas' (prawns), 'langostinos' (giant prawns), 'langosta' (crayfish), 'cangrejos' (fresh-water crayfish), 'aceitunas rellenados' (olives stuffed with an anchovy), 'cortezas' (dry pork crackling), &c., which are plentiful almost anywhere at the pre-dinner cocktail hour of 9 till 10 p.m.

Among fruits there are, naturally, grapes—black, green, muscatel, and 'rosé', cherries, the flat peaches of Madrid, fresh figs, bananas (from the Spanish Canary Islands) 'chirimoyas' (a fruit from a special cactus, translated by the dictionary as custard-apple for reasons yet to be revealed), water-melons (six different varieties of them) and, from November until April, oranges, tangerines, mandarines, clementinas, &c. The ordinary strawberries, and the finer flavoured wild strawberries, either in kirsch or cream, are available from March until June.

Do not bother with apricots, apples, and pears (except for the hard mountain variety of these last) as they are rarely good in Spain, though apples from Asturias in the north produce excellent cider.

Vegetables in Spain are infinitely varied but have a short season. Tender broad-beans ('habas'), and green peas, appear in February, and the hardy stand-by of the summer is the 'berengena', 'aubergine' or, in English (oddly named), egg-plant. These served as a cold salad, with fine oil, sliced onion, and garlic, or hot fried in batter with tomatoes and an egg in their centre, are capable of an endless variety of flavour, and cost next to nothing.

All forms of food rationing in Spain were abolished in June 1952.

APPENDIX II

SPANISH STATE TOURIST DEPARTMENTS

ANY information on such matters as Spanish art, museums, cities, summer or winter holiday resorts, hotels and pensions, railway and bus services, the state of the roads, and local shopping will be supplied at the Information Offices of the Spanish State Tourist Department, either verbally or by letter. In all of these there is at least one English-speaking employee, and no payment is accepted for any services he may render. The Information Offices will also: give the name and address of an approved local doctor on request, and if he does not speak English an official will act as interpreter; provide an English-speaking guide to places of interest locally, at a fixed fee; telephone free of charge to reserve a room at any of the Department's thirty-two Paradores or Albergues.

The Information Offices of the SSTD at present in operation are as follows:

TOWN	ADDRESS	TELEPHONE
Algeciras	On the quay	1761
Alicante	Esplanada de España, 2	2285
Almeria	Av. Generalísimo Franco, 115	2146
Aranjuez	Plaza de Santiago Rusiñol	352
Avilá	Plaza de la Catedral, 4	387
Badajoz	Moreno Nieto, 12A	1763
Barcelona	Av. José Antonio, 658	221135 and 211208
Behobia	Custom-house	
Burgos	Paseo del Espolón	1846
Cáceres	Avenida Cervantes, 40	2117
Cádiz	Calderón de la Barca, 1 dupdo	1313
Canfranc	Internat. Station Booking Hall	13
Córdova	Avenida del Gran Capitán, 13	1205
Cuenca	Calderón de la Barca, 28	171
El Escorial	Floridablanca, 6	88
Gerona	Ciudadanos, 12	1464
Gijón	Covadonga, 30	1167
Granada	Casa de los Tiros	1022
Huelva	Puerto, 40	1408 and 1409
Irún	North Station Booking Hall ⎫	
Irún	International Bridge ⎭	270
Jáca	Mayor, 22	8
La Coruña	Dársena de la Marina	1822

TOWN	ADDRESS	TELEPHONE
La Junquera	Custom-house	
Las Palmas	Casa del Turismo	2023
León	Plaza de la Catedral, 4	1083
Lugo	Plaza de España, 27	361
Madrid	Duque Medinaceli, 2	221268 and 222830
Madrid-Barajas	Airport	221165
Málaga	Larios, 5	3445
Oviedo	Cabo Noval, 5	3385
Palma (Majorca)	P.° General Franco, 38 and 40	2216
Pamplona	Duque de Ahumada, 3	1287
Pontevedra	Michelena, 27	2100
Port-Bou	International Station	81
Ronda	Plaza de España, 1	132
Salamanca	Plaza del Poeta Iglesias, 3	1655
San Sebastián	Victoria Eugenia Theatre (Ground Floor)	11774
Santa Cruz de Tenerife	Palacio Insular	2227
Santander	Paseo Alfonso XIII	1417
Santiago de Compostela	Rúa del Villar, 43	1132
Saragossa	Plaza de Sas, 7	21117
Segovia	Plaza General Franco, 8	1602
Seville	Alcázar (Puerta del León)	21404
Sitges	San Pablo, 4	234
Soria	Provincial Council (Diputación Provincial)	16
Tarragona	Rambla del Generalisimo, 50	1859
Toledo	Plaza de Zocodover	1330
Valencia	Town Hall (Ground Floor)	12585
Valladolid	Angustias, 1	1629
Vigo	Jardines de Elduayen	3057
Zamora	Santa Clara, 20	1845

MOROCCO—SPANISH ZONE

Tetuán	Tourist Bureau 'Servicio del Turismo de la Zona del Protectorado Español'. Avenida del Generalísimo, 30	

FOREIGN BRANCHES

Brussels	42, Rue d'Arenberg	125735
Buenos Aires	Florida 753 (Galerías Pacífico).	3964

TOWN	ADDRESS	TELEPHONE
Chicago, 3 (Illinois)	39, South La Salle Street. Room 613	
		Financial 6–0776
Gibraltar	1, Irish Place	A. 282
Havana	Calle Cárcel, 107 (Capdevila)	W–3030
Lisbon	Travessa do Salitre, 37	35414
London (S.W.1)	70, Jermyn Street	Whitehall 8578–9
Mexico, D.F.	Paseo de la Reforma, 1, 3, and 5	216118–20
New York, 22 N.Y.	485, Madison Avenue	Plaza 9–3842
Paris (VIIIème)	29, Avenue George V	Balzac 14–61
Rome	Piazza di Spagna, 55	681106
San Francisco, 4 (Calif.)	68, Post Street	Yukon 6–2125
Stockholm	Smalandsgatan, 11	11–90–20 and 11–90–30
Tangier	83, Calle del Estatuto	7669
Zürich	Claridenhof.—Claridenstrase, 25	279115

For everything to do with hunting, shooting, and fishing (fresh or salt water) apply to MAX BORRELL, TECHNICAL ADVISER ON SPORT, Direccion General de Turismo, Medinaceli, 2, Madrid.

INDEX

(The names of Spanish dishes are in italics.)